Nicaragua's
Other Revolution

Don Pedro: Delegado

You walk three miles
on mountain roads
to read the Word
imperfectly
with gaunt and Mayan
people of
no water
little food
less hope

You stand before them
having nothing
but your self
and faith.
They stare at you intently
comprehending
that you stand for God.
The poor (and you)
have nothing else.

Michael Dodson and

Laura Nuzzi O'Shaughnessy

Nicaragua's Other Revolution

Religious Faith and Political Struggle

The

University

of

North

Carolina

Press

Chapel Hill

and London

© 1990 The University of North Carolina Press
All rights reserved
Manufactured in the United States of America

The paper in this book meets the guidelines for permanence and
durability of the Committee on Production Guidelines for Book
Longevity of the Council on Library Resources.

94 93 92 91 90   5 4 3 2 1

Library of Congress Cataloging-in-Publication Data
Dodson, Michael, 1944–
    Nicaragua's other revolution : religious faith and political
struggle / by Michael Dodson and Laura Nuzzi O'Shaughnessy.
    p. cm.
    Bibliography: p.
    Includes index.
    ISBN 0-8078-1881-X (alk. paper). — ISBN 0-8078-4266-4
(pbk. : alk. paper)
    1. Nicaragua—History—Revolution, 1979—Religious aspects—
Christianity. 2. Christians—Nicaragua—Political activity—History—20th century. 3. Catholic Church—Nicaragua—Clergy—
Political activity—History—20th century. 4. Church and social
problems—Catholic Church—History—20th century. 5. Church
and social problems—Nicaragua—History—20th century. 6.
Catholic Church—Nicaragua—History—20th century. 7. Nicaragua—Church history—20th century. I. O'Shaughnessy,
Laura Nuzzi. II. Title.
F1528.D63 1990
261.7'097285—dc20   89-35448
                                                                  CIP

To those Nicaraguans who have tried to live their religious faith as part of a broader struggle for justice. Although they are poor, like their counterparts throughout Latin America, these humble people have profoundly influenced the shape of theology and politics in our time.

Contents

Preface   ix

Part One

Religion and Modern Democratic Revolutions   1

1   The Nicaraguan Revolution and Its Antecedents   3

2   A Crisis Erupts in Central America   14

3   The Religious Roots of North American Politics   33

4   Patterns of Political Development in the Americas   50

Part Two

The Traditional Church and the Prophetic Church   71

5   Tradition and Change in the Christian Churches   76

6   Post-Medellín Challenge and Response   102

7   Religious Renewal and Popular Mobilization   116

Part Three

Religion at the Center of Revolutionary Struggle   141

8   The Churches in a Revolutionary Society   145

9   The Churches and the Emerging Contra War   176

10   Religion, Revolution, and the Reagan Doctrine   204

11   Conclusion   238

Notes   245

Index   269

Preface

An impressive outpouring of new books has accompanied the explosion of journalistic and scholarly interest in Central America during the 1980s. This attention followed the initiatives of U.S. foreign policy, which abruptly defined Central America as being of vital importance to the security and well-being of the United States. At the same time that Central America was becoming a "hot spot," there was a surge of interest in the enduring vitality of world religions and their capacity to shape political life. The present book developed at just this point where religious renewal and political change intersect.

For a number of years the authors had done research and teaching focused on revolutions in Latin America. In the late 1970s we developed a strong interest in the popular political struggles that were emerging in Central America. We took particular interest in the events of the Sandinista Revolution in Nicaragua because the Christian churches appeared to play a prominent role in them. We had been studying the Catholic church for nearly two decades. Over that span of time we witnessed dramatic changes in the habits and attitudes of Latin American Christians, and in the social thought and institutional structures of the Roman Catholic church. Something on the order of a religious revolution took place in postconciliar Latin America, with varied but important repercussions all across the continent. We decided to examine the role played by religious change in the political revolution that swept Nicaragua during the late 1970s.

From its inception the Sandinista Revolution generated deep concern and growing controversy in the United States. Because of the importance given to it within the foreign policy agenda of the Reagan administration, Nicaragua stayed in the headlines year after year during the 1980s—and that fact no doubt contributed to the scholarly attention that was so suddenly thrust upon this hitherto neglected country. In our opinion the scholarly attention, at least, has not been misplaced. There is a great deal to be learned from the struggles of small, dependent countries such as Nicaragua to create more equitable societies and more popular forms of politics. Not the least important of those lessons is the latent capacity of religious systems to generate demands for societal justice and to invigorate popular efforts aimed at achieving that justice.

Popular struggle of this kind is inherently controversial. We have been mindful of the deeply partisan character of the subject while writing this book. Our aim has been to examine issues raised by the interaction of religion and politics within the Nicaraguan Revolution as rigorously as possible, while losing neither the sense of passion and drama that attends matters so important in the lives of a people, nor our own objectivity. The reader will be the best judge of our success.

The ideas for this book first began to take shape during the spring of 1983. At that time Michael Dodson used a sabbatical leave to begin a study of religious life at the grass roots in Nicaragua. His efforts were greatly facilitated by contact with a research team based at the Consejo Superior Universitaria Centroamericana (CSUCA) in San José, Costa Rica, who were then engaged in an ambitious empirical study of popular religiosity in Central America. The officials of CSUCA made him feel welcome, and stimulating discussions with Andrés Opazo, Rosa María Pochet, and Jorge Cáceres over a period of several years were invaluable. At about the same time (1981) Laura O'Shaughnessy visited Central America as part of a lay mission team jointly sponsored by the New York State Council of Churches and Mutuality in Mission, a program then affiliated with Cornell University. These travels in Central America at a time of intense religious ferment and political activity had a lasting impact on both authors.

We began our collaboration during that spring of 1983, agreeing to prepare a chapter on the role of the churches in the Nicaraguan Revolution for an edited volume. That chapter was published under the title "Religion and Politics" in Thomas W. Walker's *Nicaragua: The First Five Years*; Chapters 8 and 9 in the present work draw on that material. Chapter 7 draws on material published in Walker's earlier book, *Nicaragua in Revolution*, which Michael Dodson coauthored with T. S. Montgomery, while portions of Chapter 5 are based upon Laura Nuzzi O'Shaughnessy's previously published monograph, *The Church and Revolution in Nicaragua*. A Fulbright senior lectureship in the United Kingdom from January through April 1985 enabled Michael Dodson to pursue his studies of the English revolution. Special thanks go to John McClelland for his generous friendship; he arranged the terms of the lectureship at the University of Nottingham so as to allow Dodson ample time for research and writing. First drafts of Chapters 2 and 3 were produced there.

Michael Dodson also benefited from a fellowship at the Calvin Center for Christian Scholarship of Calvin College, which he held during the 1986–87 academic year. Affiliation with the Calvin Center brought the authors into association with creative scholars whose advice and critical reading of several chapters helped to sharpen the manuscript. Bill Cook, Lance Grahn, Sidney Rooy, Gordon Spykman, and John Stam exemplified a commitment to the truth and a love for Central America that continue to inspire us. Their friendship and that of their wives greatly enriched a stimulating and challenging year. Affiliation with the Calvin Center made it possible for both authors to travel extensively in Central America during the first two months of 1987. Michael Dodson wishes to express his gratitude to Texas Christian University (TCU) for providing the leave time that made the above periods of research possible. Laura O'Shaughnessy would like to thank Thomas Holladay, then director of the Latin American Studies program at Cornell University, for facilitating her stay as a visiting fellow in the spring of 1985. Special thanks go to St. Lawrence University for its initial research support and especially to Dean G. Andrew Rembert for encouraging her to continue research for the book by designing her job as associate dean in such a way as to permit continued work in the field.

It should be noted that the field research for this book was completed in January 1988 with the reaffirmation of the Esquipulas Accords in San José, Costa Rica. Since that date there have been important new developments within the Nicaraguan Revolution and in the larger international environment that impinges upon it. Most important in this regard has been the effort of the Sandinista government to achieve a ceasefire and a negotiated settlement of the Contra war. These recent events, however, lie outside the purview of this study.

Numerous friends and colleagues have influenced the book in subtle but important ways. On the faculty of St. Lawrence University, Rick Guarasci, Ahmed Samatar, William Hunt, University Librarian Richard Kuhta, and University Chaplain Dr. Theodore Linn were especially helpful to Laura O'Shaughnessy, as were Stuart Voss and Bill Culver of SUNY Plattsburgh. Dennis Gilbert, T. S. Montgomery, Rose Spalding, and Tom Walker are valued friends of both authors who always seemed able to bring a fresh perspective to interests we shared. Over a period of many years Michael Dodson's colleagues at TCU, Don Jackson and Charles Lockhart, have consistently offered the sort of support and genuine friendship that sustain one's work as well as one's spirit. Dan Levine, Meg Crahan, Tom Bruneau, Brian

Smith, and Scott Mainwaring are colleagues who have exemplified high-quality scholarship on the Latin American church. Bud Kenworthy has been a uniquely stimulating intellectual influence. His work always displays penetrating insights and is always presented in clear and graceful prose. He sets a standard to which we aspire, even though we fall short. From beginning to end our work benefited from the assistance of the Maryknoll Sisters, whose dedication to the poor of Central America is widely known and justly admired.

Both authors were graduate students in political science at Indiana University. There we relied in numerous ways on the wise and humane guidance of our mentor Alfred Diamant. We also accrued important intellectual debts and developed lasting friendships with Bernie Morris and Dick Stryker. The encouragement given us by the late James Scobie was a great boost during the early years of our careers. These teachers took the hard edge off graduate study while providing role models for what we wished one day to become.

We made more than a dozen research trips to Nicaragua between 1982 and 1988, in the course of which we accumulated debts to hundreds of Nicaraguans. These "Nicas," who came from all walks and stations of life, always received us graciously, sharing the story of their struggle and the vision of their hope. Very often we could see they were busy with more important tasks, but they took time for us anyway. This contact with a suffering but generous people was the single most valuable aspect of five years of research and writing. Among the many who helped us, we would like especially to acknowledge and thank Ricardo and Milagros Chavarría and their parents, who provided warm hospitality on more than one occasion, Gustavo Parajón, Jorge Samper, Sixto Ulloa, and Roger Zavala.

David Perry of the University of North Carolina Press has been a sympathetic and helpful editor. His enthusiasm for our project and his patience and encouragement as we labored through final drafts have been crucial to its success. Thanks are owed to Carmelita Shepelwich, who typed the first draft of the entire manuscript, and to Jim Riddlesperger and Carlos Miranda, who not only maintained their optimism in the face of successive hurdles, but actually solved the computer problems that enabled us to complete the book within sight of our deadline. Our spouses and children know better than we what costs a project of this duration can exact on family life. To Annette and Tom we acknowledge the importance of your unselfish support. To Kelly and Eric, Nancy and Ellen Clelia we raise the hope that your generation will learn to live in peace with Nicaragua.

Part One

Religion and Modern Democratic Revolutions

The Nicaraguan Revolution
and Its Antecedents

The Nicaraguan Revolution was the first popular political rebellion in modern Latin America to be carried out with the active participation and support of the Christian churches. From the late 1960s onward a vital nucleus of Catholics and Protestants found that their religious faith offered strong motives to join the cause of popular insurrection. These religiously motivated participants in the struggle against the Somoza dictatorship came from all walks of life and all sectors of society, and during a crucial period of Nicaraguan history their aspirations coincided with the goals of more secular actors in Nicaragua's political drama. The result was an unprecedented fusion of the religious and the profane in the making of a Latin American revolution.

In this respect the Nicaraguan Revolution stands apart from the other two major Latin American revolutions, those of Mexico and Cuba. The Mexican Revolution was militantly anticlerical because the church was seen by revolutionary groups as one of the most reactionary elements in society. The Catholic church had been closely allied to the dictatorship of Porfirio Díaz (1877–1910), which fell to the revolutionary movement, and it bitterly resisted the general thrust of the revolution. As a result, the Mexican constitution of 1917 dealt harshly with the church, abolishing its right to own property, reducing its control over education, denying political rights to the clergy, and giving the state legal jurisdiction over the church.

In Cuba the Catholic church played no significant role in the armed struggle that overthrew the dictatorship of Fulgencio Batista (1934–44, 1952–58), preferring to stand aside from the conflict, while occasionally criticizing both sides. However, when Fidel Castro's 26th of July Movement defeated Batista and set Cuba on the path of Marxist revolution, the church moved quickly, although ineffectively, into militant opposition. Within a few years, and particularly after the Bay of Pigs invasion of April 1961, in which some clergy were implicated, there was a mass exodus of religious personnel from Cuba, leaving an already weak church even more enfeebled. As a consequence, the church has had to struggle to establish a minimal Christian presence in Cuba's revolutionary society and has lost its predominant position in such areas as education and the regulation of family life.

It is true that the Nicaraguan Revolution shares important features with its predecessors in Mexico and Cuba. For instance, a major objective of the Nicaraguan revolutionaries was to diminish U.S. influence in their domestic politics and limit foreign control over the nation's resources. Indeed, all three revolutions were marked by this "anti-Yankee" stance, which derived in each case from a long history of U.S. intervention.[1] Similarly, in each country the revolution was driven by a powerful impulse to destroy an old order of privilege and corruption by redistributing power and wealth. Because the old regimes were closely identified with U.S. intervention, the two central features of these revolutions were mutually reinforcing. They took on the appearance of being as much revolts against the United States as they were rebellions against an antiquated oligarchy and a repressive military.[2]

In the case of Cuba the revolution moved decisively toward socialism and its leaders openly espoused Marxist doctrines. Sandinista leaders in Nicaragua, on the other hand, while candidly acknowledging the Cuban influence in their revolutionary movement, have insisted on the uniqueness of their revolution.[3] Although some top Sandinista leaders publicly professed allegiance to Marxist principles, Daniel Ortega, shortly before being elected president of Nicaragua in November 1984, took pains to differentiate the Nicaraguan Revolution from both Cuba and Chile. "We're not imitating any country in particular," he said, "but we have sought the contribution of the experiences of other countries." Ortega went on to compare the Nicaraguan Revolution to the Algerian Revolution, presumably in order to underscore its nationalist aspect. Within Latin America, he said, "we would see it as being close to what the Mexican process has been."[4] When asked whether he himself was a Marxist-Leninist, Ortega responded that the issue of Marxism was "secondary." He then proceeded to argue that strict Marxist principles could hardly be applied in a country such as Nicaragua, which, in his words, "is not a country where there are conditions for a class struggle."[5]

At this point it is not our intention to assess the merits of competing claims that Nicaragua is, or is not, "another Cuba," although Daniel

Ortega's comment causes one to wonder just what sort of Marxist he is.[6] Instead, we want to draw the reader's attention to one important way in which the Nicaraguan Revolution is demonstrably different from both the Cuban and the Mexican cases. Neither the Reagan administration's strident claims that the Sandinista Revolution is a facsimile of Cuba, nor Daniel Ortega's claim that it most closely resembles Mexico's experience some six decades earlier, should be allowed to obscure one essential fact: unlike Cuba and Mexico, there was striking support for revolution within Nicaragua's religious communities. As a consequence, the Sandinistas' attitude toward religion and the churches was quite different, being on the whole much more open and positive than was true in earlier Latin American revolutions.

At the same time, it is not surprising that the Nicaraguan Revolution provoked controversy and hostility, particularly in the United States. The Somoza dynasty was too obviously dependent on U.S. support for it to have been otherwise. Much of the frustration and rage that was vented through the popular insurrection was aimed directly at the National Guard, which was the United States' most visible link to the repressive power system in Nicaragua. Only weeks before the National Guard collapsed under the military and political pressure brought to bear by the guerrilla army, the Carter administration tried to ease the discredited dictator, Anastasio Somoza Debayle, from office while preserving military power in the Guards' hands. The Carter plan provided no role for the Sandinistas in a transitional government.[7] These machinations only added to the reservoir of suspicion with which the revolutionaries already regarded the United States and its key policy makers.

To make matters worse, the Nicaraguan Revolution took place at a time when other U.S. allies were also confronting popular rebellions. The fall of the Shah of Iran to a vehemently nationalistic and anti-U.S. revolution jolted Washington. Then, the taking of U.S. hostages in Teheran inflamed nationalist sentiment throughout the United States itself. Thus, when Nicaragua's neighbor, El Salvador, appeared to be headed for a full-scale revolution in early 1980, a sense of crisis enveloped the American body politic. Jingoistic claims about the spread of communism in America's own "back yard" suffused debates over foreign policy. Increasingly, Nicaragua came to be a focal point of American anger and frustration at the drift of events in the Third World. The Nicaraguan Revolution fell prey to bitter polemics within the American political arena. Extraordinary efforts were undertaken to prove that Nicaragua was a threat to the security of the United States.

One important consequence of these developments was that the religious presence in the Nicaraguan Revolution was first obscured, and then distorted in the mass media. Initially, in its haste to persuade the American public and U.S. allies that the Sandinistas were Marxist-Leninists loyal to Moscow, the Reagan administration repeatedly characterized the Sandinista Revolution as the work of a tiny, despotic minority who had betrayed the "true" democrats and were indifferent to the sentiments of the people. This view depreciated the popular character of the insurrection, and it ignored the prominent, ongoing role played by the churches and by individual Christians. But as scholars and journalists devoted increasing attention to Nicaragua—partly in response to the administration's cries of alarm—it began to be clear that there was much more to the story. In the course of time the undeniable Christian presence in the revolution took its own prominent place in the heated debates over U.S. policy in Central America.

As U.S. policy toward Nicaragua became more and more controversial in the early 1980s, competing claims about the nature of the Sandinista Revolution were increasingly polarized. Religious groups in the United States became heavily involved in the issue, commissioning studies and publishing reports that drew extensively on the testimony of Nicaraguan Christians who defended the legitimacy of the revolution.[8] Meanwhile, the Reagan administration, together with religious groups sympathetic to its Central American policy, organized a vigorous campaign of "public diplomacy" designed to show that the revolution was not legitimate, in part because it was antireligious. In 1983 both the White House and the State Department opened offices that were charged with publicizing this view and with shaping public opinion accordingly.[9] The result of this bitter clash of viewpoints was not to clarify the complex religious and political situation in Nicaragua, but rather to distort it by casting it within rigid ideological categories. At the level of general public discourse the issue became a set of antithetical alternatives: one voice repeated the syllogism that since the Sandinista Revolution was Marxist-Leninist, it must be antireligious and therefore an enemy of the church; another proclaimed that because the Sandinistas not only tolerated but encouraged religious pluralism and freedom of worship, their revolution must be democratic. The former view collided harshly with the fact of broad religious liberty in Nicaragua. The latter view did not seem to account for the deep divisions over the revolution that afflicted the Christian churches within Nicaragua.

The conclusion to be drawn from these preliminary observations is that religion has played a vital and far-reaching role in the Nicaraguan Revolution, but the precise nature and significance of that role have not been explained adequately. Because Nicaragua has figured so prominently in U.S. foreign policy over the past decade, this important aspect of the Nicaraguan Revolution needs to be understood. Beyond the policy implications, there is the puzzle of religion's influencing a process of revolution that is simultaneously shaped by Marxism. Is there not an unbridgeable gulf between Marxism and Christianity? To put the matter differently, can religion coexist with a Marxist revolution, and indeed influence that revolution across time according to its own values? Finally, can a revolution that professes adherence to the tenets of Marxism also be democratic? What sort of democratic revolution would it be and what influence, if any, would the religious factor have in making it democratic?

The central theme of this book is the interplay of religion and political revolution. The more closely we looked at the Nicaraguan Revolution, the more we became convinced that neither Cuba nor Mexico enabled us fully to understand the Nicaraguan case. Insofar as religion was concerned, these revolutions imitated the French Revolution: they were anticlerical, and they tended to view religious teachings and church practices as reactionary. In our search for more useful precedents, we were led to examine our own North American political heritage.

The results of our initial inquiries surprised and intrigued us, and so we have pursued them in the writing of this book. We became convinced that, from the standpoint of religion and its role in revolution, the English and American revolutions provide more interesting parallels to the Nicaraguan Revolution than do the French, Mexican, or Cuban revolutions. In both the English revolution of the 1640s and the American Revolution of the 1770s, religious belief was a strong catalyst to political action. When the layers of rhetoric are peeled away in the contemporary debate over Central America, the fusion of Christian motives with political struggle in the Nicaraguan Revolution reveals striking similarities to the English and American revolutions.

We do not say that the Nicaraguan Revolution is a copy of these two revolutions, any more than it is a copy of Cuba's. However, our perspective may foster a more historically sensitive approach to the broad forces of change that are at work in Central America by elaborating on the historical antecedents to revolution in both halves of the Americas. It may also enable us to see what is truly new and different in the Nicaraguan experience. This book examines the dramatic changes in religious life that have taken place in Nicaragua over the past two decades, placing those changes within the dynamic framework of political revolution and counterrevolution that have made this tiny country so important and so fascinating.

Studying Religion and Revolution

Historically, the Latin American Catholic church was closely identified with the status quo and was apt to oppose any sort of revolutionary movement. Roman Catholicism was a formative and sustaining element of the traditional social order, as will be shown more fully in Chapter 3. In traditional societies religion typically played a key role in societal integration: it served to buttress established authority and to justify existing distributions of power, responsibility, and privilege. In the case of Latin America, Roman Catholicism fostered "a tradition of ideas and values which are clearly antagonistic to various aspects of modernization. An integralist concept of a hierarchical society and a pronounced preference for authoritarian rule are prominent components of the Ibero-Catholic heritage."[10]

The conservative impact of Catholicism's teachings was reinforced by its mode of ecclesiastical organization. Authority within the church was centralized and hierarchical. Moral guidance, and even salvation itself, were mediated through the teaching authority of the church and the dispensation of the sacraments. This system of church organization placed "the believer in a position of extreme dependence upon the clergy."[11]

Viewed from this vantage point Catholicism was correctly seen as an extremely influential conservative force in Western society, and certainly in Latin America. A number of excellent recent studies of the Catholic church in Latin America have accepted this basic point, but without accepting the corollary proposition that is easily and commonly drawn. Writers like Daniel H. Levine, Scott Mainwaring, and Brian H. Smith argue against the conclusion that an institutionalized religion such as Roman Catholicism can only be "a conservative force that palliates the suffering of the masses and bolsters the domination of elites."[12] Their studies have shown that even as conservative a church as Roman Catholicism in Latin America can, under certain circumstances, become a source of renewal and innovation.

In this regard we have been as influenced as have the above-mentioned authors by the seminal work of Max Weber on religion and social change. We are particularly influenced by Weber's characterization of the dynamic relationship between religious ideas and the social behavior of believers. Weber rejected Marx's notion that religious ideas were merely a reflection of class interests, arguing instead that they had an autonomy of their own, and that they could stand in creative tension with individual or class interests.[13] Weber's concept of "elective affinity" is less deterministic than Marx's historical materialism in that it allows for a more open-ended relationship between religious ideas and individual or group actions.

From time to time traditional religious systems spawn innovators who reemphasize or reformulate existing elements of the faith. This often takes the form of prophetic renewal: if the ideas of the "prophet" are elected by a mass of followers (because the mass of followers have an "affinity" with those ideas), then a potent convergence of belief and material interest can take place.[14] In such instances religious beliefs become a source of social change. Explaining how and why material interests and religious beliefs converge is the task of the researcher, and the answers may be as varied as the settings where rebellion or revolution occur.

In the next two chapters we will examine the intertwining of religious and political revolutions in the political heritage of the Anglo-American tradition. We wish to show that the English and American experiences are instructive historical antecedents to the pattern of religious and political change seen in Central America today. A prophetic current set loose by the Reformation helped to instigate a strong demand for democratization in seventeenth-century England. Through the process of colonization this same religious current later helped to shape the social and political life of New England, culminating in the drive for American independence. In each of these settings changes in religious thought and action were carried along within, but also stimulated and strengthened, a wider movement for social change. The influence between the religious movement and the secular was reciprocal, each adding impetus to the other.

Consider the setting of the English revolution. At the beginning of the seventeenth century, English society was pervasively authoritarian, a fact reinforced by religious customs and teachings. The social order was rigid and static, although the forces of change were beginning to appear. Political authority was centralized and power was exercised by an aristocratic class—a landed elite that filled local offices and sent its own representatives to Parliament, where they governed in concert with the king. The Crown controlled the Church of England so that church, Crown, and aristocracy were mutually confirming authorities in a hierarchical world.

Mid-twentieth-century Central America bore a remarkable resemblance to the England of the 1640s. Political activity was the exclusive domain of a tiny minority consisting of a landed oligarchy, the military, and the urban middle class. Nicaragua varied from this pattern only in the degree to which a single family dominated the nation's political life. Elections were elitist (and invariably fraudulent). The National Guard enforced electoral outcomes whether they reflected the popular will or not. The political system was authoritarian, and the distorting character of *Somocismo* merely exaggerated the profoundly antidemocratic character of Nicaraguan politics. The vast majority of Nicaraguans were poor, illiterate, and unorganized, and lacked the means to defend their interests.

Among the many factors that conspired to alter each of these societies, two stand out. First, economic change and disruption caused significant social dislocation, thus accentuating other grievances. Second, the struggle to rearticulate religious beliefs and practices, and to redistribute religious authority, helped to turn the society "upside down."[15] In Chapter 2 we will examine these factors at work in the English revolution, suggesting some of the ways in which the English experience foreshadows that of Nicaragua.

In Nicaragua, as elsewhere in Central America, the church also became a source of revolutionary thought and action because it momentarily recovered its prophetic tradition. This recovery generated deep religious change and sharp social conflict. From that religious change grew a demand for political liberation. It is much more likely that Nicaraguan peasants and shantytown dwellers fought in the insurrection and thought of themselves as Sandinistas because of religious conviction and hatred for Somocista despotism than because they had converted to Marxism. The vibrancy of religious life in post-triumph Nicaragua is testimony to this assertion.

But how are North American scholars, particularly ones socialized in a Protestant culture and reared in the Protestant faith, to approach the complex question of religious change in a Catholic country like Nicaragua? Early on in this joint venture we decided it was essential to speak with as many people as we could from all walks of life. The Nicaraguan process afforded the unusual opportunity to observe and analyze a revolution as it unfolded. Given the extreme underdevelopment of Nicaragua, there was relatively little documentary material from before the insurrection; therefore, despite the appearance of several excellent studies of the revolution soon after the triumph,[16] we realized that to study the role played by religious actors we could not rely on documentary research alone. Our problem was compounded by the fact that much of our interest focused on change at the grass roots where few written records existed. The onset of the Contra war only made matters worse. Thus, for example, no complete inventory of Christian base communities (*comunidades eclesiales de base*, or CEBs), existed that would have enabled us to randomize a sample selection and formulate a questionnaire, the demographic and attitudinal responses to which could be tabulated and analyzed statistically. We never seriously entertained the possibility of survey research. Instead, over a period of nearly eight years we conducted hundreds of interviews that fall more properly within the domain of specialized interviewing wherein the researcher poses an initial question, which allows the respondent ample latitude to respond as he or she chooses. We did use a standardized set of questions for these interviews, with some modifications to accommodate Catholic or Protestant respondents. Wherever possible we have identified our respondents; in cases where we have not done so, we deemed it necessary to respect the respondent's confidentiality.

As our research progressed, it became apparent to us that some voices were heard more than others. It was relatively easy to determine the views of the bishops' conference on a broad range of issues—these were a matter of the public record. It was far more difficult to get a sense of what Christians at the grass roots thought in diverse regions of the country. Hence, we tried particularly to seek out persons and groups whose voice did not carry much beyond the borders of their barrio or village. This work represents a sustained effort to understand the motives of those who live at the margins of Nicaraguan society, and to place their actions within the larger context of the Nicaraguan Revolution.

We tried to enlarge upon our interviews by placing them within the social setting of the respondent's community. Wherever possible we became participant observers. We attended meetings of CEBs throughout Nicaragua, and also meetings with leaders of CEB organizational networks in Managua, Estelí, Matagalpa, and Chinandega. We attended church services of the "traditional" Catholic churches in more privileged neighborhoods, as well as the more participatory services of the "prophetic" churches. Our research has also been informed by the differing styles and perspectives of *La Hoja Dominical*, the Sunday reflection that is printed by the archdiocese of Managua and represents the views of the traditional church, on the one hand, and of *El Tayacán*, a more recent publication of the "prophetic" church, on the other.

The Protestant community in Nicaragua has also played a role in the making of the Nicaraguan Revolution, and it was essential to capture this experience as fully as we could. We have conducted many interviews over the past eight years with leaders from CEPAD (Comité Evangélico Pro-Ayuda al Desarollo), the Protestant development agency, which maintains a constructive and supportive relationship with the Nicaraguan government while carrying out its own programs and projects. At the height of the Contra war we traveled with these Protestant leaders to border areas such as Ocotal, a town devastated by Contra attack in June 1984. We attended workshops conducted for pastors working in rural areas, many of which had suffered the trauma first of the insurrection, then of the Contra war.

Other Protestant groups have advocated a more spiritual, less politically committed position for their members. Since 1983 the leaders of these groups have come together in a fledgling organization called the National Council of Evangelical Pastors (Consejo Nacional de Pastores Evangélicos de Nicaragua, CNPEN). Although it would be inaccurate to equate CNPEN with CEPAD in terms of size or strength, these pastors have voiced strong opinions and we have sought them out to hear those opinions. This grouping represents an "otherworldly" wing of Central American Protestantism that has grown rapidly not only in Nicaragua but in other Central American nations.

Our book is divided into three parts. The aim of Part 1 is to provide a historical frame of reference from which to assess both the struggle for a democratizing revolution in Central America and the role of the churches in that struggle. Chapter 2 examines the public debate over Nicaragua, highlighting the importance of competing claims about "democracy," and then offers a critical commentary on the variety of democratic experience. Chapters 3 and 4 then compare North and

Central America as "colonial fragments," contrasting the democratizing heritage of the United States' colonial experience with the antidemocratic heritage of Central America. We show that an intense surge of prophetic religious activity in England and in colonial North America stimulated the quest for democratization and for national independence, respectively.

The nature of the Catholic church and its historic impact on society and politics in Central America are treated in Chapter 4 and also in Chapter 5, which introduces Part 2. Part 2 is concerned with the historic shift within Roman Catholicism that led a deeply conservative and traditional church to foster prophetic impulses that continue to reverberate throughout Latin America. Our discussion highlights the Reformation-like character of postconciliar change. Chapter 7 details the specific nature and consequences of these changes in the case of Nicaragua, a country that underwent a social and political revolution at the end of the 1970s.

Once the revolution was under way the diverse groups that made up the revolutionary movement began to jockey for influence and control over the shape and direction of the new order. The churches soon found themselves enmeshed in this struggle to define the revolution. While Christians helped to make the revolution, they did so from diverse or even competing theological (and political) positions. Consequently, their expectations for the new society to be constructed were not always compatible. The struggle to define the Christian presence in the Nicaraguan Revolution, as well as what sort of democratic character the revolution will have, is the subject of Part 3 of this book.

Two

A Crisis Erupts in Central America

Introduction

During the summer of 1979 an unusual thing happened to Central America: it became important in the eyes of others. The focus of attention was Nicaragua—physically the largest country in Central America, but even so a tiny nation with a total population of less than three million. What attracted attention were the convulsive events of a political revolution. The Nicaraguan people were carrying out a massive popular uprising against the corrupt and repressive Somoza dictatorship, which had dominated the country for over four decades. Their struggle captured the attention and imagination of North Americans, who were able to witness its progress on the nightly news. Television brought home to those viewers the indiscriminate brutality of the Somoza regime: scenes of the National Guard beating civilians, and glimpses of the Air Force bombing civilian neighborhoods, were daily fare. U.S. audiences even witnessed the senseless murder of American news reporter Bill Stewart by a young National Guardsman. The widespread revulsion provoked by these events hastened the rift between the Somoza regime and the U.S. government, which had long been its principal benefactor.[1] Lacking essential support from abroad and facing an armed mass uprising at home, the Somocista political system crumbled throughout the month of June. When Anastasio Somoza fled to Miami in mid-July the regime collapsed totally.

Nicaragua's insurrection brought to power a political movement, the Sandinista Front of National Liberation (Frente Sandinista de Liberación Nacional, FSLN), that was committed to a revolutionary transformation of the society. In the eyes of U.S. officials Nicaragua was now perceived as strategically important—not so much in its own right, but for what it portended. Nicaragua's troubles could easily be repeated elsewhere because the conditions that had provoked the popular uprising there were equally present, even if in unique configurations, in most countries of the region. In this sense, the internal developments that produced the Nicaraguan Revolution marked a potential turning point in Central America's political history.

Within Nicaragua the insurrection raised the possibility, and the hope, that for the first time in its history the nation's political order might be constructed on a broad base of mass participation. For the region more generally it raised the specter of political change in countries where an alliance of the oligarchy and the military had long dominated, but where broadly based popular movements were gaining strength. It was this second implication that made Central America important to Washington from a strategic standpoint. The fear of spreading instability, which was subsequently overlaid with a heavy dose of anticommunism, led U.S. policy toward Nicaragua to take on the mission of "rollback," thus putting Washington's sense of geostrategic necessity on a collision course with Managua's project of "national reconstruction" and nation-building.[2] The solution that the Reagan administration attempted to implement amounted to a sustained war against Nicaragua. In that war, struggle at the ideological and diplomatic levels was about as important as military confrontation, and the ideological struggle tended to center on competing claims about who and what could promote democracy in Central America.

Not since the early days of the Eisenhower administration, when the government of Jacobo Arbenz in Guatemala was defined as a serious threat to hemispheric security, had U.S. officials shown such a keen interest in Central America. Under the Reagan administration that interest was expressed through a steady barrage of inflamed rhetoric: Nicaragua was accused of an astonishing range of political sins and described repeatedly as a dire threat to Mexico and the United States, as well as to the rest of Central America. The "rollback" policy that such rhetoric sought to justify generated intense controversy, while the rhetoric itself contributed to a polarization of views in the public discourse.

The result was an odd spectacle: a noisy, fractious debate was being conducted in a large and powerful democratic society concerning the future of democracy in a small, troubled neighbor that had scarcely known democracy in the past. And the bitter irony was that many Nicaraguans blamed their lack of democratic development on prior U.S. interventions. What made the situation even more nettlesome was the profound disagreement between outspoken U.S. officials and the Sandinistas in Nicaragua as to what form democracy must take in an underdeveloped peasant society—the same disagreement that divided ordinary citizens in each country. In short, passionate, rhetorically excessive claims were put forward concerning Nicaragua, Central America, and the security of the western hemisphere. These claims rested on conflicting assumptions about what conditions would foster democratic politics. In the public debate there was little considered discussion of what the range of democratic possibilities might be, or of what social forces give rise to democracy in the first place.

The Nicaraguan Revolution is still in its early stages, being just nine years old at this writing. For many of those nine years high-level U.S. policy makers sounded incessant warnings that democratic principles and institutions were at risk in Central America. They seized every opportunity to assert that U.S. policy was rooted in democratic values, and that it would nurture democratic institutions among Nicaragua's neighbors. This posture was exemplified vividly in President Ronald Reagan's unusual speech to a joint session of Congress on April 27, 1983, in which he contended that a crisis had burst forth in the Caribbean Basin, one that directly affected the security and well-being of the American people. Having recognized this threat, both the Carter administration and his own had shouldered the burden of defending freedom. The president made it clear that Nicaragua had caused this crisis and was the primary threat to our freedom: while the United States had tried to befriend the new government, the Sandinistas treated the United States as an enemy, threatened its neighbors, and were intent on imposing "a new dictatorship" at home. The Sandinistas, Reagan argued, were determined to abolish freedom and democratic rights in Nicaragua. Their regime was, he said, "even worse than its predecessor."[3]

President Reagan's speech to Congress served as a green light to other high officials, signaling that the war of words against Nicaragua had been declared. Subsequently, the perspective articulated in that speech was presented over and over again, at times in even more incendiary language, by other U.S. officials. As Langhorne Motley, assistant secretary of state for inter-American affairs, put it in July 1984, "[t]he export of violence by Cuba and Nicaragua with Soviet backing is the principle [sic] external threat to democracy in the hemisphere."[4] The passage of time only led to an intensification of the rhetoric. By late 1985 President Reagan described Nicaragua this way: "Nicaragua today is an imprisoned nation. It is a nation condemned to unrelenting cruelty by a clique of very cruel men—by a dictator in designer glasses and his comrades, drunk with power and all its brutal applications."[5] He went on to charge the Sandinista leaders with abuse and persecution of the church, which he implied was opposed to the revolution, and with complicity in terrorist attacks in other countries of Latin America.

These were astonishing accusations to make against the leaders of another country, particularly one with which the United States maintained diplomatic relations. The language used far exceeded the normal bounds of diplomatic courtesy. Neither the Carter nor the Reagan administration used this sort of language to portray such notorious human rights abusers as Guatemala and Chile. Apparently there was something about the Nicaraguan Revolution that made it seem especially ominous to Washington.

Let us look briefly at what U.S. policy makers have had to say about the importance of democracy in Central America and the prospects for achieving it. We should bear in mind that an important aspect of the democracy question has been the role of churches in the struggle for change. Religion (together with religious freedom) has been the subject of highly polemical charges and countercharges in the debate over Nicaragua. In no small measure this is because the churches have occupied an important place in the unfolding process of revolution.

Promoting Democracy in Latin America

The United States favors democratic government for Central America. This is an article of faith with U.S. officials. In a typically unqualified statement, Assistant Secretary Motley once said, "it is U.S. government policy to support democracy and democratic institutions."[6] President Reagan went even further, stating in a speech at Georgetown University in April 1984 that "Americans have always wanted to see the spread of democratic institutions, and that goal is coming closer."[7] Now, it is true that before 1979 as many as "two-thirds of our neighbors lived under military or military-dominated governments of both left and right."[8] However, according to American leaders there was a dramatic turnaround after that fateful year of 1979: as a result of holding nearly three dozen elections in a four-year period, "more than 90% of the people of Latin America and the Caribbean are now living in countries with governments that are either democratic or heading there."[9]

One might well ask, as Secretary Motley did, "what lies behind this region-wide upsurge in democratic politics?" U.S. officials pointed to "voter desire to repudiate both dictators and guerrillas."[10] However, the speeches and reports conveying this explanation said little about repudiating the military dictatorships that were so widespread in Latin America during the 1970s, nor did they dwell on the persistence of military control of elected governments in such friendly countries as El Salvador and Guatemala. Rather, the emphasis was placed on repudiating guerrilla movements, and attention was focused on the small nations of Central America. American leaders insisted that the dictatorship implicit in guerrilla-based movements was a major threat to Central America, even though the general populace, according to Washington, rejected the appeals of the insurgents.

U.S. officials traced the threat against democracy to "political extremism" in Nicaragua. According to Secretary Motley's report to the House Foreign Affairs Committee, right-wing extremism had few sources of external support, and therefore it posed little danger to Central and South America today. Left-wing extremism, however, had an aggressive source of external support in Cuba and the Soviet Union.[11] As President Reagan explained it, "from the moment the Sandinistas and their cadre of 50 Cuban covert advisors took power in Managua in July of 1979, the internal repression of democratic groups, trade unions and civic groups began." Sandinista rule soon became a "communist reign of terror."[12] Since this reign of terror was made for export, Nicaragua was the primary threat to democracy in the hemisphere.

Many U.S. citizens have been puzzled to hear the president and other political leaders say that a country as small and weak as Nicaragua represents such a threat to democracy. The surface implausibility of the claim probably accounts for the hyperbole. But, even though many listeners might be skeptical of the president's answer, they would nonetheless be sympathetic with the question to which it was responding: "Who shall govern and under what forms—[these] are the central issues in country after country throughout Latin America and the Caribbean."[13] Who should govern indeed, and how? In the spirit of democracy one would think that these are questions to be answered by the Latin Americans themselves. However, U.S. policy makers have urged Americans to oppose the Nicaraguan Revolution on the grounds that it represents tyranny, not democracy, while insisting that the democratization of the rest of Central America was directly threatened by the Sandinista Revolution.

In the validity of such claims as these lay the burden of United States policy toward Central America during the 1980s. A consistent effort was made in Washington to buttress these claims by arguing that the Sandinista Revolution gravely jeopardized the churches and religious freedom. The assumption is that left-wing revolutions are inherently hostile to religion. Consequently, political struggle over religion in revolutionary Nicaragua can also be blamed on the Sandinistas; it is prima facie evidence that their regime is antidemocratic. Let us examine that aspect of the issue a bit more closely.

Throughout the 1970s and early 1980s religion was highly politicized in Central America. In each country, but especially in those experiencing the severest social conflicts, church groups and clergy were prominently involved in political life.[14] Nicaragua merely exemplified the common pattern. In El Salvador particularly, a large number of religious persons were victimized in political violence. However, the Reagan administration consistently treated Nicaragua as though it were the only country where politics had a major impact on religious life, and vice versa. It portrayed that impact as one of religious persecution by an authoritarian state. For example, a February 1984 issue of the *White House Digest* contended that in Nicaragua "the self-admitted Marxist-Leninist leaders of the government are seeking to turn the Catholic Church into an arm of the government."[15] State Department spokesman Alan Romberg has referred to the "long pattern of harassment and intimidation against the Catholic Church by the Sandinistas."[16]

This perspective has been echoed widely in the U.S. media. For example, on April 20, 1984, ABC News carried a report from Managua about a Good Friday procession led by Archbishop Miguel Obando y Bravo. The procession was described as a "passionate demonstration of solidarity with the Catholic Church," as a "defiant gesture," and as "an explicit rebuff to Sandinista leaders." The report concluded by comparing the situation in the Nicaraguan church to that of Poland, suggesting that support of the Catholic church and its top leaders "means no to marxism."[17] A story in the *Washington Post* in July quoted Archbishop Obando, who was referring to tensions between church and state in Nicaragua, as saying: "Regimes that are totalitarian try to destroy the church."[18]

Whatever their source in the United States, these views have been contested energetically by a wide variety of religious groups in Nicaragua itself. Responding to President Reagan's speech to Congress, Catholics representing more than a dozen religious orders declared:

"As religious workers in Nicaragua we have found that we are free—
and encouraged—to exercise the preferential option for the poor
stressed by the Latin American bishops at Medellín and Puebla."[19] On
the Protestant side, the Baptist Convention of Nicaragua stated: "We
are convinced that the general features of the government of Nicaragua are positive and are generating a new level of life for us, one
which is more dignified and human."[20] This view is far from reflecting
the "reign of terror" depicted by President Reagan. Still more em-
phatically, five hundred members of CEBs in Nicaragua signed a declaration that said: "As part of the process of the New Nicaragua, we
recognize that there are errors and faults and we will struggle to
overcome them. But even though errors and faults exist, there is
something new, basically positive and fully in accord with the gospel—a project of the poor, a project of justice and fraternity, a search
for a new man and a new society. As Christians we recognize the
liberating presence of God in the midst of our process. . . ."[21]

These clashing viewpoints illustrate how disputed is the role of
religion and the churches in revolutionary Nicaragua. From the beginning of its tenure the Reagan administration defined the foreign policy
challenge of Central America almost exclusively with reference to
Nicaragua, which it saw as a Cuban-Soviet proxy. In choosing to view
Central America through an East-West lens, Washington forsook a
potentially fruitful alternative: Nicaragua is important, they might
have said, because of the nature of its revolution and what that
revolution suggests about the demand for new political institutions
throughout the region; because of similar conditions and possibilities
in neighboring countries, the rest of Central America is important too.

Each of these interpretive frameworks directs attention to democratic possibilities in Central America—yet the two frameworks derive
from premises that are radically different. The first defines Nicaragua
as antidemocratic using a priori, definitional criteria. The reasoning is
straightforward, if simplistic. The FSLN is a Marxist revolutionary
organization. Consequently its first loyalty must be to the larger international Communist movement. Predictably, therefore, it will ally
itself with Cuba and the Soviet Union, engage in subversive activity
toward its neighbors, and impose a totalitarian dictatorship at home.
In the face of such a regime the only sensible course of action for the
United States is to guarantee the security of Nicaragua's neighbors by
preventing "another Nicaragua" in Central America. As the administration's policy took shape in the early 1980s it also became clear that

its ultimate objective vis-à-vis Nicaragua was the overthrow of the Sandinista government.

The second scenario, however, allows for seeing democratic possibilities in the process of the Nicaraguan Revolution itself. This alternative approach would encourage curiosity about the history and the indigenous causes of the Nicaraguan Revolution, and would foster inquiry into the political conditions of popular demand-making in other Central American nations. Such an approach would enable North Americans to see the present situation in Central America as the regional crisis that it is, not as the Nicaraguan crisis that Washington imagines it to be. Nevertheless, the Reagan administration worked tirelessly to shape the domestic debate over Central America so that it was conducted within the parameters of the first scenario. Meanwhile, in Central America the second approach informed the thinking of many who sought a solution to the regional crisis.

One of the most serious deficiencies of the Reagan administration's approach was that it ignored or misunderstood the post-Medellín history of change in the Latin American churches. In Central America religious innovation galvanized millions of poor people, as well as countless clergy and religious women. New ways of understanding faith and salvation, new types of religious communities, and new styles of pastoral action organized and motivated previously apolitical Christians to demand a fundamental restructuring of the social order. Such Christians played a vital role in the Nicaraguan Revolution and are heavily involved in the political struggle in El Salvador. This new religious current has been a potent vehicle for the expression of demands for democratization.

Thus, the question of democracy seems to lie at the center of the fears and hopes that arose out of the Nicaraguan Revolution, and so too does the role of religion in promoting democratic change. When the Catholic church was implanted in Central America during the sixteenth century it played an important political role by legitimating the imposition of a centralized, authoritarian state that neither permitted dissent nor promoted the participation of ordinary people. Today new questions are being asked about the church's mission in society and its exercise of influence in the political arena. While some elements of the church cling to the authoritarian past, others appear to embrace a revolutionary present.

What does the present struggle in Central America teach us about the relationship of religion and democracy? U.S. policy makers would provide a safe environment for religion by overthrowing the present government of Nicaragua and defeating guerrilla movements elsewhere in Central America. To Nicaraguan Christians who support the revolution, Christian struggle has already produced a democratizing movement in Nicaragua and elsewhere in the region. To them the aim of U.S. policy is to bring about in Nicaragua a regime that is necessarily undemocratic because it will be imposed by an external power. Such a regime would represent profound continuity with Nicaragua's decidedly undemocratic past.

One contention of this book is that the relationship between religion and democracy cannot be conceptualized properly by formulating two mutually exclusive models: one, a model of incipient totalitarianism, guided by a Marxist ideology that uses, then discards the church and destroys religion; the other, a model of incipient democracy in which politics serves to vouchsafe religion, guaranteeing the right of churches to organize the faithful in pursuit of spiritual fulfillment. U.S. policy makers have portrayed Nicaragua as the first model incarnate—indeed, they have acted on their belief that overthrowing the Nicaraguan government is a necessary step to make possible the achievement of the second model. This view misunderstands the recent history of Central America, including the changes in the postconciliar church. It also distorts the history and nature of democracy itself.

Varieties of Democratic Experience

A first step to clearing the ground for a productive discussion of the struggle over democracy and the fate of religion in revolutionary Nicaragua is to clarify the meaning of the word *democracy* and to specify the variety of uses that have been made of it historically. Democracy is a protean term that has been used to describe diverse political experiences over time. Careful discussion of the term should help to illustrate a central theme of this book, that the debate and struggle over the Nicaraguan Revolution is more a matter of competing visions of democracy than it is a clash between democracy and totalitarian dictatorship. This underlying reality has been obscured by those who prefer simplistic judgments and reductionist approaches, in North and Central America alike.

A word must be said about the language of politics, which is enlivened by numerous terms created to describe phenomena that are particularly or uniquely associated with political activity.[22] *Democracy* is one such distinctly political word. It has an ancient lineage, having been invented by the Greeks to describe political life in those city-states wherein the common people participated in governance through the popular assemblies. The term came into use in the fifth century B.C. to refer to political activity in which all citizens, including the poor, took an active role in exercising decision-making authority. In the ancient world democracy was most closely associated with Athens, whose philosophers and historians left such vivid accounts of it—even though not all of them approved of democratic politics. Plato, for example, condemned democracy as a form of government incompatible with human nature and incapable of achieving justice. Thucydides, on the other hand, while mindful that democracy was prone to displays of excess and bad judgment, nevertheless regarded it with admiration and eloquently chronicled its virtues as well as its defects.[23]

Etymologically speaking, the term *democracy* was invented to describe rule or governance by the people, or *demos*. But what exactly was meant by "the people"? From the beginning there was a multiplicity of meanings, for "demos" referred not only to the citizen body, but also to the lower classes sociologically speaking. When "democracy" was utilized by a writer such as Aristotle it took on still another connotation, for it implied rule by the poor, including the possibility that the poor would rule in their own interest. Rule by the lower classes in their self-interest was a "perversion" of the ends of government because the purpose of government, as Aristotle saw it, was to promote the common good.[24] The common good transcended the class interests of the poor, even if they were everywhere the majority of the *demos*, or citizenry.

Despite his concern that democracy could evolve into the self-interested rule of the poor, Aristotle acknowledged the validity of the strong arguments that could be made in its behalf. What is more, the experience of two centuries of democratic rule in Athens bore him out. To begin at the most pragmatic level, he argued that if the poor were given a voice in government their participation would contribute to political stability by preempting periodic rebellion. Aristotle's own formulation of the issue would resonate compellingly with students of contemporary Central America: "a state with a body of disenfranchised citizens who are numerous and poor must necessarily be a state which is full of enemies."[25] On the more positive side, he argued the case for the collective judgment and wisdom of the many, including the poor. When the whole citizenry is gathered together they are apt to be "either better than experts or at any rate no worse" when it comes to making decisions for the whole community.[26]

Aristotle's discussion of democracy presupposed a high level of citizen participation. In the moral scheme of things, the participatory nature of democracy was its highest virtue. Not only did democracy have the potential to bring stability by incorporating the poor man into the political community, it also provided the means of his moral education. Greek democracy compelled the common man regularly to examine the changing needs of his city, to exercise his sense of civic responsibility, and to render decisions that would affect himself and others. Democratic politics was, in short, a form of moral education or, to use the Greek term, *paideia*. This emphasis on the intrinsic value of political participation lay at the core of the Greek understanding of democracy. That Athens was the most powerful, prosperous, and stable Greek state for more than two centuries while using this system of government is also testimony to its practical effectiveness.[27]

In the modern age the word *democracy* has been given a much larger range of meaning in describing political life and political institutions. It was applied to the parliamentary systems of Europe, even when they were based on a limited franchise. Similarly, in the United States it described a republican form of government in which authority was entrusted to elected representatives rather than exercised by the citizens themselves. In the United States, furthermore, democracy was linked to the notion of limited government—meaning that it was as much what government could *not* do to you as what it could do *for* you or how directly involved you were in its decisions, that determined whether people understood it to be democratic. In the same vein a distinction was introduced between "responsive" government and "responsible" government;[28] some "democrats" preferred the latter, even though it implied less citizen participation in government. John Locke's doctrine of consent, especially tacit consent, and his claim that legitimacy in government meant having "a standing rule to live by," came to be seen as the very essence of democracy.[29] In practice, however, the doctrine of tacit consent is far removed from the Greek conception of democracy. Political obligation is inferred from the mere enjoyment of government's protection rather than being associated with active participation in the exercise of political authority, and political legitimacy derives from constitutional restraints on government action. A system of government whose legitimacy rests only on this ground need not be democratic in the original Athenian sense of the term.

The term also has been extended into other areas of human activity so that it is no longer confined strictly to governmental or political activities and institutions. For example, people speak of democratizing education when they refer to expanding the base of education to take in the lower classes or racial minorities. Or they speak of democratizing industrial relations when they refer to efforts to give factory workers a greater share in running industrial enterprises. In this book we will discuss at length the democratization of religious thought and religious institutions, which has been a vital element in earlier political revolutions just as it is in the present Central American revolutions.

R. R. Palmer has argued persuasively that the frequent and positive use of the term *democracy* in the twentieth century, particularly since World War I, is a much more unusual development than most people realize. Although Palmer traced a great democratic revolution in the West from the end of the eighteenth century, he argued that the actual term was in fact little used and little admired in England and her colonies at the time of the American Revolution. In America this was notably true of some key leaders during the fight for independence. In that time and place the word *democracy* had negative connotations; certainly, few gentlemen regarded democratic ideas in a positive light. As Palmer put it (albeit with some exaggeration, but not where the political elite was concerned), "No 'democrats' fought in the American Revolution."[30]

This assertion is supported by James Madison's treatment of democracy in the *Federalist Papers*, a decade after the Declaration of Independence. When it came to founding a government for the new United States of America, Madison was prepared to understand democracy in the ancient Greek sense, as direct rule by the people. So understood, he wanted no part of it—for he regarded it as a pernicious and dangerous form of government. In taking this position Madison rested his argument in part on the notion that, contrary to what has been said above about the relative stability and success of the democratic experience in Athens, democracy was inherently unstable. He put the matter forcefully:

... such democracies have ever been spectacles of turbulence and contention; have ever been found incompatible with personal security in the rights of property; and have in general been as short in their lives as they have been violent in their deaths. Theoretic politicians, who have patronized this species of government, have erroneously supposed that by reducing mankind to a perfect equality in their political rights, they would, at the same time, be perfectly equalized and assimilated in their possessions, their opinions and their passions.[31]

Madison did not say what theorists he had in mind, although he may have been referring to Rousseau and the democratic tradition associated with the French Revolution, which will be discussed below. However, if we take Aristotle as a fair-minded analyst of popular democracy in the ancient world, then Madison's argument is overstated, if not incorrect. Comparatively speaking, Athenian democracy was admirably stable. Moreover, it never rested on assumptions about the need to equalize property or opinion, nor did the enjoyment of equal political rights and direct participation in decision making lead to those outcomes.

Despite the historical inaccuracy of Madison's claims, his argument gave cogent expression to the prejudices of educated, propertied men in 1787. Under such leadership the United States was established as a republic, with a narrow franchise and restricted participation. Only gradually, and through political struggle over a period of two hundred years, has that republic been "democratized" by extending the franchise, thereby broadening the opportunities for ordinary people to participate.

In the twentieth century, with the rise of competitive and hostile political systems such as fascism and communism, it became obligatory to use the word *democracy* to define and justify the kind of representative political system that has evolved in the United States. This revisionism was facilitated by writers such as Joseph Schumpeter, who redefined democracy so as to restrict its meaning to the electoral process that in fact characterized the political system of countries like the United States. To Schumpeter, democracy was nothing more than the method by which the mass of ordinary people chose from among competing parties and candidates those few individuals who actually held power.[32] Not even the selection process itself had to be democratic. This view was reinforced by voter studies revealing that there was a high level of voter apathy and nonparticipation in some Western democracies, especially in the United States. Schumpeter's conceptualization, in short, transformed the original meaning of "democracy" by emptying it of the classical content that implied an active, informed, and involved citizenry.

Following Schumpeter, it is easy to equate democracy with elections, a tendency that has been pronounced in Washington's efforts to persuade the U.S. public that there was a genuine democratic transition under way in Central America during the 1980s. This approach is problematic even for advanced Western societies, where stable electoral systems are well established, because it masks serious inequalities of power and privilege. In Third World societies like those of Central America, where inequalities are pervasive, enduring, and even life threatening, and where elections have historically been a facade for perpetuating such inequalities, this revisionist approach is wholly inadequate.

These reflections lead us to another set of observations. The democratic experience in modern Western history is not limited to the Anglo-American tradition. A number of writers have suggested that, broadly speaking, there are two democratic traditions in the modern era—one characteristically Anglo-American, the other more typically French, or continental.[33] The first tradition follows the ideas of Locke and Madison, while the second follows Rousseau and Bosanquet. The Anglo-American tradition incorporates Locke's restricted notion of consent. Locke envisioned legitimate political authority as the product of a contract between the people and the government in which the people agreed to obey in return for the government's pledge to protect their rights, including especially their property rights. Such a system was entirely compatible with sharp social class differences in which only the propertied minority actually participated in government. The poor majority was left only with the right to rebel if governmental authority became oppressive.[34]

Madison added to this Lockean approach an explicit critique of democracy for its alleged tendency to foster a "tyranny of the majority." He argued for a republican form of government in which "checks and balances" were established by a written constitution and designed into the structures of government to thwart the participatory excesses of "majorities." In short, the Lockean-Madisonian approach placed greater emphasis on liberty and the protection of individual rights and constitutional stability than on the equality of citizens and the active expression of their consent through participation in the exercise of political authority. The political theories of Locke and

Madison, like the English and American revolutions with which they are associated, were "never detached from a theory of society which accepted status as a matter of course and which regarded status as not only compatible with political freedom but even as a condition of it." The democratic tradition they represent grew out of "a political rather than a social revolution."[35]

The second democratic tradition can be traced to Jean Jacques Rousseau and is epitomized in the historical setting, goals, and underlying philosophy of the French Revolution. The French Revolution was directed against privilege and status as manifested both socially and politically. It attacked a governing aristocratic class that used political power to promote its own interests, corrupting political life and oppressing the peasant majority. Inspired by Rousseau, the revolution sought initially to incorporate the lower classes into political life. To this end, it abolished legal privileges of the aristocracy and of such corporate bodies as the Catholic church, while at the same time encouraging popular participation. It promised, without fully delivering, a redistribution of land on the grounds that land ownership promoted the freedom and independence of the peasantry.

Rousseau himself had focused attention on the psychological importance of being included through participation. Active involvement of the people in political affairs elevated their own sense of dignity and provided opportunities for moral education. In other words, the Rousseauian approach implied a social revolution as well as a political one. It placed as much value on political equality and participation as it did on individual liberty and constitutional stability; indeed, it saw these values as correlative and mutually reinforcing.[36] This tendency in modern democratic theory and practice captures the participatory emphasis of the original Greek concept more fully than does the Anglo-American tradition.

The Church and Popular Mobilization

This historical perspective helps us to see why U.S. policy makers' efforts to explain political change in Central America often distort, even invert, reality. Each of these democratic traditions has its exponents in Nicaragua, El Salvador, and other countries. (For the most part we will ignore groups that espouse explicitly antidemocratic visions.) In these countries the Anglo-American tradition so ardently promoted by U.S. policy makers may have little appeal for the common people because it does not fit well with the conditions that confront the peasantry and working classes. We must remember, also, that the two traditions are not mutually exclusive: they share certain values and institutions. Each believes in liberty, for example, although they disagree on how it is best promoted. Each tradition also places a high value on consent as the proper foundation of legitimate government, but they disagree as to what constitutes consent. That is, the two traditions coexist in tension with one another, particularly as concerns such issues as political equality, participation, and privilege.

To offer a concrete example, during the period of the popular insurrection everyone in Nicaragua spoke the language of democracy as they united in opposition to the corrupt system of privilege and oppression represented in *Somocismo*. But some envisioned a transition to a new democratic system constructed in the image of the Anglo-American model, in which the competition of political parties through regular elections would guarantee the rights of all citizens. Others had in mind a system designed to accommodate what many Central Americans today call "the logic of the majorities." A partial sense of what this latter model entails was captured succinctly in Daniel Ortega's speech announcing the presidential elections that were held in November 1984. He said: "For us, democracy is organization of the people. For us, democracy is agrarian reform. For us, democracy is rights for the workers. For us, democracy is sovereignty and self-determination."[37]

Organizing the common people through the creation of associations that enhance participation and a sense of equality is an important theme treated in the pages that follow. It is a theme that calls attention to the church and to religious change. As we will see, churches stimulated and facilitated the creation of grass-roots popular organizations through which participation became possible for the poor in Central America. Through the sorts of experiences described in this book, Christians by the thousands came to an appreciation of the need for greater and more authentic participation in order to promote meaningful democratic change.

Prior to the surge of political upheaval that began in the late 1970s the general populace of Central America had been quiescent for decades. In Nicaragua the great bulk of the population had long been politically apathetic. Regular elections were never seen by the poor as a vehicle of popular expression. Under *Somocismo* political parties lacked a mass base and made appeals to the peasants and urban lower classes only in the days immediately before elections. Cynicism pervaded the body politic. The absence of political institutions designed to serve the masses, or in any way controlled by them, reinforced the natural disposition of the poor toward conservatism and political indifference. Widespread illiteracy only compounded the problem. Within this setting the Somoza dynasty ruled Nicaragua as a fiefdom, utilizing the National Guard as a personal police force to protect the interests of the ruling elite. These elements of the nation's history suggested the absence of democracy in either of the two senses discussed above.

And yet, by early 1978 Nicaragua was poised to enter a phase of transformation. The masses who previously had stood aloof from politics underwent a period of intense politicization. Their customary apathy gave way to active participation in opposition politics. For many, the path to political involvement originated in a religious awakening. Thousands of Christians, many acting from well-thought-out religious motives and with the support of grass-roots Christian communities, participated actively in the popular insurrection. Sandinista leaders later acknowledged this participation and its importance to the success of the revolution. Comandante Tomás Borge, the only surviving founder of the FSLN, has said: "both organized and unorganized Christians participated in all aspects of the revolutionary struggle that brought the Sandinista Front to power. Many, indeed, came to the revolutionary process through Christian organizations."[38] How and why it happened that Christians became an important force in the Nicaraguan Revolution is the subject of this book.[39]

To conclude this chapter we should mention three important factors that distinguish the Nicaraguan Revolution from the English and American ones. First, among the three revolutions we stress the similarity of religious motivation as a catalyst for democratizing political action. But we should not expect precisely the same outcome from revolutions separated by several centuries and by different colonial legacies. Historical perspective enables us to see that the Levellers did not see their goals realized in their own generation; indeed, the democratization of English society and politics took centuries to complete. By contrast, in Nicaragua the revolutionary forces seized the reins of power: they not only shattered the Somocista system that had prevented democratization, but found themselves in a position to push the popular, democratizing project in a radically egalitarian direction. Because the Nicaraguan Revolution is still young, it is too soon to tell where these efforts will lead.

Second, the English and American revolutions took place in settings where Protestantism was rapidly becoming, or already was, the dominant religious influence. Like the rest of Latin America, Nicaragua is still a predominantly Catholic country, even if Protestantism is spreading rapidly. We have noted that both Protestants and Catholics joined in the revolutionary struggle. Those Protestants who did so could find precedent for their actions in the Reformation, and in the English and American revolutions that were associated with it. Roman Catholics found inspiration in much more recent, though equally powerful, sources: they were stimulated by changes in the church that were introduced after the Cuban Revolution. Because these changes are recent and momentous, they have not yet been resolved. Therefore, the Nicaraguan Revolution has become a focal point, a lightning rod, for the stresses and strains within Roman Catholicism itself. This means that the religious situation in Nicaragua is highly fluid and emotionally charged. The situation has been attributed to religious persecution by an atheistic revolution, but it is much better understood as the result of authentic religious ferment in the midst of rapid political change.

Third, when a revolution succeeds, political actors assume new positions in relation to one another. In the Nicaraguan case the popular classes now have a greatly expanded voice in political decisions, while former elites have found their voice comparatively reduced by the change in power structures. The roles of individual Christians and of institutional churches are an integral part of the new relationships that demand definition. These relationships would be problematic even if the revolution were allowed to develop according to its own lights, free from outside interference—but the Nicaraguan process is caught in the vortex of the Cold War struggle, and that brute reality may determine the direction of the revolution as much as the internal dynamics of the revolution itself.

By contrast, the English and American revolutions were much less enmeshed in the major power conflicts of their day. For instance, the Loyalists, those who opposed the American Revolution and subsequently fled to Canada, were not funded and armed by the British to overthrow the fledging American republic. On the contrary, the Americans benefited from the fact that there was relatively little foreign meddling in their internal affairs as they set about the tasks of nation-building. Nicaragua has enjoyed no such luxury. From its inception the Nicaraguan Revolution was beset by foreign intervention, above all from the United States. Since early 1981 Nicaragua has been subjected to an intense application of the Reagan Doctrine. It has been the target of a bitter, costly, and destabilizing counterinsurgency war, which has disrupted Sandinista efforts at nation-building.[40] The struggle for democratization in the revolutionary process, including the role of the churches in that struggle, must be set within this superimposed Cold War framework.

Three

The Religious Roots
of North American Politics

Puritanism in Early Seventeenth-Century England

Almost overnight, United States policy makers became deeply preoccupied with political events in Central America in the late 1970s. Because the United States has immense economic and military power, it is in a position to exert strong influence over such events; consequently, the precepts and prejudices that U.S. leaders bring to Central American policy can have great impact on the region's political development. Following other writers, we contend that U.S. leaders lack historical perspective on the present crisis. We further argue that they lack a sense of the origins and heritage of the United States' own development as a democratic nation. Hence, these leaders do not appreciate the important role played by a religious revolution in generating the democratic tradition that so benefited North Americans, nor do they draw from their own colonial heritage lessons applicable to Central America.

In order to see how the present political crisis in Central America has been generated and is being shaped by democratic impulses arising in both religion and politics, it is helpful to examine the United States' own religious and political heritage. That heritage can be traced to the Protestant Reformation in sixteenth-century Europe, and particularly to the seventeenth-century English revolution. The present chapter examines these early roots of North American democracy. Chapter 4 then compares the North American colonial experience with that of Latin America, highlighting the very different roles played by religion in the political development of the two halves of the Americas.

English society in the reign of James I (1603–25) was "authoritarian from top to bottom," and the authoritarian structure of society was strongly reinforced by religious customs and teachings in which "obedience was inculcated from an early age."[1] The society was traditional in the Weberian sense of the word: the social order had long been sharply stratified and was relatively unchanging. Political authority in this predominantly feudal and rural society was exercised by the aristocracy. "Gentlemen, from peers of the realm to small landowners, were the natural rulers of the countryside"; these were the men who owned the land, filled local administrative offices, and sent their own representatives to Parliament.[2] Three and a half centuries later, Nicaraguan society was a caricature of this earlier model. A landed elite shared power with a family dynasty and used that power to promote its own self-interest. The impressive economic growth that benefited the oligarchy in the 1960s and 1970s did little to improve the lot of the peasantry.[3]

Jacobean English society was also pervasively religious. Queen Elizabeth had placed governance of the church in the hands of the Crown late in the sixteenth century. The church thus depended on political authority for its institutional well-being, while the Crown enjoyed the imprimatur of religious authority. In short, church and Crown were mutually reinforcing authorities in a hierarchical, authoritarian world.[4] Similarly, in mid-twentieth-century Nicaragua the Roman Catholic church was a reliable ally of the Somoza regime. However, in seventeenth-century England, as in twentieth-century Nicaragua, the traditional society was about to come unraveled under the onslaught of new ideas, the movement of new social classes, and a bitter struggle to reconceptualize and redistribute religious and political power. The political struggle and the new political ideas and values that it cast up were deeply informed by the religious struggle.

The glue of ideas, customs, social stratification, and concentrated political power that held this traditional English society together dissolved as the result of corrosive forces that accumulated over the period of a century. In the economic realm, a long and sustained period of inflation placed increasing pressure on the institutions of the agrarian economy. Landowners who had become accustomed to giving over substantial tracts of land to copyholders, or tenant farmers, found themselves squeezed by the inflationary spiral; to make their land more productive, they were forced to dispossess copyholders. Thus, in the early decades of the seventeenth century, economic exigency brought severe stresses to bear on rural society. As Howard Shaw has observed, in some instances the "smaller copyholder frequently was ejected from land his family had farmed for centuries."[5]

In this way, economic upheaval produced a growing reservoir of casualties whose once-secure status was jeopardized. In Nicaragua in the three decades prior to the revolution, a similar wave of displacement of peasant smallholders took place. The development of coffee and cotton production in particular led to a concentration of rural landholdings and to the transformation of once-independent farmers into a "rootless rural proletariat."[6]

On the other side of the coin, the economic chaos of Jacobean times also produced the new institutions, practices, and attitudes of early capitalism. The growing spirit of entrepreneurship enabled some men to exploit opportunity and gain leverage for social advancement. Some individuals were growing rich and elevating their social status, while others were descending on the social scale. In short, early seventeenth-century England was the scene of rapidly increasing social disorganization and social mobility: "In the upper ranks of society high social mobility generated jealousy, envy, and despair among the failures, and status anxiety among the successful. In the lower ranks extraordinary geographic mobility and periodic catastrophes due to epidemic disease, combined to shatter the traditional ties to family, kin, and neighbours, and to wrench men away from their familiar associations and surroundings."[7]

At the lower end of the social scale the process created, in Christopher Hill's words, a mass of "masterless men." Conflating somewhat the categories into which he divides them, we can identify three types of people newly released from the status boundaries of the old society. One group were the rural and urban poor who had lost their access to land or their places on estates. They became casual laborers in the city, or cottagers and squatters in the wastes and forests. Some became rogues and beggars. A second group were the "itinerant trading population, from pedlars and carters to badgers, merchant middlemen. The number of craftsmen in villages, in those days of restricted markets, was vastly greater than it is today."[8] The third group were members of the new Protestant sects who had left the state church, which so closely reflected the hierarchical nature of the society at large. The sectarians were concentrated in the towns and tended to be highly motivated carriers of a new set of individualist principles, the working-out of which accelerated the remaking of English society. Puritanism, by which we mean the aggressive strain of English Protestantism that passionately struggled to live out the principles of the Reformation, may have been a refuge for the socially dislocated.[9] At the same time, some individuals found new opportunities in this social upheaval. As Hill observed: "a masterless man was nobody's servant: this could mean freedom for those who prized independence more than security."[10]

In prerevolutionary Nicaragua the pattern of social change and dislocation was remarkably similar. We have already mentioned the proletarianization of those peasants who lost access to the land and became a migratory labor force serving the large coffee and cotton producers. Many of these gradually moved to the cities in search of employment. At the same time, in the late 1960s new religious groups appeared that had a leavening effect within this new social mix. The Delegados de la Palabra and the *comunidades eclesiales de base*, which spread rapidly throughout Nicaragua as part of a more general process of religious renewal, played a catalytic role comparable to that of the Puritan sects in the period leading up to the English Civil War.

In England, Puritanism contributed a potent new ideology and new forms of social organization to the forces changing the face of society. Despite the efforts of Queen Elizabeth and her successors to maintain a state church and to thwart the rise of independent, self-governing congregations, the Puritans enjoyed considerable freedom in the generations before the Civil War. Though they kept within the bounds of the established church up to 1640, by 1632 they had established a brotherhood of preachers working independently of constituted authority. They had developed their own sources of funding and had begun to buy up impropriated tithes to provide for Puritan lecturers. By the time of Charles I (1625–49) their growing autonomy and numbers represented a threat to the established authority of church and Crown. The king felt obliged to move against them in order to retain control over the church. He encouraged Archbishop Laud to "stamp out Puritanism by forbidding lectureships, by suppressing the scheme for supporting lecturers out of impropriated tithes, and by punishing critics who assailed his authority in the press"; however, by this time Puritanism had advanced far enough that these efforts "merely served to spread the fire."[11]

The "fire" referred to here was the growing importance given to individual conscience. Even if one follows Lawrence Stone's interpretation that much of the subversive character of Puritanism came about accidentally, it remains true that Puritanism penetrated society with ideas that had an explosive impact for change in the midst of social turmoil. The mainstream Puritan believed in the traditional values; he may not have objected to existing social and political inequalities. But the Reformational emphasis on conscience and personal interpretation of the Bible, over against the dictates of church law and established orthodoxy, led inexorably to doubts about the legitimacy of the established system, first of the church and then of government. The attack on the bishops evolved into an attack on hierarchy in the society much more broadly considered.[12]

Puritanism contributed two Calvinist doctrines that challenged English tradition, even though they were in tension with each other. One, the doctrine of the elect—a sort of spiritual aristocracy—posited a religious elite. However, according to the second doctrine, in the sight of God the elite were equal among themselves.[13] Calvinists believed that God spoke directly to the elect. But precisely who were the elect? In time the boundaries of the elect broadened irresistibly: "under the law of Moses all were condemned for the sin of Adam, but under the Gospel some were saved through the grace of Christ. The one doctrine made all equal. The other set a limited number free. Both were said to be plainly set forth in the Scripture."[14]

The direct impact of these ideas on English society was enhanced by the Puritan emphasis on reading the Bible, and by a revived emphasis on prophetic interpretation. The Puritans fostered the spread of popular literacy to enable members of the congregations to read the Scriptures themselves. Printing, together with the translation of the Bible from Latin into vernacular English, furthered the process. The decentralized Puritan system also encouraged popular preaching to assist in the correct interpretation of the Scriptures. And it was not only a trained Puritan clergy that engaged in biblical scholarship; "mechanic laymen [began to] put their own allegorical constructions on a vernacular text available for all to read."[15] In this respect the Puritan clergy themselves were unable to contain the spread and impact of ideas they had helped unleash. Whereas the clergy sought to create a single religious community, unified in doctrine, that would stand in opposition to the established Church of England, they ended by producing a separatism that spawned a proliferation of sects.

The use of the Bible as a historical and prophetic text during the period reinforced these trends, particularly the democratizing consequences of Puritanism in practice. What Hill calls "eschatological prophecy" became a major element in Puritan literature. By means of such prophetic interpretation of the Bible, ordinary readers sought to democratize its mysteries. As Hill puts it: "the Bible, if properly understood, really would liberate men from destiny, from predestination. By understanding and cooperating with God's purposes men believed they could escape from the blind forces which seemed to rule their world. . . . They believed, on good Protestant authority, that *anyone* could understand God's word if he studied it carefully enough, and if the grace of God was in him. And then the Bible could be made to reveal the key to events of his own time."[16] In short, the Bible became a key point of reference by which to evaluate the unfolding political struggle. In the eyes of Puritans generally, it did not justify the pretensions of the traditional ruling class to superiority and dominance. For the lower ranks of Puritanism it became, in the course of the Civil War, the basis for a broad-scale demand for democratization in society.

Thomas Hobbes, one of the seventeenth century's most penetrating political thinkers, regarded the wide distribution of the Bible during the 1630s and 1640s as a chief cause of the rebellion against political authority that led to war in 1642. He did not approve of the trend, as this wry and biting comment makes clear: "after the Bible was translated into English, every man, nay every boy and wench, that could read English thought they spoke with God Almighty and understood what he said."[17] No doubt those of Hobbes's contemporaries who wished to defend order and stability shared his alarm over where these democratizing trends could lead.

Finally, while Puritanism unleashed a hitherto unknown degree of individualism into English society, it was not the totally undisciplined, anarchic individualism that its most vehement critics imagined. It is true that the doctrine of the "inner light" led to private interpretation of the Bible and direct communion between God and believer. But the believer was a member of a congregation (often separatist, to be sure—hence the threat to those committed to centralized control), and it was within the congregation that individual interpretations were tested and gained currency.[18] Furthermore, it was the very context of the congregation (and during the Civil War, the context of the New Model Army) that gave concrete substance to prophetic interpretation of the Bible. The members of the congregation typically shared the stigma of being a religious minority, and they generally had a similar economic background; consequently, they nursed common grievances against the political order under which they lived. The Bible spoke to them as a group, or as a class, that had been treated unfairly by the system. In this way new perceptions of religion led directly to new attitudes in politics. At the same time, the gathered churches represented a new model of religious organization that foretold the emergence of the more radical political organizations that soon appeared, attempting to press democratizing demands in the political arena. As Stone has suggested, it is doubtful that many Puritan leaders favored participatory democracy for its own sake, ". . . but their actions certainly encouraged it."[19]

Nicaragua's own process of religious change, and the impact of that change in the political arena, will be the subject of extended discussion in Chapters 6 through 10. For the moment we wish only to point out that the process bears striking resemblances to the Puritan experience in England. We will show how new religious teachings produced, in each setting, a heightened appreciation of individual conscience. The importance attached to conscience, and hence to individual dignity, was sustained by ordinary people's increasing access to the Bible. Bible study, in turn, was done in community, whether it was the Puritan congregation of the 1640s or the Nicaraguan Christian base community of the 1970s. In each case the political repercussions pressed in a democratic direction.

The Coming of the Civil War

The English revolution unfolded in stages, the first of which was essentially a struggle among political elites rather than a full-scale challenge to the existing social order. During the 1630s and early 1640s it took the form of a rapidly intensifying rivalry between the Puritan gentry, on the one hand, and the king, his royal supporters, and the established Church of England on the other. The conflict moved from Parliament to the battlefield. It began over issues of taxation and the rights and privileges of landed interests in the Parliament, issues that were reinforced by religious differences between Presbyterians and the leaders and supporters of the state church; but it ended in a struggle over the locus of sovereignty in the English political system, with the result that the defeat of the king led to the reconstitution of sovereignty in Parliament. The political and religious leaders of this revolutionary movement sought to redistribute royal power among the propertied and intended to use that power to guarantee the rights of private property, to disencumber the Presbyterian church system, and to foster their own ethic of religious and political conduct. The vitality of their efforts broke down the ideological props of the old order, while the strength of their competition eroded the "unquestioning and habit forming faith of the past."[20] In this they were greatly assisted by the intransigence of the government and the church, which resolutely spurned all criticism.

The parliamentary forces in the struggle with the Crown were themselves divided, however. The Puritanism that had helped give coherence to their cause against the king also stimulated a multiplicity of viewpoints; shaped by the same Puritan energy, these viewpoints were carried to their logical conclusions as well, resulting in political movements opposed to the newly triumphant Puritan leaders. Apart from the sects and mechanic preachers, the primary vehicle for this revolution within the revolution was the New Model Army.

The New Model Army was the decisive force in the Civil War. Parliament, in its struggle with the king, effectively lost control of the army, which came to be led by the Independents—most notably, Oliver Cromwell and his son-in-law, Henry Ireton. These men and their followers in the army were prepared to be more radical on key issues than their Presbyterian allies in Parliament who wanted to preserve the old order, but without the king and with their own religious orthodoxy replacing that of Archbishop Laud and the state church.[21] The Independents were prepared to accept greater religious freedom and toleration, and would push somewhat wider the boundaries of sovereignty within the populace—but in the final analysis, these men represented the gentry, and they intended to use the increased power of Parliament to protect the property rights and franchise of this class.[22] However, the New Model Army organized other interests, divergent from those of Cromwell and his generals.

Let us look briefly at the major events of that revolutionary decade. In the hands of Charles I, the English monarch's power had become perilously strained by 1640. His government had become financially dependent on the counties, which were governed largely by the gentry. Although landowners, the majority of these men were not nobility; in the eyes of the law they were commoners. Even though their world view was substantially compatible with that of the king and his courtiers, important lines of cleavage had developed. The king pursued policies they did not approve of, and when they resisted such policies Charles took to dismissing Parliament and asserting royal prerogative. He increased Crown monopolies that facilitated corruption and profiteering by those in royal favor, but did nothing to benefit the gentry. He sought to raise taxes and borrow money without their approval. When they protested these actions, there was the threat of arbitrary arrest. These grievances were reinforced by religious issues and differences. Charles favored the Arminian divines, or leaders of the Anglican church, whose leader was William Laud. Laud's attempt to bring back altars, vestments, and elaborate liturgy recalled popery, while his open hostility to Calvinist theology alienated the Puritan gentry. To make matters worse, the king placed Laud and two other bishops on the Privy Council, which violated established tradition. He also used the court of Star Chamber, a prerogative court, to enforce a galling censorship that deeply offended the Puritans.[23] As will be seen in Chapter 6, these actions and policies were similar in broad outline to those of Anastasio Somoza in Nicaragua, which led to alienation and rebellion not only by exploited peasants but also by important sectors of the church and the privileged classes.

In 1640 Charles went to war with the Scots but suffered a humiliating defeat that left the monarchy nearly penniless. He was forced to call Parliament together and come to it hat in hand. During this famous Long Parliament, the tide of power shifted toward the gentry. Parliament abolished Star Chamber, asserted the supremacy of common law over royal prerogative, and allocated to itself the vital power of taxation. Despite these serious concessions, the king still governed and there was no intention at this time to depose Charles or to abolish the monarchy. However, behind these political and economic issues lay serious disagreement over religion; that disagreement came to a head following the outbreak of rebellion in Ireland.[24]

The Irish rebellion required that a new army be raised. Parliamentary leaders were determined that raising an army and prosecuting the war in Ireland would be the occasion for requiring that all the king's ministers had the confidence of Parliament. But would Parliament actually control the army? Could it bring about religious reforms that would satisfy its Puritan constituency? Over issues such as these England now divided along royalist and parliamentary lines, and the Civil War began. The landed gentry played the crucial role, but its members were arrayed on both sides. In 1643 the parliamentary forces made an alliance with the Scots that pledged England to establish a Presbyterian church. When the decisive battle of the war was fought at Naseby in June 1645, Charles surrendered to the Scots rather than to Cromwell and his New Model Army. The king intended to play off against each other the factions that had developed within Parliament.

He counted on the Scots to help restore him to the throne in return for his promise to install Presbyterianism as the national church of England.[25] These intrigues made sense only when set against the background of the evolving religious struggle, and in terms of the decisive role played in the Civil War by the gentry and the New Model Army.

In the early stages of the Civil War a split developed between the Presbyterians and the Independents in Parliament. The Presbyterians were the more orthodox faction in religious matters. They wished to impose the "godly discipline" of early Calvinism on the entire church.[26] They were sympathetic to the restoration of the king, committed to retaining hierarchy and rank in society, and distrustful of the New Model Army. The Independents were a less cohesive group. Their primary religious goal was to see churches established on the basis of "covenants" made among the members of the congregation. This goal led the gentry in the Independent party to ally themselves with the sects, whose roots were in the classes below their own in the social hierarchy; it also pushed them toward a position of toleration that clashed with the orthodoxy sought by the Presbyterians. Despite falling into opposing camps in the Civil War, Puritan leaders in Parliament accepted inequality and had no intention of carrying out a social revolution. Puritan ministers were generally of gentry stock and depended on the patronage of Puritan squires or peers. However, the exigencies of war drove them into an alliance with individuals who were developing much more radical and egalitarian views of what the present struggles should bring to religion and politics in England.

Following Charles's defeat at Naseby, the Presbyterian faction in Parliament moved to disband the New Model Army, fearing its potential political power. But the leadership of the New Model was dominated by Independents. Some of these men—military chaplains such as William Dell, Hugh Peters, and John Saltmarsh—were leaders of the separatist tendency of the sects that had flourished in the army during the war. These leaders were rapidly pushing Puritan teachings in a radical egalitarian direction.[27] While such New Model generals as Cromwell and Ireton had moderate religious views, the heavyhanded efforts of the Presbyterian majority in Parliament to disband the army threatened to cut their power base from under them. In this context, the New Model Army went into revolt against Parliament, which was incapable of resisting it. The New Model began to speak in the name of the people of England. For a brief moment, with the dramatic rise of the Leveller movement, the Agitators threatened to

take control of the army and England stood at the brink of a potentially sweeping democratization of society and polity.[28]

The Rise of the Levellers

Christopher Hill has characterized the New Model Army as "a body of
masterless men on the move."[29] Its ranks were filled with itinerant
craftsmen and merchants, and with mechanic preachers. During the
Civil War the sects "multiplied amazingly."[30] They flourished particularly in London among the newly masterless men who were swelling
the population of that city, and in the New Model Army. The way the
sects were organized, and the subjective experience of their members,
had a marked influence on the course of events. Organized around a
covenant to which all agreed and by which all were bound, the sect
provided a measure of security and identity for people uprooted from
the English countryside. Sects organized in this manner were brought
under the discipline of the New Model Army wherein, despite the
efforts of the commanders to control it, there was "free discussion of
religious ideas, ideas frequently leading to the extreme individualist
position of free will and universal grace. Given the right circumstances, it was but a short step from the demand for religious freedom
to the demand for political freedom also."[31] In this way the religious
activist in the army was in the process of becoming "the secular revolutionary springing out of the Puritan reformer."[32] At the same time,
the New Model brought together previously inconsequential and politically voiceless groups scattered throughout England and gave them
a new confidence. The Leveller movement sprang from this source.
    The example of William Walwyn illustrates what happened—how
far Puritan doctrine could be carried and how religious radicalism led
to political radicalism. Walwyn was a principal organizer and spokesman of the Leveller movement, and exerted a powerful influence over
the officers in the New Model, such as John Lilburn, who emerged as
Leveller leaders.[33] In widely circulated pamphlets Walwyn argued
persuasively that being free and equal in the sight of God implied
having equal rights on earth: "by the grace of God which brings the
possibility of salvation to all men and by the law of nature to which all
are subject, all men should be equal also under the laws of England
and have equal voice in making them."[34] The free circulation of Calvinist ideas, hastened as it was by the revolutionary situation of the

country, encouraged the notion that grace was universal. This principle, in turn, had become a basis for the demand for democratic rights. The first notion democratized religion; the second sought to democratize the polity.

This interpretation was spread throughout the New Model Army by such preachers as John Saltmarsh and William Dell, and it was heard by men who were about to be cashiered from the army by a parliament eager to be rid of them. It marked a long step beyond where Cromwell and other gentry leaders of the army were prepared to go. This was not merely the Independent demand for religious toleration, but a call for "the promotion of justice in the body politic."[35] In the end Walwyn's theology served as the basis for constitutional proposals put forward in the Agreement of the People. H. N. Brailsford has called the Agreement "the first rough draft of a written constitution in the history of democracy."[36] These proposals were debated by the Levellers and the army commanders at Putney church in the fall of 1647.

The Levellers were a people's party, representing radicals both within and outside the army. They sought to establish the supremacy of Parliament over king and lords by pushing legal reforms that would have brought about an extensive democratization of mid-seventeenth-century English politics. At Putney their chief spokesmen, Colonel Rainsborough and John Wildman, urged three broad proposals. First, they argued that seats in Parliament should be redistributed according to population, and that this should be done by the Long Parliament before it dissolved in September of the following year. Second, they argued that Parliament was subordinate to the sovereign people who chose it, but was superior to kings and lords; because the people themselves were sovereign, certain "matters" were reserved exclusively to them, including their form of worship. Third, "all are equal before the law and none is exempted from the ordinary course of legal proceedings."[37] These central proposals of the Agreement of the People, itself a product of mutual consultation, debate, and consent within the rank and file of the New Model, rejected the older "mixed monarchy" scheme that allowed king and lords to limit the power of the common people. Instead, it vested parliamentary power in the House of Commons and based the authority of the Commons on the consent of the people.

The Agreement of the People rested on the following logical propositions: God made all men equal, endowing them with an inner light of reason. By the exercise of that reason each could discern God's justice. Therefore, the only means by which one man could acquire the right to exercise authority over another was by the other's consent. "We conceive . . . no authority being of God, but what is erected by the mutual consent of a people."[38] This logic pointed to universal manhood suffrage, which was a radical proposal indeed at the time. Neither the House of Commons nor the army high command was prepared to accept it. At Putney, Ireton challenged the Levellers to say whether they were intending that "every man . . . is to have an equal voice in the election of those represerters?" The answer was yes: "We judge that all inhabitants that have not lost their birthright should have an equal voice in elections." During the course of debate this answer was put more poignantly in the famous lines of Colonel Rainsborough: "I think that the poorest he that is in England hath a life to live, as the greatest he; and therefore, truly, Sir, I think it's clear that every man that is to live under a government ought first by his own consent to put himself under that government."[39] This point of view expressed a faith in common people and in their capacity to participate in a more popular form of government that was shared neither by Parliament nor by the army commanders at Putney. Indeed, these men regarded such views as subversive of the civil order.

Ireton spoke for the grandees. He thought it essential that the franchise be restricted to men of property. In his opinion propertyless men had no rights, and he feared that the Leveller proposals led in the direction of an attack on the right of property itself, which was the cornerstone of stable government. Defining property as a "permanent fixed interest," Ireton put his position as follows: "No person hath a right to an interest or share in the disposing the affairs of the king-dom, and in determining or choosing those that shall determine what laws we shall be ruled by here—no person hath a right to this that hath not a permanent fixed interest in this kingdom. . . ."[40] In other words, only those who held property should vote, and from their ranks should come those who govern. In Ireton's view the doctrine of consent, taken to the democratic extreme that it was by the Levellers, constituted a prescription for anarchy. As G. P. Gooch has pointed out, he held a much more Hobbesian view of human nature than did the radicals: "men as men are corrupt and will be so."[41] For this reason Ireton, together with the class for which he spoke, was fundamentally "suspicious of a doctrine which allowed to each individual the right and duty to decide according to the light of his own conscience what was just and what was unjust."[42]

The debate at Putney marked the beginning of defeat for the Leveller party and for the democratizing demands they represented. In the immediate future lay not democracy but the Protectorate of Oliver Cromwell. The Levellers lacked the political skills to build on their popularity or to outmaneuver their opponents; as a result, in England their impact was to be felt in the long term, not immediately. Abroad, their ideas came to fruition only later in the American and French revolutions. Had they been more successful the consequences might have been far-reaching for seventeenth-century England.

> In practice the difference between Ireton and the Levellers was between a constitution which placed power in the hands of the gentry and the merchants, and a constitution which placed power in the hands of small property owners. And the difference is important, since more than half the population consisted of small property owners. In seventeenth-century England democracy could not be based on the wage earners, whose conditions were close to beggary. The Levellers would have created a political system based on the mass of shopkeepers, craftsmen, and farmers; and that would have been indeed a democratic system.[43]

The democratic system called for by the Levellers was not achieved at this time. The established elites were already closing ranks against it. The Agreement underwent revisions that weakened it while its opponents played for time and dealt with another pressing issue— what to do with the king. By January 1649 the Rump of the Long Parliament and the army commanders had sentenced the king to be executed, and they had shelved the Second Agreement of the People.[44] In the final analysis, the Levellers had confronted the decisive power of "an oligarchy of calculating politicians, many of them elected more than eight years ago, and all sustained by the sharp swords of the grandees."[45] In the face of such odds their quest for democratization failed.

The Democratic Legacy of the English Revolution

Let us sum up what has been argued thus far. First, it is clear that religion was a primary source of inspiration for the more radical democratic movements that were spawned by the Civil War. The correlative Calvinist doctrines of the elect and of the equality of the elect before God fostered two competing strands of Puritanism. The former doctrine took hold in Presbyterianism, whose ministers became "leaders of the reactionary wing of the alliance that had defeated the king."[46] They stoutly resisted the democratizing impulses of the Levellers and strove to impose a new religious orthodoxy. The Puritanism inspired by the latter doctrine took the form of independent congregations organized on the model of the voluntary covenant. This tendency built upon the central activity of reading the Bible, thus accentuating the direct, personal relationship between ordinary people and God, and so highlighting the importance of individual conscience. "Here in the equality of the elect and the elevation of the individual lay the origins of Leveller thought."[47]

Second, it is evident that politics overtook religion as the Civil War progressed, and that in the short run it was for compelling political reasons that the democratizing initiatives were suppressed. The Leveller program implied a sweeping extension of political rights to the broad mass of English citizenry. Indeed, the Levellers were the first political movement that sought to incorporate "inalienable rights into a proposed constitution."[48] Their approach drew on the theory of the "Norman Yoke," which asserted: "Before 1066 the Anglo-Saxon inhabitants of this country lived as free and equal citizens, governing themselves through representative institutions. The Norman conquest deprived them of this liberty and established the tyranny of an alien king and his landlords. But the people did not forget the rights they had lost."[49]

Nevertheless, the Levellers added significantly to the folklore of a golden age of self-government and ancient rights. Blending biblical and constitutional interpretations, they saw Anglo-Saxon men per se as by nature free and equal under God. The words of Leveller leader Richard Overton are remarkably similar in expression to the idea of natural rights made famous, and acceptable, by John Locke forty years later. In 1646 Overton wrote: "To every individual in nature is given an individual property by nature not to be invaded or usurped by any: for everyone as he is himself, so he hath a self propriety, else he could not be himself. . . . For by birth all men are equally and alike born to like propriety, liberty and freedom."[50] This is, as Christopher Hill has pointed out, a portentous innovation in political thought: "from the recovery of rights which used to exist, to the pursuit of rights because they ought to exist: from historical mythology to political philosophy."[51]

The democratic political philosophy formulated by the Levellers represented a profound threat to men of property, who saw quite clearly the potential consequences of these broadening concepts of liberty. Once the Independents had purged Parliament, executed the king, and established the Commonwealth, they determined to crush the radical movement. At Putney, Henry Ireton had made clear just how narrow the limits of reform were to be for the time being—for him "the people" in the body politic were men of property, not the whole of the adult male population. In the post–Civil War constitution it would be the gentry who would enjoy political rights and access to political power.

In the short run, then, the revolution of the 1640s ended with social and political radicalism being suppressed. The proposed Leveller reforms were blocked. Even religious dissent and experimentation were brought under control with the Restoration and the revival of Anglicanism in 1660. Within the political settlements achieved toward the end of the century, the Leveller proposals were modified to become the core of Whig doctrine that emerged from the Glorious Revolution of 1688. The political events of 1688 established that "only the economically independent are free; that property confers both political and personal responsibilities and political privilege; that property is the principal security for liberty; and that the duty of the state is therefore carefully to preserve and protect it."[52]

Although the democratizing impulses of the revolution failed to come to fruition in the short term, in the much longer term the revolution left a potent legacy. In the words of Lawrence Stone, this legacy was "an immensely rich reservoir of ideas that were to echo and reecho down the ages."[53] Liberalizing elements showed up in the Bill of Rights and the Toleration Act, but these measures did not carry democratization very far. With the passage of more than a century, however, the political ideas of the English revolution found expression in the American and French revolutions. In England's own history of political development, Leveller ideas achieved full fruition only in the twentieth century. Similarly, their working-out in the American experience took place over many generations. But as we return to the Americas with our analysis, we are in a position to appreciate the depth of the impact that England's religious and political revolutionary heritage had upon this working-out: "When . . . the American colonists became too similar to their English parents, they staged an oedipal revolt, inspired by pamphlet and pulpit rhetoric that involved the same ideas hammered out in the fires of England's revolutionary century."[54]

The English revolution thus presaged America's own colonial rebellion of just over a century later. It constituted a powerful precedent for revolt against authoritarianism and provided a rich fund of justifying ideas and principles. As we will show, in late twentieth-century Central America similar conditions generated new revolutions that conformed much more closely than is commonly recognized to these earlier landmarks in the American democratic tradition.

Four

Patterns of Political
Development in the Americas

The Heritage of the Americas

When speaking to Latin Americans, presidents of the United States are fond of stressing that a common heritage unites the Americas. It is understandable that they would do so since diplomatic protocol requires that a basis for good relations be acknowledged. Of course, the matter goes deeper than this because U.S. presidents often find themselves addressing Latin Americans in response to a perceived crisis that affects mutual relations. They enter into such situations under the venerable shadow of the Monroe Doctrine, which has done yeoman duty justifying U.S. intervention for a century and a half. At least since the days of James K. Polk the Monroe Doctrine has been a cloak for the pursuit of U.S. interests in Latin America: it was helpful to think of that pursuit as always being for the mutual benefit of the United States and Latin America.[1]

A typical example is provided by President John F. Kennedy who, in response to the Cuban Revolution, created the Alliance for Progress, a foreign policy initiative by the government of the United States to promote economic and political development in Latin America. Just weeks before the CIA-sponsored invasion of Cuba at the Bay of Pigs, President Kennedy formally announced the Alliance program to a gathering of Latin American ambassadors, appealing for Latin American cooperation in these terms: "We meet together as firm and ancient friends, united by history and experience and by our determination to advance the values of American civilization. For this new world of ours is not merely an accident of geography. Our continents are bound together by a common history—the endless exploration of new frontiers. Our nations are the product of a common struggle—the revolt from colonial rule. And our people share a common heritage—the quest for the dignity and freedom of man."[2] Certainly there are ways in which the two halves of the hemisphere are "united by history and experience," but the harmony and mutual understanding of that history implied in President Kennedy's speech were greatly exaggerated.

Let us consider for a moment what historical features North America and Latin America do share in common. In the first instance, each is the product of European colonization during the great age of exploration and discovery in the New World, extending from the late fifteenth century to the early seventeenth century. Each, therefore, has had a long period of colonial rule. Each half of the Americas also began its own quest for nationhood with a war for independence. In this respect, both Latin America and the United States came into being as "new nations" that were culturally European due to colonization. However, they were separated from Europe not only by a vast ocean but also by a sense of distinct identity and a belief in a unique destiny, as will be shown more fully below. Finally, the Americas were also linked by the spread of Christianity to the New World. Each of these new societies was founded in important measure as a religious undertaking of great scope and ambition. This point can hardly be emphasized too strongly, because all the nations of the Americas are ultimately products of a wave of European colonization that was deeply inspired and informed by the Christian religion. When all of these points are taken together, the two halves of the Americas do appear to have a great deal in common in their historical development. Each was founded and grew originally as a "fragment society" born of European colonialism.[3]

In practice, however, their colonial experiences were sufficiently different to lay the basis for a historical relationship plagued by misunderstanding. To take only the religious example for the moment, it is essential to recognize that North America was colonized by Reformed Protestants while Latin America was conquered and settled by pre-Reformation Catholics—both were representatives of European Christianity, but their religious world views and sociopolitical orientations were sharply divergent. In both cases the colonizers were impressively successful at founding societies in the New World after their own image. The societies so founded, together with the churches established and the political institutions built up over time, were quite different. Before discussing those differences, it will be helpful to say something about the concept of "fragment societies."

The theory of the "colonial fragment," as developed by such writers as Louis Hartz, holds that the path of modernization followed by a new society is apt to be heavily conditioned by the nature and timing of its colonial experience. If Hartz is correct, the fragment society, due to the relative isolation within which it evolves, tends to lose continuity with the cultural and political development of the mother country. The fragment leaves, as it were, the moving stream of its own history, with the result that the strongest tendencies of the culture implanted by the mother country tend to take deep root, persisting and flourishing more powerfully than in the mother country itself. So long as the fragment remains isolated from the broader currents of world affairs, its development will reflect the strongest tendencies of the originating culture, including the most prominent characteristics of the colonization process itself.[4] Consider how such an approach illuminates the history of the Americas. Both the United States and Latin America originated as fragment societies, and the long-term development of each was profoundly influenced by the stage of development of the culture and politics of the mother country at the time of colonization. In this vein, our point of departure is to ask of both North and Latin America: When did colonization take place, what was going on in the mother country at the time, and how closely supervised, or independent, was the fragment society during the period of colonial control?

From the angle of vision provided by these questions a number of points stand out clearly. In the first place, Latin America was colonized fully a century before North America, and its colonial experience lasted roughly twice as long as North America's, covering about three centuries as opposed to a century and a half. The United States achieved its independence first, approximately four decades before Latin America, and certainly helped to inspire the independence struggle in the nations to the south. The length of colonial control is in part a reflection of the differing agendas carried to the New World by Spain and by England. For its part, Spain was intent on extending Iberian influence and control by quite literally incorporating the New World into the kingdom of Spain.[5] The society of the New World was to be made over in the exact image of Iberia itself, and this would be accomplished under the direct supervision of the monarchy; the New World colonists, better known as the conquistadors, were all agents of the Iberian monarch and were understood to be carrying out his agenda.[6] The situation was quite different in the English colonization of North America: there, the colonial project was carried out by dissidents in the English body politic, by Puritans who sought to escape from the constraints of English political and religious life. Generally speaking, the English king was only too glad to be rid of the dissidents, and paid scant attention to them during much of the colonial era. In terms of future political development, this "salutary neglect" by the British state proved a blessing for North America—while the efforts of the Iberian state to achieve tight control and centralized direction were a liability for Latin America.

The second salient factor helps to explain the first. Latin America ✓ was colonized by a state that was profoundly Roman Catholic. Its colonial venture was undertaken prior to the Protestant Reformation and was carried out in an atmosphere that actively precluded Reformation influence. Hence, the Iberian half of the New World was conquered and grew in an environment of strictly imposed religious orthodoxy. North America, on the other hand, was colonized during a period when the Reformation was well advanced in England and had exerted a deep influence over English life, especially in the areas of religion and politics. The English colonists left behind the authoritarian, hierarchical, tradition-bound world of seventeenth-century England when they crossed the Atlantic, and their colonial experience reinforced their sense of separateness from that world. What took root in North America was a religious and political experiment derived from the more radical tendencies of the Protestant Reformation. In Latin America, what became established were the most pronounced tendencies of religious orthodoxy and political centralism associated with the early sixteenth-century Iberian state and its assiduously cultivated, pre-Reformational Roman Catholicism. Let us now trace out and contrast these two quite distinct colonial experiences in somewhat more detail in order to appreciate the very different legacies they have left behind in the political development of the Americas.

The Puritan Character of English Colonization

The American Revolution occurred more than a century after the English Civil War. The Levellers were by then hardly remembered in the English-speaking world. England had gradually resolved its political crisis by diminishing the powers of the king, increasing the powers of Parliament vis-à-vis the king, and effecting a piecemeal accommodation of the newly ascendant gentry. The Glorious Revolution of 1688 ratified the new balance of power in the English constitution and the

eighteenth century saw the rise of political parties to voice the demands of the newly dominant groups. These parties did not articulate
the political goals first enunciated by the Levellers; rather, they preserved the existing narrow base of political power right through the
eighteenth century.

We have seen how deeply the turmoil of the 1640s was influenced by
the demands of the Puritans. It is a familiar fact of American history
that one way of coping with the tensions provoked by Puritanism was
to allow the dissidents to migrate to the New World. The origins of
New England are to be found in the powerful religious convictions of
these dissident Puritans, who were driven by two motives: first, the
desire simply to be left alone to worship after their own fashion, to
escape the crushing orthodoxy that was reasserting itself in England;
and second, the desire to pursue a divine mission—that of establishing a spiritual community in the wilderness.

The earliest English migration to North America came in two waves
of settlement during the first decades of the seventeenth century. The
Pilgrims arrived first by way of Holland, whither they had fled earlier
to escape religious persecution. Pilgrim churches were based on a
covenant theology that informed both religious and political life. This
group intended to complete their break with the Church of England
through colonization in the New World. These future Congregationalists were of lower middle-class origin and brought with them to the
New World a tradition of democratic governance within the church.[7]

The second and much larger wave of settlers were the Puritans
who founded the Massachusetts Bay colony. They were chartered by
Charles I in 1629, shortly before he dissolved Parliament and set his
government on the course that led to the Civil War. This group was
not as intensely separatist as the Pilgrims, since the majority of its
members still regarded themselves as belonging to the Church of
England. They enjoyed higher social status than the Pilgrims and their
mode of governance was more aristocratic. But they too founded their
church government on a covenant, and they also embraced the concept of congregational autonomy. As one writer has put it, they embraced "the equality of all believers and the independence of all
churches."[8] Their religious views centered on "sainthood," or personal conversion, as the prerequisite for church membership. Those
who met this criterion represented a cross-section of English society:
they were farmers and craftsmen, as well as members of the profes-
sions and the landed gentry. They were bound together by the com-

mon core of their religious beliefs.[9] To their good fortune, once in the New World they were all far removed from the conflicts associated with feudal land tenure in England. They were also less constrained by the commercial monopolies sanctioned by the British state, and less affected by the ascriptive norms of the hereditary social order.

As the decades passed and civil conflict and religious persecution deepened in England, the pace of migration to America increased, bringing with it a growing diversity of religious viewpoints. Despite the implicit egalitarianism of their theology, early leaders of the Bay Colony, such as John Winthrop, held traditional, hierarchical views of authority. They sought to root their authority in popular consent without really making it subject to popular control. They instituted a system of elections but sought to limit the vote to church members and the actual exercise of political authority to the clergy. Eventually, however, their own experience led them to abandon these practices.

The Puritan movement, as we have already seen through its experience in England, harbored inherent schismatic tendencies due to both its theology and its organizational principles. Elite control implied the imposition of a new orthodoxy on people who were dissenters by tradition and who therefore strongly resisted it. In the course of time the Bay Colony generated new settlements headed by its own dissenters who formed new churches based in new covenants. Some of the leading theologians in the Bay Colony had themselves justified this by arguing from the Old Testament, as John Cotton did in 1645, that all "civil relations are founded in covenant."[10] Certainly the idea of congregational autonomy strengthened this process since it meant that there was no body—say of bishops or Presbyterian elders—to enforce orthodoxy. The tendency was further reinforced by a theology that encouraged all believers to read the Bible for themselves rather than merely to accept an established dogma from the clergy. In America as in England, the internal logic of Calvinist doctrine encouraged decentralizing and democratizing trends in church and politics. Whereas in the first decades of colonization the churches had tried to limit political rights to church members, by 1669 all such laws had been fully repealed.[11]

Looking back it is clear that the thoroughly Protestant character of colonial America was one of its most significant and decisive features. Catholic immigration was never significant, even though Maryland was founded in part to grant refuge to persecuted English Catholics; on the other hand, there was a great variety of Protestants: Congregationalists, Presbyterians, Anglicans, Baptists, and Quakers were the largest groups and comprised the majority of churches. Toleration of this diversity gained ground steadily, with England itself showing the way in the late seventeenth century. In the end, some colonies in America never had any established church.[12] By the turn of the century the colonists had firmly established a settlement pattern that facilitated the building of diverse local communities. Such communities were linked by shared religious principles but were autonomous and self-governing.

This settled pattern was disrupted in the 1740s by the Great Awakening, which Bruce Catton has called America's "first evangelical movement."[13] Linked to economic change and to social dislocation and stress similar in kind, if not in degree, to the crisis in England a century earlier, the Great Awakening was marked by the revival and spread of a reinvigorated religious impulse in America. It was spearheaded by an Englishman named George Whitefield, whose preaching directly challenged the lingering influence of the hierarchical principle in society and church. While the clergy had long since incorporated the doctrine of natural rights into their theology, they had not accepted the corollary principle of natural equality or endorsed it for civil society. Indeed, there was a fear of "levelism" and the clergy spoke out against it, just as the Presbyterians had in England during the Civil War.[14]

Whitefield challenged this accepted vision in a manner reminiscent of the Levellers. He "taught that all men, rich and poor, wise and ignorant, shared in the Gospel of Christ. Conscious of the indwelling spirit of God, the 'new birth' was the one thing needful. No man, however rich, however powerful, but must share the common experience; and all men, having this experience, were equal in the fellowship of Christ. So common men, 'the rabble,' crowded to hear him."[15] But at the same time that such teachings revitalized religious faith—particularly among the lower classes, but by no means only among them—they also caused division and led to a new wave of persecution in some areas. The Awakening accentuated the division between Old Lights and New Lights, splitting some denominations down the middle. Old Lights tended to oppose the movement, while New Lights supported it.

There is no consensus among writers on the colonial period as to what degree of impact the Great Awakening had on the American Revolution: some see its influence as indirect, while others see it as direct. But all writers seem to agree that the Awakening instilled in the common people a belief that it was their right to assert themselves and to participate in political causes that bore upon them. As Catton has put it: "For some of these humble folk . . . the experience of self-assertion and participation would prove lasting."[16]

The Awakening revived the original Calvinist emphasis on the centrality of each individual's direct personal relationship with God. This individualist strain had always been present in the Puritan society of the colonies, but it had been submerged within the settled pattern of belief in authority and obedience to it. It had lain dormant while the mass of the people accepted the dominant position of the established clergy and acquiesced in the hierarchical, and therefore inegalitarian, structure of society, church, and government. Now that people were reminded that they themselves might be better judges of God's will than any clerical elite, the impulse to broaden and democratize rights and status was itself rekindled. In this way the notion that all colonists were entitled to enjoy certain basic rights was raised to the level of conscious demand. In religious terms it took the form of "a passionate conviction in man's right to freedom of conscience"; within the churches, such thinking led to "a revulsion against undemocratic methods of ecclesiastical control and state interference and a more determined devotion to the old Congregational way of local self-government in religious affairs."[17]

The revitalization of Calvinist doctrine harbored the same challenge to political authorities that it raised to religious authorities. The Awakening created fertile ground for the influence of Whig political ideology with its great emphasis on avoiding the tyranny latent in hierarchical authority. In other words, it encouraged colonists to consult not only their Bibles as a guide to action, but also "Sydney, Locke, Milton, Hoadley, and other writers to find arguments to support their cause."[18] After the Awakening, religious and secular themes were increasingly blended together in response to specific conditions and grievances that seemed to lead inexorably toward the war with England.

One result of this blending was to lay the foundation for a national political community that soon would have to be built. The combining of a "popular spirit of pietistic self-righteousness with a new commitment to inalienable natural rights" helped to establish the spiritual and ideological core that would lie at the center of America's identity as a nation; to put it differently, the Awakening broke the "apolitical pietistic shells" of the mainstream colonial churches and brought them out into the political arena.[19] At mid-century, on the eve of the events that led to separation from England, renewed religious competition in the form of mission efforts by the Anglican church gave further impetus to the growing nationalism among the Puritan churches.

The Churches and the American Revolution

At the time of the Stamp Act in 1765, Jonathan Mayhew declared that religious faith was the best guarantee of the political liberty enjoyed by New Englanders. Mayhew was expressing a view that had long been held by Puritans, and that had enjoyed a new resonance throughout the colonies since the Great Awakening. The inseparability of religious and political rights was proclaimed constantly from the pulpit during this period. Such preaching frequently recalled the earlier Puritans of the 1640s, thereby forging a symbolic link between the English revolution and the impending American Revolution.[20]

Between 1763 and 1776, as prospects deepened for war between England and the colonies, the New England clergy—and particularly Congregationalists—worked diligently at stirring and sustaining an active resistance to the British reassertion of authority in America. They helped to develop and disseminate the principles on which resistance would be based. After 1774 their role was an open and influential one. Their sermons, which were published as patriotic pamphlets, sought to establish legal and moral justifications for resistance. They worked with colonial legislatures to obstruct British political initiatives, and they helped in the recruitment of colonial militias as the prospect of war came closer.[21]

In short, in the eyes of many colonists, Puritan theology provided compelling reasons to resist Britain's violations of their God-given rights. As Alice M. Baldwin has shown, the "most fundamental principle of the American constitutional system is the principle that no one is bound to obey an unconstitutional act [and] . . . this doctrine was taught in fullness and taught repeatedly before 1763. . . . He who resisted one in authority who was violating the law was not himself a rebel but a protector of law."[22] All the rights asserted in the Declaration of Independence had been formulated much earlier in the Puritan churches, and had been vigorously promoted and defended throughout the colonies by the Puritan clergy.

Separation from England, then, together with religious pluralism and a more egalitarian social condition, enabled the colonists in North America to develop the distinctive tendencies latent in the Protestant Reformation generally, and present in specific ways in the English revolution. These tendencies were facilitated by the economic circumstances of New England. Most families who made the journey to America found opportunity awaiting them: wages were high in comparison with England; even more importantly, there was an abundance of land. Although North America lacked the immediate riches of Latin America in the form of gold, silver, and other precious metals, it did afford the typical lower-middle-class immigrant the possibility of obtaining a stake in the land. The "moving frontier" permitted separatist churches to go their own way, it enabled new communities to be founded as groups of families and worshipers saw fit, and it made economic opportunity available to a broad cross-section of the society. In this way North America provided a different kind of wealth from that available in Latin America—an abundance that was much more spontaneous, decentralized, and ultimately democratic in character.

This is not to suggest that colonial government in the English colonies was democratic; but it *was* substantially free of direct central oversight and control from Britain. Under terms of the royal charters each colony was ruled by a royal governor in concert with a colonial assembly. The governor, who was appointed by the king, headed the Anglican church where it was established, summoned and dissolved the assembly, had the power to veto legislation of the assembly, and commanded any armed forces. As the colonial era advanced, however, the assemblies, which were elected and controlled by the colonists themselves, tended to dominate the colonial governments—above all by providing the revenues upon which government depended.[23] The royal governors suffered the same sort of financial dependence that had weakened the position of the English monarch prior to the Civil War. As a consequence, the North American colonists enjoyed a long period of de facto self-rule. When the movement for independence arrived they were well prepared for it.

Hartz argues that for the North American colonists the rebellion to achieve independence was less a repudiation of colonial political arrangements and principles than an application of doctrines that were thought to inform and justify the colonial experience itself. Put differently, the Lockean ideas of natural rights, limited government, and a right of rebellion against tyranny that grew out of England's seventeenth-century revolution were seen by the colonists as having direct application to their own colonial situation. When the drift toward separation began in 1763 North Americans already thought of themselves as self-governing and already acted as an independent people.[24] All that remained was to articulate the principles that would make this clear to the rest of the world, and then to fight for that independence if necessary. The justifying principles would be drawn directly from English tradition.

In a brilliant work Bernard Bailyn has shown that the movement for independence arose out of what amounted to a constitutional crisis within the British empire. Despite generations of neglect toward the colonies, the British view was that Parliament represented all Englishmen, including those in the New World. In English constitutional thought, Parliament was the locus of sovereignty in Britain. That sovereign authority was exercised through a process of virtual representation. Consequently, all laws passed for the administration and taxation of the colonies were valid and authoritative. The colonists could complain and appeal the various "stamp acts" of the day, but they could not override the decisions of Parliament.[25]

This entire approach clashed with the historical experience of the colonists. They had long enjoyed a de facto actual representation in their own assemblies. Suddenly, their laws were being "contradicted" by those of Parliament and their immediate interests were being submerged in the broader interests of Britain as a whole. The struggle to assert their claim to, or demand for, actual representation in these circumstances was correctly seen by the king and by Parliament as a repudiation not only of virtual representation but also, in effect, of Parliament's sovereignty. The problem was compounded when the colonists began to speak as though their rights were not a grant from Parliament, but prior even to Parliament's authority: it was Parliament's duty to protect and guarantee rights that Englishmen in America already held. When the Stamp Act was repealed but was followed by the Declaratory Acts, which asserted that Parliament had supreme authority under the British constitution, the colonists' position was rejected—and the die was cast.[26]

From this vantage point the Declaration of Independence can be seen as the colonists' response to the central tenet of the Declaratory Act, which was necessarily nonnegotiable. Either Parliament was sovereign, or it was not. The colonists had reached a point where Parliament's exercise of sovereignty seemed incompatible with their own. This impasse was reached precisely because the colonists had been effectively self-governing for so long. All that remained was to find the appropriate arguments in support of their cause and adequate means to defend themselves if the arguments failed. As Hartz says, they found their arguments in Britain's own Whig tradition, and specifically in the writings of John Locke, which were so ably and eloquently reformulated by Jefferson in the Declaration of Independence.[27] They pressed their arguments skillfully in the form of a "Radical Whig ideology" that was articulated with great energy and determination in the pamphlet literature of an opposition press.[28] By doing so, they fulfilled the inner logic of their own dissenting tradition and lengthening history of self-government. The war of independence, then, was neither a cause nor a sign of social revolution in North America. It was, rather, a final act of violence to guarantee the continuity of American colonial development. It represented, not a breakdown of legitimate authority, but a dramatic declaration of where legitimate authority actually lay.

The Religious and Political Character of Spanish Colonization

Iberian colonization of the New World began during the reign of King Ferdinand and Queen Isabella, who united the kingdoms of Castile and Aragon through their marriage in 1469. These were the first European monarchs to create a dynastic state with absolutist pretensions. In their drive to unite Spain and expel foreigners they pursued an active policy of political and administrative centralization. Since the nobility was a serious obstacle to unification, they strove to undermine the nobility's independence and to subordinate them to Crown control. Their efforts were remarkably effective. By creating a militia loyal to the Crown, by denying the nobility a wide variety of symbolic and ceremonial trappings that suggested their coequal status with the monarch, and by threatening to withhold the financial perquisites available only to the Crown as a weapon against disloyalty, Ferdinand and Isabella succeeded in removing this large obstacle to their authority.[29]

Their second target was the church. In this regard, their most effective strategy was the provision of badly needed support to the papacy in its wars with France. In return, in 1508 Pope Julius II issued a papal bull granting the Spanish monarch "the privilege of founding and organizing all churches . . . in all overseas territories which they possessed or might acquire in the future."[30] This grant gave the Spanish king complete control over religious affairs in the New World and opened the way for a "union of altar and throne" in Spanish America that has no parallel in other experiences of European colonization.[31] As J. Lloyd Mecham has written, "it is difficult to conceive of a more absolute jurisdiction than that which the King of Spain exercised over all ecclesiastical affairs in the Indies."[32] Without the king's authorization, no church could be founded; he granted permission for the clergy to travel to the New World, and he appointed all bishops. The Iberian domains in the New World were formally titled "The Indies of the Crown of Castile," and appropriately so: by 1510 Ferdinand had achieved a strong centralized control over the Iberian peninsula, and he therefore was able to transfer that model of government to the New World. Let us look for a moment at one of the key measures taken by the Crown to assure implementation of its societal vision for the New World. We may then conclude our discussion of the colonial era with a word about the collaboration of the Roman Catholic church in the process.

The colonization of the Indies was undertaken essentially as a private initiative of the Crown. The conquistadors, on whom so much attention is normally focused, were in fact little more than agents of the monarch. The king made every effort to control them and to provide as direct a supervision of their activities as distances and communications allowed. One astonishing measure of this fact is that something on the order of 400,000 decrees concerning the New World were issued by Spain between 1500 and 1635; this averages out to about 2,500 per year![33] This reality of close supervision from Spain, which stands in such striking contrast to English colonial rule in North America, resulted from the way Spain's exploration and settlement of the New World were conceptualized. The Indies were thought of not so much as a colony, but as "New Spain." The king's mission was to incorporate the Indies into the realm, to extend or re-create the church and the sociopolitical order of Spain in new territory. It followed that the unity of ecclesiastical and political power that Ferdinand and Isabella had achieved in Iberia would also be reproduced, insofar as possible, in the Indies, and that the king would strive to direct the colonial church and government administration in the same autocratic fashion utilized in the mother country.

Perhaps the most famous and enduring mechanism used by the

Spanish monarchs to maintain a centralized control in the New World was the *encomienda*. To appreciate how it worked we need to consider the incentives that attracted conquistadors to undertake the king's mission. One familiar incentive was the prospect of fame and fortune through the discovery of gold and silver; some such fortunes were indeed made, but these opportunities did not go very far. A more lasting source of wealth was in grants of land. Since all land belonged to the king, it could be exploited by conquistadors only with the king's permission, which was granted on the basis of service and loyalty to the Crown. Both the exploitation of mineral wealth and the effective utilization of the land required an ample, manageable labor force. This was provided through the *encomienda*, a grant of Indian labor made available only to persons (*encomenderos*) deemed worthy of employing such labor on the basis of their service to the king. Thus, the *encomienda* assured centralized control of the colonies.[34]

The Catholic church actively supported the colonial policies of the Iberian monarchs—in part because of a shared world view, and in part because the church was so clearly subordinate to the king's authority. On one side, the Crown assumed the responsibility of seeing that the church prospered, granting it such privileges as its own courts, control over schools, hospitals, and charitable services, and extensive opportunities to acquire lands and other sources of wealth.[35] The church's special position was reinforced dramatically when Philip II introduced the Inquisition into the Americas in 1570.[36] Thus shielded by royal authority from religious competition, the church was free to play a diffuse, multifaceted role in the settlement of Latin America, serving, in effect, as an agent of social control for the Crown: "Since Catholicism was indissolubly united with royal authority, the church was quite as effective an instrument in the conquest and domination of the Indies as the army. It was one of the principal agents of the civil power in America for over three centuries. The clerics, being beholden to the King . . . served him without the slightest inclination to rebel. They felt more closely attached to him than to the pope. They were more royalist than papalist."[37]

This portrait of Iberian centralization should not be exaggerated. No European state had developed the bureaucratic structures necessary to effect complete centralization of political control at this time. In Spain's instance, government consisted of the totality of such agencies as courts, treasury juntas, and the church hierarchy, each of which was independent of the others. These agencies competed to define public policy. Many office holders held their office for life. At the same time, such officials were appointed by the Crown and were understood to be "direct representatives of the Crown."[38]

In extending its control to the New World, the Crown had its greatest success in the capital cities where its own appointees were concentrated. From a bureaucratic point of view, the task was more difficult in the countryside because the monarchs had less leverage over the *encomenderos,* while the latter had immediate and powerful economic interests to protect. For example, a major issue in the early Conquest period was treatment of the Indians, whom the *encomenderos* wished to exploit as agricultural laborers and mine workers, and whom the Crown wanted to protect from abuse and to Christianize. As one writer has put it, in resolving this issue "the vested interests of the colonists" had to be balanced against "the paternalistic idealism of the Crown."[39] In this manner the policy initiatives of the Crown were often moderated or altered when they met determined resistance or criticism from affected groups in the New World. "The king recognized no superior inside or outside his kingdom; he was the ultimate source of all justice and all legislation. . . . The laws that bore the royal signature, however, were not the arbitrary expression of the king's personal wishes."[40]

Despite these qualifications, the Iberian pattern of colonial settlement differed notably from that of North America. Iberian colonization created a society in Latin America that was religiously orthodox and intolerant of dissent. As Claudio Véliz puts it, "Latin America . . . never had the formative historical experience of religious nonconformity."[41] Colonial society was strongly hierarchical and status conscious. Its pervasive inequality and corporatist nature afforded distinct privileges and rights for various social groups. Despite some fluidity in the social structure, the overall character of Hispanic society in the New World displayed remarkable staying power through three centuries of colonial rule. Thus, at the moment of independence in Spanish America, the social and religious situation was quite different from that of North America forty years before. The independence movement did not represent the fruition of a long period of autonomous political development geared toward achieving national sovereignty so much as it reflected Spain's inability to maintain control over its colonial empire.

The struggle for Latin American independence from Spain took place over a period of sixteen years, from 1810 to 1826. It was fostered by a variety of external factors, including the currents of Enlightenment thought that encouraged a liberalization in religion and politics and were used to justify the American and French revolutions. Perhaps even more important was the waning capacity of the Spanish government to retain influence over its colonies in economic as well as political and administrative terms. Spain's war with Britain in the first decade of the nineteenth century encouraged among the colonies a high degree of "commercial independence from Spain in advance of any moves toward political separation."[42] The impact of weakening commercial ties and communications between Madrid and the colonies was reinforced by the difficulties the monarchy soon experienced at the hands of Napoleon. French pressure forced the abdication of King Charles IV and then of his son, Ferdinand VI, in 1808. The imposition of a French king undermined the authority of the existing Spanish administration in the Americas, paving the way for the wars of independence, which brought an end to Spanish rule in the Americas by the mid-1820s.

Independence did not bring about a substantial social or political revolution in Spanish America. Creole elites took the place of the Crown-appointed officials who had exercised authority previously. The aspiration to create republican institutions of government was undermined in practice by the lack of prior experience with them, and Caudillistic rule soon began to make its appearance. As to the religious sphere, the Catholic church had to renegotiate its relationship with state authorities. Initially it turned to Rome for assistance, but it received little help in its struggles with the emergent governments, which sometimes had a strong anticlerical bent. Yet although the church's legal status changed, it was neither dispossessed of all its privileges nor compelled to accept religious competition, because the new political elites themselves did not want such competition. Their anticlericalism was not primarily a religious phenomenon, as in the Reformation, but rather a drive to limit the church's ability to exercise independent political power.[43] Eventually the new governments arranged patronage rights over the church in return for making Roman Catholicism the state church.[44] Thus Roman Catholicism remained the dominant religious institution and was "the only de facto national religion."[45] Even with the coming of Protestantism in the late nineteenth century, the church continued to play an important role as guarantor of the values of a Catholic society.

The Arrival of Protestantism: The Early Years

Protestantism played no role in Latin America during the period of the Spanish conquest. As we have seen, the Catholic clergy came to the New World at the request of the Spanish Crown, and as an integral part of the extension of Spain's dominion over its colonies. The pervasive religious orthodoxy of the Spanish meant that distribution of the Bible was inhibited in Latin America until the late seventeenth century. It was not until the national period that Protestantism began to play an important part, as the bearer of "modernization."

In the early 1800s the first Protestants to arrive in the Spanish New World came to resettle in ethnic-cultural enclaves. These "transplant churches"[46] were fleeing discrimination in their own nations and did not want to suffer the punishments of the Spanish Inquisition in Latin America. Hence, they were not missionary churches actively engaged in spreading the gospel or challenging Roman Catholicism.

Evangelizing Protestantism grew slowly in Latin America after independence. In regions such as Central America, which were controlled by conservative forces in the initial postindependence period, Catholicism was restored to legal primacy; the *patronato real* became the *patronato nacional*. The 1824 constitution of the Central American Confederation stated: "Her religion is the Roman Catholic Apostolic with the exclusion of the public exercise of any other."[47]

At the same time, postindependence liberals advocated trade with northern European nations and viewed favorably the quality of life in these northern Protestant nations. They encouraged the influx of Protestant missionaries and tried to remove the obstacles to Protestant colonization by granting religious freedom as part of commercial treaties. Under liberal guidance, by 1832 the provisions of the Central American Constitution were amended to allow freedom of worship.[48] In part the liberals saw Protestantism as a countervailing force that could challenge the hegemony of Catholicism. In a more positive sense, they viewed Protestantism as an important component of the "modernist project"—an integral part of the success of the westernized industrializing nations. Thus, the liberal elite welcomed the dedication to schooling that the missionaries brought in their attempt to extend the knowledge of the Bible to the local populations. The earliest missionaries, who came under liberal sponsorship, exemplified a missionary approach that had great impact on Protestant development in Central America. Their objective was to work with the more privileged classes.

A most interesting case is that of Guatemala, where liberal president Justo Rufino Barrios returned from a diplomatic visit to the United States in 1882 accompanied by Presbyterian missionary John Hill. Barrios was convinced that Guatemalan society could be improved by the infusion of Protestant values, and the Presbyterian Board of Foreign Missionaries of the United States was willing to accommodate him.[49] The Guatemalan government paid Hill's passage from the United States to Guatemala; President Barrios personally accompanied him to Guatemala City and donated the land upon which the Guatemalan Presbyterian church still stands. Hill became the pastor of an English-speaking congregation in Guatemala and founded the Colegio Americano, which the children of Rufino Barrios attended.[50]

The denominational churches were not the only Protestant organizations to see Latin America as a fertile ground for evangelization: the Bible societies also played an important role in bringing the gospel to Latin America. In the nineteenth century, both British and American Bible societies performed an invaluable service by their distribution of the Bible to rural as well as urban areas. These Bible colporteurs were among the earliest Protestants to risk persecution at the hands of the Catholic church. Despite the risk they persevered, and by the early twentieth century their interdenominational work was supported also by the growth of faith missions. The independent Central American Mission was founded to "spread Bible teachings throughout Middle America."[51] By 1902 the Central American Mission had missionaries in all five Central American nations.

Both the Bible societies and the faith missions helped to give Central American Protestantism the distinctive personality that it maintains to this day. In contrast to the liberal "top-down" strategy of missionaries like John Hill, the spiritual and emotive use of Scripture was employed by many faith missions to convert the popular classes. Of particular note was the Latin American Mission founded by Harry and Susan Strachan in Costa Rica in 1921. The Strachans were dismayed by the slow growth of Evangelicalism in Central America and devised an unconventional strategy of tent meetings, fireworks, popular music, and oratory to reach the faithful.[52] This approach to conversion has remained a dominant characteristic of several important and expanding forms of Protestantism such as Pentecostalism, which arrived in Latin America in the 1930s.

The Strachans were unconventional in another way: They voiced a social and political awareness not usually associated with the privatized missionary work of the nineteenth and twentieth centuries. For example, they sent a letter to President Calvin Coolidge criticizing American intervention in Latin America.[53]

Thus, unlike the case of Catholicism, whose origins and interpretation can be traced exclusively to the Spanish Crown, the arrival of Protestantism in Central America was characterized by substantial variations that have remained in evidence to the present day. One contemporary missionary has said that the Protestant mission in Latin America was more difficult than that of the Far East.[54] American missionaries in China were encouraged to minimize their differences and unite against a foreign culture—but in Latin America, Christianity was already established. From a common core of shared belief, differences emerged more readily between and within the established churches and the faith missions.

Despite these determined beginnings, Evangelical growth in Latin America was slow and difficult. Catholic resistance was strong, and many missionaries had little prior knowledge of the arduous conditions of a life of poverty in a different, Hispanic culture. More importantly, the mission boards of many North American and European churches considered Latin America to be Christianized, so that substantial missionary effort was not concentrated there. Due to this mental image of "Catholic" Latin America even moderate Protestant growth went largely unnoticed by the mother churches in Europe and the United States. It is estimated that by 1916 the Protestants in Latin America numbered 10,442 communicants.[55]

Against these modest numbers there was in Central America a marked continuity with the colonial past, particularly as concerned church-state relations and the role of Roman Catholicism as legitimator of the existing social order. Well into the twentieth century, the Latin American Catholic church clung to traditional methods of assuring its influence in society. Rather than relying on evangelization, it sought "legal bases of privilege and the support of political elites."[56] The church counted on structural relationships to political authority rather than on its pastoral presence among the people. In this sense its broad religious presence masked its religious weakness and institutional dependence. Although Latin America contained nearly a third of all the world's Catholics, its Roman Catholic church was static, cautious, and largely isolated from broader developments in world Catholicism. When, under the leadership of Pope Leo XIII, the Roman church began to try to come to grips with the changes brought on by industrialization and to reassert itself in European society, the Latin American church remained aloof. Panamanian Archbishop Marcos McGrath has pointed out, for example, that Leo's great encyclical *Rerum Novarum* was not approved for publication in Chile until after World War I, three decades after its promulgation.[57]

In sum, at the turn of the twentieth century neither Catholicism nor Protestantism exerted a very dynamic influence in Central American society. The Catholic church retained some of its former privileges and lent its moral authority to preservation of the status quo, even though some of its power had been curtailed by liberal regimes. Meanwhile, owing to its small numbers and its general orientation, Protestantism did not have the potent influence for change that it had demonstrated earlier in England and North America. As we shall see in the next chapter, when North American Protestant missionaries did arrive in large numbers, they did not bring with them the challenging religious legacy of their ancestors.

Part Two

The Traditional Church
and the Prophetic Church

Prior to the popular insurrection that initiated the Sandinista Revolution, the Nicaraguan Catholic church was a remote and neglected outpost of the Roman church. It was severely understaffed and heavily dependent on foreign clergy to carry out its pastoral mission and its educational work. During the period of the Nicaraguan insurrection the Latin American Bishops' Conference (Consejo Episcopal Latinoamericano, CELAM) gathered in Puebla, Mexico, for the sequel to its important meeting at Medellín (see Chapter 5, below). At this Puebla conference Archbishop Miguel Obando y Bravo was not permitted to address the assembly concerning the drastically deteriorating political situation in Nicaragua. It seems fair to say that, as far as Roman Catholicism was concerned, the local problems and challenges of the Nicaraguan church were insignificant among the larger priorities of the universal church. However, the onset of revolution rapidly and drastically altered this situation. Nicaragua came to be seen as a crucial testing ground for the defense of the church's most important goals, especially the preservation of church unity and the guarantee of freedom to pursue its religious mission.

Part 2 of this book examines the historical background to these momentous changes in the religious life of the country. We will show how Christian churches—both Catholic and Protestant—that were very traditional in outlook underwent a period of intense change to become leading actors in the social and political arenas. In the years prior to Vatican II the Nicaraguan Catholic church had exhibited the profile typical in a small Latin American country laboring under authoritarian rule: it had largely acquiesced to dictatorship and was seldom seen to denounce government abuses. It enjoyed a privileged position in society, particularly in the area of education. Yet it had a weak pastoral presence among the populace.

Vatican II and Medellín introduced Reformation-like changes into this static and torpid religious setting. The reexamination of religious principles and the reordering of pastoral goals that so characterized these two church councils found a fertile soil in Nicaragua. One objective of Part 2 is to clarify the nature of the most important changes initiated at Vatican II, and to show how they were articulated more fully and more radically at Medellín. A second objective is to explain how and why these changes took hold with such force in Nicaragua—as they also did, we may add, in other parts of Central America. We will attempt to show why religious renewal brought vital new energy to the church, leading to a much more dynamic presence in society. Our focus will be on the prophetic character of religious renewal.

The prophetic edge to religious renewal led not only to a heightened sense of spiritual integrity and vitality, but also to increased conflict between the church and its former ally and patron, the Somocista regime. Our third objective, therefore, is to explain why, in the Nicaraguan case, religious renewal led to strong identification with a broader movement for political change. As in Puritan England, this was especially true at the grass-roots level where, over the course of a decade, thousands of Christians gradually embraced the cause of revolution. The Christian base community was a causal agent of great importance in this transition.

Ironically, these changes also carried the seeds of a powerful backlash. In the case of the Roman Catholic church, the prophetic dimension that gave vibrant new life to the church soon provoked a strong reaction against the "politicization" of the church that it seemed to entail. As we shall see, when CELAM III was convened at Puebla in late January 1979, an important sector of the Latin American hierarchy was mobilizing to halt, if not reverse, the prophetic tendencies that had been unleashed at Medellín. This movement reflected more than merely the antiquated theology of a few reactionary bishops: it reflected a growing concern, shared by many church authorities, that the pace of religious renewal engendered by Medellín had begun to career out of control—that it might soon threaten the very institutional integrity of the church itself.

This too was a Reformation-like phenomenon. Change that rejuvenated the church was good, so long as it could be controlled and managed by those possessed of the church's authority. But in Latin America the progressive social teachings of Vatican II had issued in a theology of liberation that spread rapidly across the continent, implicating the church in all manner of social and political rebellion. These events vividly recall the experience of Martin Luther, whose doctrine of the universal sainthood of all believers led to Anabaptism and peasant rebellion—consequences he did not anticipate, and which he tried aggressively to thwart. As we tried to show in Part 1, they are also quite similar to the experience of the English Puritans during the Civil War. In a setting where authoritarian rule and social injustice were being challenged, in part on the grounds of religious principle, those very religious principles became a means of advancing far more radical political demands than the Puritan gentry ever intended they should.

Liberation theology was accompanied, and even inspired, by religious changes at the grass roots. Nicaragua exemplified the sort of changes that were taking place. Christians responding to the prophetic challenge laid down at Medellín had mobilized for change. In so doing, they had entered into the revolutionary process that overtook their nation, contributing to its energy and direction. However, in the eyes of those entrusted with the authority to govern the church, this Christian activism posed new challenges and a potential threat to the church's institutional integrity. For this reason the Nicaraguan church became much more important to CELAM and to Rome after the triumph of the revolution. Indeed, the Roman church hierarchy's intensified interest in Nicaragua paralleled that of the Reagan administration.

Five

Tradition and Change
in the Christian Churches

Roman Catholicism and the Challenge of Modernity

While the Latin American Catholic church functioned at the margins of the universal church, and looked to the state to protect its religious status and social prerogatives, it depended on Rome for its doctrinal orientation. This dual dependency posed a dilemma for the church in Latin America when Pope Leo XIII and such successors as Pius XI and Pius XII pushed the church in Europe toward an accommodation with industrialism and the social and political changes brought on by modernization. The concern for the working class articulated in *Rerum Novarum* (1891), for example, implied a strong critique of the economic and political elites upon whom the institutional church relied so heavily in Latin America. To take up the pope's critique was to jeopardize the very foundation of the church's position in society. For this reason, the social doctrines of the Roman Catholic church that emerged in Rome during the seventy years between *Rerum Novarum* and Vatican II found only a faint echo in Latin America. While that teaching reached Latin America, it lay dormant for decades awaiting conditions that would bring it to life.

At the end of the nineteenth century the Catholic church in Europe still viewed society through a largely medieval lens. As a religious institution the church had once been coextensive with secular society, and that aspiration persisted across the centuries that brought the Reformation, the French Revolution, and the Industrial Revolution to challenge the church's historic "Constantinianism."[1] The church's response to these challenges had long been one of hostility and resistance because each of these "revolutions" attacked fundamental aspects of the church's very identity, as well as its authoritative role in society. Yet society continued to be transformed by these events, and the traditional Roman Catholic church became more and more anachronistic, refusing to relinquish its "Christendom" world view long after that world view had ceased to describe its actual relationship to society.

Symbolic of the impasse at which the church had arrived were the *Syllabus of Errors* issued by Pius IX in 1864 and the First Vatican Council, held in 1869–70. The *Syllabus* explicitly undermined the program of such Catholic reformers as Robert de Lamennais by opposing freedom of religious conscience, separation of church and state, and ecumenism.[2] In all, some eighty propositions covering a broad range of issues concerning faith, church, and society were "condemned as erroneous by Pius IX." Seventeen of these had to do with the church's relationship to civil society.[3] In the same vein, Vatican I "was preoccupied with protecting the church's authority and property against rising tides of nationalism, anticlericalism, and revolutionary ferment sweeping through mid-nineteenth-century Europe."[4] To that end it proclaimed the dogma of Papal Infallibility. With such severe pressures for change in society, this seemed necessary in order to affirm the continuing validity of a Thomist world view with its natural hierarchies and their corresponding lines of command and obedience, together with its fixed, immutable principles of morality and right reason.

But then, just when the church seemed to draw a definitive line against the advance of modernity, Pope Leo XIII reversed course, however tentatively, in the direction of reconciliation. The new point of departure was Leo's encyclical, *Rerum Novarum*, which focused on the frightful condition of the urban working class brought about by rapid industrialization. The encyclical opened with these ringing declarations:

> . . . there can be no question whatever that some remedy must be found, and found quickly, for the misery and wretchedness pressing so heavily and unjustly at this moment on the vast majority of the working classes.
>
> For the ancient workingmen's guilds were abolished in the last century, and no other organization took their place. Public institutions and the very laws have set aside the ancient religions. Hence by degrees it has come to pass that workingmen have been surrendered, all isolated and helpless, to the hardheartedness of employers and the greed of unchecked competition.[5]

There can be little doubt that Pope Leo "intended his encyclical to be a major intervention in defence [*sic*] of the poor."[6] He was deeply concerned with the plight of workers and he spoke harshly of the "callousness of employers and the greed of unrestrained competition."[7] However, while Leo XIII was pushing the church toward a stand for the poor, he was not urging it to take sides in the broader political conflicts emerging in European society. He opposed the "fact of exploitation," but he did not "attempt to put the Church on the side of the working class *against* another class" (emphasis in original).[8]

It is fair to say that *Rerum Novarum* was in fact a Catholic response to the "mounting tide of socialism."[9] Socialism represented some of the worst evils of modernity: secularism, class conflict, egalitarianism, and democratization. The church taught that violence, disorder, and leveling were inappropriate and involved a "striving against nature."[10] Social justice was to be achieved through the fulfillment of mutual obligations already inherent in the social order. The rich had their rights and their authority, and they had to be called to conversion; the poor had their rights too, but they were to be patient. The church acted as intermediary, preserving stability while seeking justice. Therefore, the church had little sympathy for the creation of unions that would be run by workers themselves and that set them in conflict with the owners of capitalist enterprises: such a vision clashed with too many traditional principles to which the church still clung. Let us look a bit more closely at Pope Leo's case against socialism.

According to Leo XIII, the socialist remedy to working-class ills was contrary to justice as the church understood it. This was because "every man has by nature the right to possess property as his own."[11] Socialists would deprive the worker of his freedom by controlling his wages, and in the final analysis this would not improve his conditions of life. A socialist state would destroy the stability of the family, establish state supervision of children, and encourage class conflict. The church, by contrast, sought to "bind class to class in friendliness and good feeling. The things of earth cannot be understood or valued aright without taking into consideration the life to come, the life that will know no death."[12]

It was in this spirit that Leo XIII warned workingmen to beware of the false promises of socialism. There could be no perfect life on earth, and, more importantly, in God's sight poverty was no disgrace. The pope reminded workers that Jesus became poor for our sake, that he called the poor "blessed and offered the tenderest charity towards the lowly and the oppressed."[13] Leo went on: "To suffer and endure, therefore, is the lot of humanity; let them strive as they may, no strength and no artifice will ever succeed in banishing from human life the ills and troubles which beset it."[14]

If socialism was not the answer to the problems of the working class and the church staunchly defended the rights of property, how then could the workers' lot be improved? Leo XIII argued that even though poverty was consistent with the image of Christ, still the rich should be inclined to generosity with those who were less fortunate. More importantly, owners of property and workers should agree upon a just wage: the owner must then provide the agreed wage, and the worker must complete the necessary work. In the event that either party failed to comply with the agreement, only then could the state intervene to see that "each obtains his due—but not under any other circumstances."[15] Apparently the pope believed that workers should organize Christian workingmen's guilds in order to provide both material and spiritual help to their members. He was concerned that workers' associations might seek to improve only the physical conditions of men, thus becoming "little better than those societies which take no account whatever of religion."[16] It is evident that Pope Leo's proposal for the working class continued to reflect the medieval Catholic ideal of a society regulated by guilds and bound together by vassalic relationships. He did not say what the worker should do if the rich were not inclined to generosity and moral persuasion, and if the poor did not accept the "meek resignation" that was offered them.

At the same time, even though the word *liberalism* was not mentioned in this famous encyclical, the papal argument was grounded in eighteenth-century philosophical liberalism: the role of the state was regulatory to a minimal degree—it must guarantee the "natural" right to property and intervene only if owners and workers did not comply with the wage bargain they had justly agreed upon. This tacit Catholic acceptance of liberal principles seems ironic given the historical disposition of "liberal" regimes toward the church. In both Europe and Latin America, such regimes were among the first to call for the abolition of church property and power. We must assume that, faced with what seemed the greater threat of socialism, church leaders decided to make an accommodation with liberalism in the hope of turning some tenets of liberal doctrine to the church's own advantage.

The perception that socialism was a more serious threat to the church may also be attributed to the fierce anticlericalism of the French Revolution and to the events of the Paris Commune that had occurred just two decades earlier, in 1871. In this brief and violent episode, Parisian Communards tried to establish their own government. Although many of the rank-and-file Communards were workers, the Commune was not a socialist or proletarian revolution—despite the legendary status it later received from Karl Marx.[17] Eventually the Communards fought against the army of the French National Assembly. Before their defeat, they defiantly shot their own hostages, including the archbishop of Paris, rather than surrender them to the national government. This left a frightening and bitter memory in the Vatican.

Insofar as *Rerum Novarum* encouraged the church officially to address itself to the social questions posed by modernization, it must be seen as an innovation in Catholic doctrine. It was even prophetic in the degree to which it denounced existing injustices and called for conversion. But it did not ally the church with the broad tendencies that industrialization had unleashed, which were irrevocably altering the face of modern society. In the aftermath of *Rerum Novarum* the church encouraged Catholics to form associations of their own, separate from the rest of the working class.[18] Similarly, it refused to accept the view that political authority should be democratized. The rights of workers did not extend to self-governance, or to equal representation, either in the work place or in the state. As Pope Leo XIII himself put it in the encyclical *Immortale Dei*: ". . . every civilized community must have a ruling authority and this authority, no less than society itself, has its source in nature, and has, consequently, God for its author. Hence it follows that all public power must proceed from God. . . ."[19]

In short, Christendom remained the ideal that inspired the church's social vision. Christendom necessitated that the church interpret God's will in temporal as well as spiritual affairs and continued to place all social questions within a framework that accepted hierarchical authority and inequality as given in the social order. With only limited concessions to the ongoing process of modernization, this remained the church's position until the Second Vatican Council (1962–65).

Protestantism and the Congress of Panama

We have seen that the Latin American Catholic church was largely removed from the mainstream of Catholic thought but that it relied upon the European church for its general orientation. In contrast, geographic proximity to North America and missionary zealotry afforded Latin America no such luxury where its Protestant community was concerned. Because of the schismatic tendencies within Protestantism, the major influx of North American missionaries during the heyday of "Manifest Destiny" made the Latin countries a fertile ground for competing evangelizations. The presence of North American missionaries had a particularly strong influence on, and control over, Protestant churches in Central America. By 1916, North American inroads into Latin America were such that major Protestant denominations were able to coordinate their missionary work throughout Latin America.

In 1910, Protestant churches from Europe and North America held a great "Conference on Missions" in Edinburgh, Scotland. At this conference Latin America was neither represented nor included for discussion. The significance of this omission was soon recognized by some of the North American churches with missions in Latin America, and in 1913 they organized a meeting to discuss the region and set up a "Committee on Cooperation in Latin America." Despite its title, however, this committee was not engaged in North-South American cooperation; rather, the cooperation was among North American leaders of the various denominations that had missionaries working in Latin America.

Thus, the historic Congress of Panama, convened in 1916, was composed mainly of representatives from North American churches who met to plan strategy and share resources in their missionary work. This conference was organized by the largest Protestant denominations working in Latin America: Methodists, Presbyterians, Lutherans, United Brethren, and Baptists. Four hundred and eighty-one delegates attended: 230 as official delegates, 74 as official visitors; the remaining 177 did not have official status. Of the official delegates and visitors, 159 came from the United States, Great Britain, Canada, Spain, and Italy; the remaining 145 came from eighteen Latin American nations—but of these "Latin American" delegates only 21 were Latin American by birth. Although several presentations were offered in Spanish, English was the official language of the congress.[20] There was also little formal Catholic participation. Indeed, the congress was divided as to whether Catholics should be invited at all. Many feared that an invitation to Catholics would be the first step toward an accommodation with Rome, which they opposed in light of the persecution they had suffered.

The concerns of the North American mission boards dominated this historic congress. Issues such as the relationship between science and religion, the impact of the distribution of the Bible in Latin America, and the sharing of printing costs among the various denominations were an important part of the conference agenda. The congress also recommended that a distribution of Protestant labor should be agreed upon—if one mission was founded in a specific area, other missions should begin work in another area.[21] Thus, by means of "comity agreements" Latin America's territory was divided among several denominations. In Central America, for example, El Salvador, Honduras, and Nicaragua were assigned to the northern Baptists, while the Methodist Church was assigned Panama and Costa Rica.[22]

The pastoral message of the congress was a product of its time and allows us a historical measure of the Protestant self-image and "top-down" evangelizing strategy of the early twentieth century. Three major reports—"On Exploration and Colonization," "The Role of Women," and "Education"—sketch out this orientation, which was clearly directed toward the upper classes. In the first document the congress traced the history of Latin America from its Catholic-Spanish origins. In their view the introduction of liberalism with its modern system of education was beneficial for the upper and middle classes. Liberalism helped to undermine the Spanish-Catholic system and made the upper classes more receptive to the Protestant message. Recognizing the importance of these classes, the congress vowed to improve the quality of their missionaries so that the privileged might be converted in greater numbers.[23]

The congress documents that dealt with education and the tasks of women also made similar points. The gospel must be brought to the more educated women in Latin American society by improving the programs and the physical buildings of the Protestant schools.[24] Education for the poor was not viewed as a necessity; what was important was to convince the intellectuals. Thus, Protestantism, on the eve of its greatest period of numerical growth in Latin America, assumed the values of the middle and upper classes in Latin America. In a theological version of "trickle-down" theory, missionary concern was directed toward the upper middle classes in part because of the missionary belief that a general improvement in the level of education would benefit society as a whole.

Finally, there was the question of what posture the churches should adopt toward social injustice. The Congress of Panama conceded that it was impossible to remain silent if religious liberty was threatened or if indigenous tribes were threatened with extinction—in such cases, Protestants should speak out. But in all other cases, missionaries were to use extreme caution—not because other injustices should be ignored, but because as foreigners their intervention in political issues could lead to harmful consequences both for local peoples and for the churches.[25] Curiously, the authors of these documents made no mention of the contradiction between their statements of noninterference in the internal affairs of a host country and their proud analysis of the Protestant role in the "modernizing project" and in the weakening of the Spanish-Catholic state (see Chapter 3, above).

The Anomaly of Central American Protestantism

As we shall see, during the 1960s Latin American Protestants began a difficult journey toward unity and toward the formulation of an authentic Latin American Protestantism that responded to local concerns. In the southern cone of Latin America the main denominations were relatively open to this prospect and to the opportunities they saw in interdenominational cooperation. In Central America, however, due to the greater impact of North American fundamentalist churches and nondenominational faith missions, the movement toward an indigenous Latin American Protestantism was less successful. To set the background for the rich and sometimes volatile dynamics of Central American Protestantism, which will come into play in subsequent chapters, we must analyze the reasons for its distinct character in Central America. This discussion is especially compelling if, as we have argued, the prophetic possibilities inherent in Protestantism were a catalyst for the development of a radically different political vision in England and the United States.

The question is, why did Central American Protestantism not lend itself to the democratizing impulses that characterized British and North American Protestantism? If the belief system that English Protestants carried to North America was essentially the same as that which North Americans subsequently brought to Central America, then would the social and political consequences not have been similar also? Indeed, in each of these historical cases, Protestant faith was characterized by four affirmations: the primacy of the individual, the authenticity of Scripture, the priesthood of all believers, and the gift of grace. As the Brazilian Protestant theologian Rubém Alves has argued: "The opposition between persons and structures, which is so characteristic of Protestantism, could and should have produced an ethic by which men would accept as their vocation the transformation of those structures to which they were opposed, in order to be reconciled to them."[26]

One explanation, advanced both by Alves and by the Argentine theologian José Míguez Bonino, is that instead of understanding the antagonism between man and social structures in dialectical terms, Protestants insisted on interpreting it in dualistic terms.[27] To see the world in dialectical terms means that one's understanding of the world is historical and conflictive. From such a perspective, Protestant freedom encourages the believer to work toward structural changes in the belief that changes can be for the better. A dialectical view thus locates the individual within the community and insists on responsible membership in that community: "I am my brother's keeper."

On the other hand, while a dualistic view is cognizant of social structures, it encourages withdrawal from them because it does not see the possibility of reconciliation between the individual and social structures. Protestant freedom is used, not to change an immutable world, but to withdraw from it in order to concentrate on one's personal salvation. The harsh realities of life do not build solidarity with others; instead, they signify trials sent by God. The earthly world is a place of suffering where one adapts to social institutions, maintains personal discipline, and converts others. If personal conversion and personal discipline are necessary to improve an individual's life, structural problems are essentially personal problems that the individual can overcome. Poverty is not conceptualized in terms of economic and political relationships, but in terms of one's personal life decisions. In this sense Protestant dualism, in its refuge of privatized religion, has been nonstructural in its world view while at the same time it has accepted the existing social structures as immutable.

How can we explain the incompatibility between the democratic imperative of the Puritans who settled the New World in the seventeenth century and the dualism that North American Protestants brought to Latin America in the twentieth? Part of the answer lies in the powerful and enduring character of the Hispanic colonial legacy. Arriving in Latin America, Protestantism confronted authoritarian religious and political structures within which a Catholic tradition was deeply entrenched, despite the formal separation of church and state. Yet this is at best a partial answer: seventeenth-century English society was also characterized by authoritarian religious and political structures, but these were challenged by dissenting Protestants. A full answer must examine the character of North American Protestantism at the turn of the century.

H. Richard Niebuhr's discussion of the relationship between established denominations and sects is helpful in this regard. He argues that throughout Protestant history the sect has been "the child of an outcast minority."[28] Led by those who are without effective voice in the governance of their church or polity, these dissenters turn to the only form of association that they can utilize—the democratic pattern. Yet as generations pass, the vitality and isolation of the original members cannot be maintained. Moreover, if the sect submits itself to the aesthetic rigors of hard work, wealth will ensue. With growing wealth comes the possibility of greater participation in the economic life of the nation. The separateness and autonomy of the religious community become harder to maintain, and typically a trained, professional clergy replaces the original lay leaders. The result is that the sect begins to compromise and to adapt to the wider social and political environment.[29]

Niebuhr argues that the rise of sects is a way of calling Christianity back to its roots in the gospel message. The sects are an indication of the churches' inability to transcend social conditions that gradually transform them into organizations whose primary goal is self-preservation. The imperative of institutional survival takes on additional importance when the established churches become part of the "caste system," for it leads to an ethical weakness that is particularly evident in times of war or social upheaval. The slackening of commitment to the gospel mandate renders Christianity susceptible to those social forces or ideologies that formulate an effective rationale for action. In a society where the norm strongly favors the acquisition of material goods, and where nationalist or chauvinist sentiments run high, it is inevitable that the churches will adopt the rationale of the groups with which they are allied. As Niebuhr himself put it, the churches "usually join the 'Hurrah' chorus of jingoism, to which they add the sanction of their own 'hallelujah'; and, through their adeptness at rationalization, they support the popular morale by persuading it of the nobility of its motives. Christian ethics is allowed to fade into the background while the ethics of the social classes takes its place, unless, indeed, it is possible to re-interpret the Christian ideal in such a way that its complete accord with social morality is demonstrated."[30] Niebuhr's argument is not that the churches function merely as political institutions; they do pursue religious objectives. But they also represent the accommodation of religion to the social class system.

What light does Niebuhr's analysis shed on the values and attitudes of the North American Protestants who arrived in Central America?

First, it seems clear that by the late nineteenth century they no longer resembled the dissident, prophetic sectarians who had come to the New World over two centuries earlier. The sects had become established churches embodying the values of the status quo. Although their roots lay in prophetic upheaval, and even though they had played an important role in the abolitionist and feminist movements during the nineteenth century, they did not carry this tradition of prophetic criticism to Central America.[31] The dissenters were now fully "Americanized." They had improved their socioeconomic status and considered themselves to be a vital part of the North American success story.[32]

Also pertinent is the fact that during this period North American Protestantism was caught up in a major theological battle between fundamentalists and modernists over the authority of the Bible. This dispute had far-reaching repercussions on the interpretations of Christianity that missionaries brought to Latin America. A brief look at the debate will help to clarify why this was so.

Modernists believed that biblical teachings should be reassessed in specific historical or social periods. Although they did not use phrases like "reading the signs of the times," this was in fact what they advocated. They also tended to emphasize the ethical aspects of the Scriptures more than the spiritual, and they were receptive to using sociological approaches to biblical study.[33]

Against the modernists were the fundamentalists, who believed that they must defend and preserve the most basic elements of historic Christianity. Ernest R. Sandeen has argued that fundamentalism rested upon two nineteenth-century theologies, "dispensationalism" and the "Princeton theology." These two theologies were united until about 1918.[34] While the Princeton theology gave a logical and rational ordering to dispensational belief, what is important for our understanding is the concept of dispensationalism itself. This term refers primarily to the division of history into periods of time, or dispensations; seven such periods are specified. The seventh dispensation is called the Kingdom, or Millennium, in which the church will reign as Christ's bride and Israel will be restored to its ancestral homeland.

Dispensationalists had a very negative view of the material world and placed their hope in God's direction of life on earth. They also believed in God's ultimate, cataclysmic judgment of the world and the arrival of the Millennium. A dualistic theological position, such as that outlined previously, flowed easily from this premillennial view. Premillennialist theology discouraged interaction with a sinful world. The practical result was a reduced emphasis on earthly concerns that led to individual passivity and collective acceptance of the status quo.

In all likelihood both modernist and fundamentalist missionaries evangelized Latin America during the early twentieth century, since these tendencies cut across denominational lines (as they still do); two North American denominations that were deeply divided by this controversy were the northern Baptists and the Presbyterians, both of whom sent missionaries to Central America. However, given the legendary "zealousness" of the missionary, fundamentalists from the faith missions and Bible societies probably had the greater success in the first half of the twentieth century.

John XXIII and the Second Vatican Council

In the aftermath of World War II and the struggle against fascism, which had posed such painful dilemmas for the church's traditional view of authority, and in the face of European decolonization, a host of new social and political questions troubled the Roman Catholic church at mid-century. In 1959 Pope John XXIII announced his intention to call another council, one that would approach the relationship of the church to society with a much more positive attitude toward modernization. Convinced that the church could no longer cling rigidly to the past, Pope John urged that it "shake off the dust of the imperial era" and learn from the modern world.[35] He brought to the council a three-fold agenda. First, open the church to the world. No longer could the church rely only on "timeless" principles from the past, and no longer need it fear and resist modernity. On the contrary, in order to have a good understanding of its role in society it needed to stand with an open, inquiring mind before the concrete situations of progress and poverty in the contemporary world. Only then would its mission be grasped adequately. Second, the church must seek to be an agent of Christian unity. This meant entering into dialogue with other Christian confessions—which implied, of course, coming to terms with the Reformation, a view that had been anathema for centuries. Third, there was the question of the renewal of the church itself. What did faith require of the church in the modern world? If a "Christendom" view of the world was to be relinquished, what then would be the church's relationship to the social classes and the political conflicts of industrial society, or of the underdeveloped societies presently emerging in the postcolonial era? The response of Vatican II to this set of questions launched the church on a voyage in uncharted waters and brought an end to "ghetto Catholicism."[36]

The Second Vatican Council (1962–65) was a world council, with representatives not only from Europe and North America but from Latin America and other parts of the Third World as well. Moreover, it was called, not to deal with one specific issue vexing the church, but rather to address the whole problem of change in the world and the church's role in this modern, secular, technological age.[37] Specific issues set for debate included moving away from Latin to utilize local languages in worship, collegiality within the hierarchy, revitalization of religious life, and ecumenism. As Donal Dorr tells us, "The main drama of the Council was the struggle between liberals and conservatives on these issues."[38] To a large degree the council developed progressive positions on these matters: Bible reading was given new importance in Catholic worship, the clergy were authorized to say Mass in the vernacular, religious freedom was acknowledged, and the principle of collegiality was indeed embraced.[39] At the same time, the bishops became increasingly aware of the immense Christian presence in the Third World, especially in Latin America, and eventually some of the concerns of that presence were incorporated into the deliberations. Of particular significance were the issues of poverty and injustice. The council's preliminary efforts to address these issues in *Gaudium et Spes* (Pastoral Constitution on the Church in the Modern World) were the first halting steps toward transformation.

Vatican II approached its task of church renewal in a spirit of optimism about much that had once been valued negatively by church leaders. Pope John XXIII himself was optimistic about the benefits of modernization and the new possibilities it opened up for mankind. In that sense he began to move the church away from its traditional orientation toward the status quo and its ancient alliances with the most reactionary social and political groups.[40] In *Mater et Magistra* the pope carefully but clearly directed the church toward acceptance of state intervention in society and the economy in order to defend the rights of individuals and to promote justice. In instances where private property rights led to extensive hardship and suffering among the poor, he accepted the necessity for "socialization," which had been so fiercely rejected by the church in an earlier era. Such innovations pointed toward an "option for the poor," and they were given serious attention by the Vatican Council.

Gaudium et Spes adopted a penetrating and critical attitude toward poverty, inequity, and powerlessness, both within and among nations. In this document the council recognized the paradox of growing wealth and growing poverty: "Never has the human race enjoyed such an abundance of wealth . . . and economic power. Yet a huge proportion of the world's citizens is still tormented by hunger and poverty."[41] At a moment when unqualified enthusiasm for the benefits of development ran high, the Vatican Council injected a cautionary note—one that was picked up by the Latin American church and turned into a serious challenge both to local elites and to the rich nations. The prevailing model of development was producing unexpected anomalies and harsh moral dilemmas because "excessive economic and social differences between the members of one human family . . . cause scandal, and militate against social justice, equity, [and] the dignity of the human person."[42] The council insisted that "the immense inequalities which now exist" must be removed as rapidly as possible.[43] It also drew a direct connection between these conditions of economic inequality and the absence of political rights or representation. In a passage that strikingly anticipated the critique soon to emerge from Latin America, and which stood as an apt description of life throughout that region, the council said:

> It is not rare for those who are hired to work for the landowners, or who till a portion of the land as tenants, to receive a wage or income unworthy of human beings, to lack decent housing, or to be exploited by middlemen. Deprived of all security, they live under such personal servitude that almost every opportunity for acting on their own initiative and responsibility is denied them, and all advancement to human culture and all sharing in social and political life are ruled out.[44]

With these observations in view the council began to refocus the Catholic church's pastoral mission toward a conscious concern for those who are made and kept poor by conditions of injustice. An option for the poor would be "eloquent proof of [the church's] solidarity with the entire human family."[45]

A second area of innovation at the Second Vatican Council concerned the way in which the church endeavored to discern its proper role and mission in society. Traditionally that mission had been deduced from principles of natural law, which were taken to be fixed and eternal; history was merely a passive setting for the application of these principles, the validity of which was in no way dependent upon existing contexts. Without abandoning this tradition entirely, the council followed the pope's suggestion in *Mater et Magistra* to examine real-life situations before adapting traditional norms to them. Thus, church discernment involved "three steps [that] are at times expressed by the three words: observe, judge, act."[46] *Gaudium et Spes* followed this direction by asserting that the church had the "duty of scrutinizing the signs of the times and of interpreting them in the light of the gospel."[47] This new, more critical and prophetic posture had great impact in Latin America, where its application wrought momentous changes in the church.

③   The third area of innovation had to do with the internal structure of the institutional church and affected the relative authority and responsibility of hierarchy and laity. Prior to Vatican II there was no official theology of a lay apostolate; therefore, discussions of a more collegial sharing of authority and a more significant role for the laity in pastoral work broke new ground. Centralized structures of authority in the church had caused it to lose touch with the laity. Renewal meant recovering the ancient conception of the church as the "people of God." As the council put it in *Lumen Gentium* (Dogmatic Constitution on the Church): "Christ conferred on the apostles and their successors the duty of teaching, sanctifying, and ruling in His name and power. But the laity, too, share in the priestly, prophetic, and royal office of Christ and therefore have their own role to play in the mission of the whole People of God in the Church of the World."[48] Such statements provided an opening, of unspecified scope, for lay participation that had not existed in the church, especially in Latin America. Of course, the council was also careful to reaffirm that the bishops "have supreme authority in the church";[49] the "co-responsibility" offered the laity was assumed to be harmonious with the magisterium. But how would shared responsibility work out in practice if authority remained in the hierarchy and the laity only followed clerical direction? New structures and attitudes had to be established within the church to facilitate these changes. In Latin America the effort to do so received a great stimulus at the Second Council of Latin American Bishops, which met at Medellín, Colombia, in 1968 (CELAM II).

The Prophetic Church at Medellín

Vatican II was a great turning point in the history of the Catholic church, not least because of its repercussions in Latin America. Yet the council was dominated by West European bishops and theologians who could take for granted a stable political order, economic abundance, and a pluralistic society; its discussions of poverty and development could assume a broad consensus that would facilitate reform. When the Latin American representatives at the council returned home intent on holding a conference of their own to discuss the issues of Vatican II, they confronted a very different sort of world. The next three years were a time of intense reflection, study, and communication across diocesan boundaries. The traditional isolation that had so typified the Latin American diocese began to break down.

As bishops and their advisors delved into social issues in preparation for Medellín, they entered into an unprecedented dialogue with social scientists and other "secular" experts. They came into contact with new perspectives and a new language of self-description in Latin America: the language of dependency and domination. The language of dependency spoke to their daily experience as they pursued their pastoral mission among the peasants and urban migrants who were flooding into the cities at a stunning rate. They groped for ways to implement their broadened pastoral mission in a setting marked by economic exploitation, social marginalization, and political repression. In that setting they discovered just how weak the church's presence was, and how anachronistic the Christendom model of church and society. Thus, the seeds of a new vision of the church and its role in society were planted and nurtured, waiting to blossom in the most astonishing way at Medellín.

The Second Council of Latin American Bishops convened in 1968 in order to interpret Latin American reality in the light of Vatican II. What took place, however, was a rereading of Vatican II in the light of Latin American reality. Neither the church's historic body of social doctrine, nor even the pronouncements of Vatican II, were adequate to the situation of profound underdevelopment that Latin America's bishops surveyed at Medellín. The condition of the people was even worse than most had imagined. The church sought renewal in a society where oppressive poverty was widespread and growing and where the vast majority of people lived out their lives in utter powerlessness. Foreign corporations dominated local economies, and domestic elites were indifferent to the needs of most citizens. Aided by two important innovations—one structural, the other methodological—the bishops at Medellín attempted to come to grips with a church renewal oriented to the poor.

Edward Cleary's discussion of Medellín helps to highlight the two innovations in question. First, the council was organized so as to have pastoral representation, meaning that delegates were chosen from within functional divisions of the church. This yielded much broader representation than had been true of earlier bishops' conferences, with voices not previously heard at high-level church councils: "it meant that the church would be analyzed and defined from the bottom up."[50] In this decision lay one origin of the democratizing process that has generated enormous vitality and hope, as well as widespread conflict and fear, during the last twenty years.

Second, it was agreed that at Medellín the council would adopt a new methodology for carrying out its work. Following *Gaudium et Spes*, the participants shifted from a deductive, dogmatic method to an inductive, exploratory approach to religious and social issues. This choice encouraged unprecedented, critical self-examination. The shift in method reinforced the organizational shift, giving increased impetus to its democratizing potential. The church began to make room for new voices to be heard, including those of the laity. Church leaders engaged in dialogue with diverse groups in society, encountering Marxism as a widely used and practical tool of social analysis. They also began to see more clearly what clergy and religious women at the grass roots already understood experientially: Latin America was advancing irrevocably along the path of underdevelopment.[51]

The actions and statements of the bishops at Medellín (which reflected the strong influence of their clerical advisors) led the church almost immediately into political controversy. One reason for this can be seen in the very organization of the final documents, which placed such topics as poverty, peace, and justice at the front of the agenda, leaving more strictly church-related topics for last.[52] In their substance, the Medellín documents reveal an underlying logic that very much altered the church's historic stance toward society, its own pastoral strategy, and implicitly its relation to political authority.

For the Latin American bishops, clergy, and invited observers gathered at Medellín the overriding problem of their continent was the profound, deepening, and degrading problem of poverty, which they judged to be an insult to the human spirit. Throughout the official documents the bishops spoke passionately of the pervasive "structural" sin of economic and political institutions and relationships that maintained a vast chasm between rich and poor. They spoke of the need for the liberation, not the "development," of their continent, because for many Latin Americans "development" was no longer an objective term; rather, it was a concept tainted by a long history of imperial domination. Some of the flavor of this new approach is suggested by the following excerpt:

> The lack of socio-cultural integration, in the majority of our countries, has given rise to the superimposition of cultures. In the economic sphere systems flourished which consider solely the potential of groups with great earning power. This lack of adaptation to the characteristics and to the potential of all our people, in turn, gives rise to frequent political instability and the consolidation of purely formal institutions. To all of this must be added the lack of solidarity which, on the individual and social levels, leads to the committing of serious sins, evident in the unjust structures which characterize the Latin American situation.[53]

As the preceding quotation demonstrates, the Medellín documents, especially the sections concerning "Justice," "Peace," and "The Poverty of the Church," offered a causal analysis of the economic, cultural, and political conditions of Latin America. The bishops portrayed their continent as violent, as dominated locally by national elites and more globally by international capitalism, and as the victim of both internal and external colonialism. They condemned the marginality of much of the population, the flight of capital, and tax evasion by those individuals and companies who were most able to reinvest in the "progressive development of our countries."[54] These documents also had an unmistakable sense of urgency and a comprehensive, encompassing quality: no one aspect of Latin American life could explain the totality of Latin America's reality; by extension, all sectors of society, both civil and religious, had to be involved in the solutions.

In assessing their continent the bishops also evaluated their church and the role they wanted it to play in the future liberation of their nations. Despite the church's poor record in the past, it must now strive to be a sign of solidarity with the poor in their struggle for liberation. The bishops were aware of the *patronato real* and the special position that the Catholic church had enjoyed since the days of the Spanish conquest. They did not exonerate the historical church; instead, they admitted that the church must give up its privileges to become the authentic church of the poor. In their exhortation to the Latin American church, these bishops reaffirmed the position taken by the European bishops in *Gaudium et Spes*: "The church does not rest its hopes on privileges offered to it by civil authorities; indeed it will even give up the exercise of certain legitimately acquired rights in situations where it has been established that their use calls into question the sincerity of its witness or where new circumstances require a different arrangement."[55]

To vindicate their conviction that the church must relinquish its privileged status, the bishops attempted to clarify different meanings of poverty. They made a vital distinction between spiritual poverty and material poverty, arguing that the latter form of poverty is "in itself evil . . . and the fruit of the injustice and sin of Men."[56] In contrast, spiritual poverty is an attitude of opening oneself to God. One's trust in God permits a devaluation of the goods of this world and a valuation of the riches of God's Kingdom. In an important sense all Christians are poor in spirit and should bear witness to the evil that material poverty represents.

The bishops called for an urgently needed transformation of societal structures in which Christian belief and commitment must play an integral part. Conversion to the Gospel would facilitate needed change in Latin America. As the bishops put it, "the uniqueness of the Christian message does not so much consist in the affirmation of the necessity for structural change as it does in the insistence on the conversion of men which will in turn bring about this change."[57] They also stressed that temporal progress and the Kingdom of Christ should not be identified as one and the same thing. Nevertheless, the former, "to the extent that it can contribute to the better ordering of human society, is of vital concern to the Kingdom of God."[58]

Latin America's bishops wanted to see a change in which all the peoples of the continent, "but more especially the lower classes," had a creative and decisive participation in building the intermediate structures that could lead to a new society. They called specifically for the creation of a Latin American economy that was not dependent on either the capitalist or the communist world for inspiration or support. The authentic Latin American economic model they envisioned would foster the dignity of the human person while avoiding both excessive individualism and undue collectivization. To this end, labor organized within intermediary structures and worker participation in the running of industry were essential.

Especially identified as urgently needing change was the condition of the extensive peasant and Indian class. A thoroughgoing reform of agrarian structures was called for. Land reform was not enough; technical aspects of production must also be addressed, as well as the organizing of peasants into cooperative associations that could assure their participation in the local and national economic decisions that affected their lives.

In order to empower intermediary structures such as peasant cooperatives, the reform of political institutions and the development of an increased social awareness would be necessary. The bishops saw that the proper role of government was not to favor a few privileged groups, as had traditionally been the case, but to facilitate broader participation and legitimate representation for all groups. They hoped that this political reform would start at the communal or municipal level, and spill over to the regional and national levels. But in order to achieve these objectives the populace needed a "realistic perception of the problems" confronting them.[59] Interestingly, the bishops ascribed an important educational role to the church. Through the national bishops' conferences, pastoral plans would be drawn up by teams comprised of clergy and laity. A special effort would be made to reach out to the privileged classes, which was thought to be essential in order for peaceful change to occur.[60]

At the same time, the bishops realized that programs could not simply be created *for* the peasantry and that a balance must be established between privileged groups and the poor. In the final analysis, peasants must develop their own organizations, small basic communities, so that "they might come to know their rights and how to make use of them."[61] The church committed itself to this task of empowerment so that a national dialogue could take place among all classes of Latin American society. In adopting these positions the Latin American bishops at Medellín sanctioned creation of the new religious structures that came to be known as Christian base communities.

Having staked out these positions, the bishops recognized that there were risks inherent in calling for an authentic plan of broadly based national development. Although there might be enlightened exceptions, dominant groups were apt to "characterize as subversive activities all attempts to change the social system which favors the permanence of their privileges."[62] These groups could be expected to appeal to anticommunism or the need for order and stability in order to justify their resistance to any reforms that threatened their power. But because the social and economic conditions of the majority were growing steadily worse throughout the continent, while the likelihood of political violence was increasing, reform was necessary and in the interest of all.

The bishops cautioned Latin America's Catholics that peace means more than the absence of violence: lasting peace must be built upon social justice. They realized that the changes they advocated, and the conscientizing education they called for, would bring a tension to their societies that might seem to threaten social peace. They were now convinced, however, that a lasting peace could only be built on the foundation of a more equitable distribution of society's resources. Peaceful solutions were clearly to be preferred because changes brought about by violence would be superficial; authentic change must come from personal conversion and majority participation. Yet the bishops also cautioned: "One should not abuse the patience of a people that for years has borne a situation that would not be acceptable to any one with any degree of awareness of human rights."[63]

The statement on peace was concluded by a repetition of the words of Pope Paul VI as expressed in his encyclical *Populorum Progressio*.[64] However, the bishops' recitation gave greater force to Paul's views. Like Paul, they argued that social transformation by peaceful means was far superior to change through violence:

If it is true that revolutionary insurrection can be legitimate in the case of evident and prolonged "tyranny that seriously works against the fundamental rights of man, and which damages the common good of the country" whether it proceeds from one person or from clearly unjust structures, it is also certain that violence or "armed revolution" generally "generates new injustices, introduces new imbalances and causes new disasters; one cannot combat a real evil at the price of a greater evil." [Therefore,] we earnestly desire that the dynamism of the awakened and organized community be put to the service of justice and peace.[65]

In short, the effect of the Medellín documents was to clarify the options before the Latin American church.[66] The bishops acknowledged the structural relationship of violence and exploitation that bound an impoverished majority to a privileged minority, and they defined the church's mission as a defense of that "voiceless" majority. The church could no longer assign poverty to an exclusively spiritual domain. At the same time, liberation took on a rich new dimension of temporal significance to complement its more traditional transcendent meaning.

Protestant Renewal

The Catholic renewal of Latin America that burst forth at Medellín was inspired by Vatican II and by the "conversion" experiences of priests and religious who lived and worked in grass-roots communities. Latin America's Protestants, on the other hand, did not have the immediate reference point of a Vatican II. Thus, in their search for an authentic Latin American understanding of their faith they had to cast off the garments of the mother churches in the United States without a unifying directive. They relied primarily on the life experiences of their own pastors and congregations, and upon their reading of the Bible. Given their divisions and lack of doctrinal consensus, their search was fraught with difficulty.

During the 1960s, when Latin American Catholicism was experiencing a period of intense renewal, there was also unmistakable pressure upon the Protestant churches to reexamine their role and mission. Discussion groups were formed within the main-line churches to address Latin American concerns. These groups began to reinterpret their faith based on the prophetic traditions of the Old Testament. At the same time, they began to posit a dialectical relationship, not a dualistic one, between individual faith and social mission. Protestant leaders were challenged by the young people in their congregations to reexamine their faith. In effect, the renewal in the Catholic church was a catalyst for the Protestants.

The search for unity centered around two issues: the working out of an indigenous identity as Latin American Protestants, and the achievement of a unifying consensus on what their role should be in society. We will argue that as Protestantism evolved in Latin America its mission changed from an original privatized, inward-looking sense of faith, to one in which social commitment played an integral part. This new idea of mission, to the extent that it gained a foothold, has in turn aggravated the fundamentalist-progressive divisions within Protestantism. As Latin Protestantism developed a Latin American theology based on its own reality, the unity it sought became ever more elusive.

The Latin American Evangelical Conferences (Conferencia Evangélica Latinoamericana, CELA I, II, and III) attest to the evolution of a progressive Protestant mission in Latin America.[67] Before discussing CELA I, it should be noted that after the 1916 Congress of Panama several preliminary conferences were held in Latin America that attempted to bring the continent's Protestants together for discussion. Of particular note was the Havana Conference of 1929 because it was called and organized by Latin America's Protestants, not by the mission boards of the North American churches. The Havana steering committee wanted to initiate a dialogue between North and South Americans and to form an international Protestant federation composed of national councils that would meet on a regular basis.[68] Twenty years later this proposal of the Havana conference was realized at the first CELA conference, held in Buenos Aires in 1949. Significantly, the theme of CELA I was "Who Are We?" This meeting also saw the formation of an organization called Church and Society in Latin America (Iglesia y Sociedad en América Latina, ISAL), which would have a great impact on ecumenical cooperation and the formation of a new religious consciousness in Latin America.[69]

By the time of CELA II (held in Lima, Peru, in 1961), Protestants were being challenged to discuss a new model and a new evangelizing role for their churches. The theme of this conference was "Id por el Mundo" (Go out into the world). One keynote address was a working paper prepared by José Míguez Bonino, who challenged the conference to deal with this issue: "Has not the insistence on the personal character of salvation resulted in an individualism obsessed with one's own well-being, and arrogantly disinterested in the fate of the world? Has this not been the case of our Christian joy deteriorating into an insolent self-sufficiency, and a proud self-assertion?"[70]

What distinguished CELA II from previous conferences was its initial foray into socioeconomic analysis and its attempt to relate this analysis to its Protestant mission. This conference demonstrated an awareness of the conditions of underdevelopment and of the need for structural change. But it has been argued that the basic solutions put forth at CELA II were part of the modernizing, "trickle-down" perspective.[71] The conference endorsed a model of economic growth associated with capitalism and increased capital investment, as well as educational reforms, the expansion of democracy, and the reconciliation of social classes.[72] In its turn, CELA III would attempt to move the Protestant perspective to more controversial solutions.

In July 1969, Protestants from all over the continent met in Buenos Aires to celebrate CELA III. Orlando E. Costas called this conference "a landmark in the ecumenical history of Latin American Protestantism."[73] Representatives of Pentecostal churches, as well as faith missions such as Evangelism in Depth (which evolved from the Latin

American Mission) and World Mission, joined the denominational churches, the World Council of Churches, and ISAL at this meeting. Forty-three churches and ecumenical organizations sent representatives to CELA III, where the growing social consciousness in Latin American Protestantism was manifested. While committed to developmental ideals, CELA III was more realistic in its appraisals. The conference acknowledged the value of the democratic ideal but also noted "the failures and . . . frustrations, the disillusionments and distrust [which] many regimes that call themselves democratic have produced."[74] Instead of accepting the call for democracy at face value, CELA III argued that the church should work to promote Protestant participation in the transformation of existing unjust political systems.

The participants of CELA III acknowledged the renewal in the Catholic church, and a subcommittee report was prepared on the subject of the Protestant debt to the Catholic church. The report looked to further understanding and cooperation between Catholics and Protestants through mutual study of the Bible. In light of the historic animosity between these groups and the resistance of some Protestant groups to an endorsement of Catholicism, these statements were a startling departure. As a partial concession to the more traditional Protestants the CELA III report stated that an improvement in ecumenical relations should not be interpreted as " 'a giving-in to' or 'rejection' of our Protestant tradition. . . ."[75] For the first time, two official Catholic observers were invited to participate in a major Protestant conference.

At this conference Christians continued their search for an indigenous model of a Latin American Protestant church. Several committee reports urged the churches to reject "foreign garments" and begin to share in the life of their own continent.[76] In this context the theme of CELA III, "The Message of Jesus Christ for Latin America," explored the concept of the incarnation and what it signified for their continent. What emerged from the discussion was a conscious rejection of a passive Christology in the face of evil and an unwillingness to speak of reconciliation instead of acknowledging tension and conflict.[77] It was admitted that "instead of transforming Latin American Protestants into committed agents of change, Protestant preaching has alienated them from their society and further disfigured the already blurred image of God present in every human being."[78]

How could the churches move from what they were doing to what they should be doing? How could they make the incarnation present in every individual? The answer given by the conference was to invoke the power of the Holy Spirit that was present in all. Costas interpreted this response as an ecumenical attempt to legitimate one of the central beliefs of the Pentecostal church, whose member churches were deeply divided by CELA III.[79]

If we can argue that CELA III represented a determined thrust toward a new social awareness, we must also realize that the forceful-ness of this position was opposed by the more conservative Protes-tants in attendance. This disagreement was sharply drawn in the deliberations of the Youth Commission, which presented two conflict-ing reports to the conference plenary session. The majority report (which was influenced by ISAL) called for a fundamental change in political and economic structures and expected "the church to 'com-mit itself' to the liberation process, thereby taking 'the gospel to its ultimate consequences' rather than continuing to be an institution that 'maintains the status quo.' "[80] The minority report, fearful of the implications of the majority report, condemned all dictatorships of the right or the left, and wanted the conference to endorse a more "bal-anced" course of action.[81] In the plenary discussions of these reports CELA III eventually decided to refer both documents to the churches for further study.

Thus, if CELA III revealed a new consciousness it was not uni-formly accepted. However, in order to continue the dialogue within and between churches, it was proposed that CELA IV be scheduled and that an interim "organism of continuation" be established.[82] Ac-tually, an earlier body, called UNELAM (Movimiento Latinoameri-cano Pro-Unidad Evangélica, or Latin American Protestant Unity Movement), had been established as a result of CELA II. This group was given the charge of maintaining the channels of communication between the churches in attendance at CELA III and of organizing future ecumenical conferences such as CELA IV. But because UNELAM attempted to be an all-inclusive ecumenical organization it was inef-fective, and momentum was growing to establish a Latin American Council of Churches.[83] Realizing that its role should at least be that of facilitator, UNELAM called for a meeting in Panama to discuss estab-lishing a Protestant council; the proposal to create such a council would then be placed on the agenda at a meeting to be held in Oaxte-pec, Mexico, in September 1978. What was not clear was whether this meeting would actually establish a Latin American Council or merely discuss its formation at a future date.[84] The stage was thus set for an ecumenical conference dominated by the accumulated tensions within the Protestant community.

To conclude, the decade of the 1960s in Latin America was a period of intense ferment and change within Christianity. The failures of development programs, which were heralded with much optimism in 1960–61, increased the gap between rich and poor. This reality prompted Christian leaders and lay persons to reevaluate the conditions of their continent. By different routes both Catholics and Protestants began to define their role in terms of the struggle to overcome regional poverty. Yet, as we shall see in the next chapter, a commitment of this magnitude was a potentially dangerous one for the institutional church as well as life-threatening for individual Catholics and Protestants.

Six

Post-Medellín Challenge and Response

The Struggle to Define the "Option for the Poor"

The conference at Medellín thrust the Latin American church into new commitments in the same way that Vatican II had done for the universal church. Within the church itself, the changes proposed by each council met resistance from those who found the shift in orientation too sudden, or too far-reaching. What would happen to the authority of the magisterium in a pluralistic church? In *Octogesima Adveniens* (1971) Pope Paul VI wrote of the need to recognize the diversity of the world's Catholic population, and acknowledged the church's inability to offer a universal solution for all times and all peoples. But could this diversity eventually weaken the universal church? He had strongly encouraged a participatory role for the laity—but was it not ultimately the hierarchy, and especially the pope, who were entrusted with preserving the integrity of the institutional church?

From a historical perspective it is evident that an important source of strength in the church has been the maintenance of a strict traditional, or hierarchical, authority structure. Since Leo XIII, most encyclicals have relied on the teachings of previous popes and most papal statements have referred extensively to earlier papal documents.[1] The maintenance of papal authority was deemed vital to the integrity of the church. Despite the sincere statements of many popes concerning pluralism there was a strong tendency to see diversity as a threat to authority, just as unity was considered a source of strength. This attitude was dominant until the Second Vatican Council, where church authorities seemed to endorse the idea of promoting strength through diversity. Yet it has been difficult to adhere to that path. Often, the rhetorical support for pluralism has not been realized in the concrete actions of the hierarchy, from the Vatican to local bishops. This gap between rhetoric and practice is vividly demonstrated by the events surrounding the Nicaraguan Revolution, as we will see in Chapters 7 through 10.

An equally difficult dilemma grew out of efforts to define the meaning of the "option for the poor." How does the church judge and respond to the reality of social injustice? How can it achieve an integrated pastoral solidarity with the poor? From a position of solidarity, how can the church serve the poor as they struggle for justice against the terrible odds posed by a sinful society? High-level church officials soon found the commitments implied in the new official positions on these issues difficult to fulfill without adding qualifications—but the qualifications failed to simplify the problems or resolve the issues.

For example, the 1971 statement of the Synod of Bishops, *Justice in the World*, was a strong endorsement of the church's option for the poor. In that document the bishops affirmed "the Church's mission for the redemption of the human race and its liberation from every oppressive situation."[2] They specifically criticized the social injustices that oppressed humanity and argued that the church must be the voice of those who suffer injustice and are voiceless. They further argued that social structures placed obstacles in the way of the conversion of hearts and the realization of charity.[3]

Justice in the World sounded the same theme as Pope Paul's *Call to Action*, which appeared earlier the same year. It was issued in the name of all the bishops, yet it soon became obvious that some bishops regarded the document as too radical and felt that the synod was presenting a one-sided, overly politicized view of the church's mission on behalf of social justice. These more cautious bishops felt that one of the key propositions of the document—"Justice as a constitutive element of the gospel"—was too strongly formulated; the spiritual mission of the church was minimized to a degree that they found unacceptable. They argued that it was possible for the church to be prevented from taking action on behalf of justice without losing its integrity as church or its capacity to perform its other functions. For these bishops, action on behalf of justice should be an "integral" but not a "constitutive" dimension of the preaching of the gospel. This debate over words masked a deeper debate over the meaning of liberation and salvation, and how and where they could be achieved.[4]

Thus, the topics of liberation and salvation became the focus of the next Synod of Bishops, which was held in 1974, as well as the subject of Pope Paul's apostolic exhortation *Evangelii Nuntiandi* (On Evangelization in the Modern World). At the 1974 synod the bishops could not reach consensus on a final document, and it remained for the pope to try to reconcile some of the differences among them in his encyclical. This papal directive was significant because Paul VI was not able to clarify the different meanings of important theological concepts: the relationship between salvation, liberation, and the option for the poor remained ambiguous. A further significance of this directive is that much of its reasoning and its ambiguity influenced Pope John Paul II and the Latin American bishops at Puebla.

On the one hand, *Evangelii Nuntiandi* offered a strong affirmation for work on behalf of justice as a constitutive element of the gospel. Paul VI argued that when speaking of the gospel we must take into consideration three related concepts: (1) the Kingdom of God proclaimed by Christ, which is of such importance that everything else is secondary to it; (2) evangelization, as the duty of Christians to bring the good news of the Kingdom to all people; and (3) liberation, which is inclusive of, but more expansive than, economic or political liberation. Christians must proclaim the good news of the Kingdom, but they must also witness—showing by word and by example—how Christ wants us to live. They must work to liberate people from all forms of earthly oppression, the end result of this liberation being salvation, which comes from God. In the pope's own words:

Evangelization will also always contain—as the foundation, center and at the same time summit of its dynamism—a clear proclamation that, in Jesus Christ, the Son of God made man, who died and rose from the dead, salvation is offered to all men, as a gift of God's grace and mercy. And not as immanent salvation, meeting material or even spiritual needs, restricted to the framework of temporal existence and completely identified with temporal desires, hopes, affairs and struggles, but a salvation which exceeds all these limits in order to reach fulfillment in a communion with the one and only divine Absolute: a transcendent and eschatological salvation, which indeed has its beginning in this life but which is fulfilled in eternity.[5]

Human action and divine grace work together to bring about liberation or "action on behalf of justice," in the words of the 1971 synod. Human activity contributes to the salvific work of God but salvation itself is a gift of God, which has its beginning, but not its end, on earth.[6]

Having thrown his support to the 1971 synod statement, Paul VI then proceeded to identify some of his concerns about the misuse of the concept of liberation. In doing this he supported those bishops who were most concerned about the politicization of the church in its quest for justice. For the pope, political and economic considerations were vital aspects of liberation, but liberation "must take account of the totality of the human person in all its aspects and elements."[7]

Pope Paul was concerned lest the term *liberation* be reduced merely to an earthly understanding devoid of its otherwordly quality. He was afraid that if liberation were viewed as something to be achieved here on earth the term could easily become overly politicized in its usage, being associated with certain types of political regimes and not others. Therefore he attempted to broaden the Christian meaning of the term to include both a transcendental dimension and an all-inclusive earthly sense of the liberation of culture in its entirety. He argued that structural change alone was not enough, but that liberation must "envisage the whole man, in all his aspects."[8] External structural reforms could easily become another form of oppression *if* an interior change did not occur also. Thus, for an integral liberation to occur, a whole culture—its values, its collective attitudes and traditions—must be transformed.

While it is certainly true that values influence the development of culture, the reverse is also true: the existing culture influences the system of values—a trend that Pope Paul neglected to point out in his discussion of cultural liberation as the complete, integral liberation. It could be argued that through its individualism and consumerism, Western culture reflects and reinforces the cultural values of capitalism. Similarly, Communist culture, in its conformity and collectivism, reflects the cultural values of Marxism. By not recognizing the influence of structure on culture, the structural analysis of *Evangelii Nuntiandi* has been weakened. Moreover, priority given to the universality of the Gospel for all mankind in the absence of structural analysis obviates the question of poverty.

One can only surmise that to emphasize structures would have led the pope to emphasize economic and political considerations, which he had previously said would be an incorrect interpretation. This leads us to another of Paul's concerns: If this "incorrect" interpretation of liberation were to prevail, could one then justify the use of violence to bring about the "correct" liberation? In anticipation of this perceived danger Paul attempted in strong, unconditional language to dissociate the church from the use of violence:

The Church cannot accept violence, especially the force of arms—which is uncontrollable once it is let loose—and indiscriminate death as the path to liberation, because she knows that violence always provokes violence and irresistibly engenders new forms of oppression and enslavement which are often harder to bear than those from which they claimed to bring freedom. We must reaffirm that violence is not in accord with the Gospel, that it is not Christian; and that sudden or violent changes of structures would be deceitful, ineffective of themselves, and certainly not in conformity with the dignity of the people.[9]

It should be noted that this discussion of violence in *Evangelii Nuntiandi* was different from that of *Populorum Progressio,* written in 1968; in the latter pronouncement Pope Paul did allow for the possibility of justifiable violence against prolonged tyranny. How does one explain the difference in tone in these statements by the same pope? What had happened between 1968 and 1975? Dorr has suggested that Paul VI was not happy with the way in which the Latin American bishops had included his teaching from *Populorum Progressio* in the Medellín documents: they gave more emphasis to the exceptional circumstances (in which violence could be justified) than the pope himself had done.[10] It may also be argued that the pope, as a European-educated intellectual, was ambivalent about Third World violence. He also may have seen his primary responsibility as head of the church to be that of maintaining consensus within the church, and thus he spoke of liberation of the *whole* culture.

Many church officials in Latin America shared Pope Paul's reservations about the option for the poor and the meanings of liberation and salvation. By the time of the Puebla conference (February 1979) many Latin American bishops were equally concerned about the forceful statements they had endorsed at Medellín. What had happened in Latin America during the decade from 1968 to 1979?

The Road to Puebla in the 1970s

If, as we have argued, the Medellín documents clarified the options before the Latin American church, there can be little doubt that this clarification has caused and continues to cause great consternation within the Latin church. In 1973, barely five years after the Medellín conference, Sergio Méndez Arceo—then bishop of Cuernavaca, Mexico—acknowledged that many of his fellow bishops at Medellín

had not fathomed the implications of the documents they were signing.[11] To become a church of the poor was to make a radical break with
the past accommodation of the Latin American church to temporal
powers. This was a difficult adjustment for many church leaders—
especially during the 1970s with the rise of what came to be known as
"national security states" in Latin America. In the setting dominated
by such regimes, the defense of the poor brought the threat of direct
physical violence on the church itself. Under repressive military regimes many religious workers—priests, nuns, and laypersons—lost
their lives because they encouraged the training of lay leaders and
because they supported land reforms or worked with trade unions or
peasant organizations.[12] In these nations individuals disappeared,
torture was routine, and efforts toward peaceful change were violently
suppressed.

In the face of aggravated state repression and with the appearance
of guerrilla activity in some Latin American countries, what position
should the church take? Should it continue to defend the option for
the poor, risk the life of the church, and appear to justify guerrilla
violence on the basis of the church's teaching in *Populorum Progressio*
and the Medellín documents? Or should church leaders argue that
reconciliation, not armed class struggle, was the mission of the
church? Could they not also argue on the basis of *Populorum Progressio*
and *Evangelii Nuntiandi* that violence begets violence and armed insurrection may replace one tyrannical regime with another?

The Roman Catholic church will probably never resolve such dilemmas on a theological or practical level, especially given the rich ambiguity of its social teaching. These dilemmas were especially compelling for the Latin American church because of their immediacy. Given
the profound class divisions in Latin America and the violently repressive nature of many regimes, armed struggle was more and more
readily identified with the "liberation" of the poor. Thus, there was
much opposition, both direct and subtle, to maintaining the commitment to the poor because of the church's fear of appearing to defend
guerrilla or Marxist-inspired insurrection.

In the years immediately following the Medellín conference the rise
of guerrilla movements was not a pressing concern. The national
security states were the problem for the church of the poor. But by
the end of the decade, with the success of the Sandinista Revolution—inspired by nationalism, Marxism, and Christianity—liberation
through armed struggle came to the fore and became a more problem-

atic issue for the Latin American church, as well as for the Roman Catholic church as a whole.

As in Europe, Latin America's bishops were divided over the changes that had taken place in their churches and their societies in the ten-year period between the Medellín and Puebla conferences. The events of the intervening decade—the intrachurch conflicts and the deaths of two popes, Paul VI and John Paul I—cast a different perspective on the Puebla meetings. It had been one thing to endorse an option for the poor, and to encourage the participation of the poor in their own development, back in 1968; at that time few CEBs had actually been created. But by 1979 hundreds of CEBs had been set up, and their ambiguous relationship to the church hierarchy was beginning to cause concern.[13] Thus, with caution and apprehension apparent within both the European and the Latin American Catholic churches, the stage was set for the 1979 Puebla Conference of Latin American Bishops.

At the onset of the Puebla conference the 360 delegates were not of a single mind as to what direction their church should take in future years. To the majority of delegates the church should become more "balanced" in its positions: they accepted the assumptions of the preliminary drafts written by the CELAM secretariat, which argued for prudence on the part of the church and warned against the dangers of deviations. At the same time, a significant minority of the conference delegates was committed to continuing and even deepening the concepts of Medellín. The documents that evolved during the plenary sessions of the conference (at which participation was more open) weakened the theological predominance of CELAM. Thus, the final documents of Puebla would represent a compromise between those who argued for a reaffirmation of Medellín and those who wanted to place the Latin American church in a doctrinal mold that was European in nature. This ambivalence within the conference and within the documents accounts for much of the conflicting evaluation of the Puebla conference.[14]

In his analysis of Puebla the Salvadoran theologian Jon Sobrino admitted that there were many "lacunae" in the documents, which issued a generalized call for unity instead of exploring why there was no unity within the church. He argued that the theological frameworks were inadequate to support the conclusions of the final documents. He also noted that the Puebla documents failed to mention the martyrdom of many Latin American Christians during the previous decade. He lamented this failure, suggesting that the church had missed an important opportunity to clarify the implications of siding with the poor against oppression and injustice.[15] Nevertheless, the documents praised the CEBs as the "hope of the church" and affirmed the preferential option for the poor. The delegates also left no doubt as to who constituted the poor in Latin America: laborers, slum dwellers, peasants, and Indians. Yet their reaffirmation was a cautious one, which gave witness to their uncertainty. The bishops were afraid to stand squarely behind the Medellín documents because of their forceful implications. At the same time, as bishops they could not abandon the church's commitment to the poor.

This ambivalence was also shared by Pope John Paul II, whose role at Puebla cast a long shadow over the conference deliberations. For example, the addresses delivered by the pope in Mexico during his visit for the Puebla conference can be interpreted in different ways. His address to peasant and working-class groups in Oaxaca expressed a fervent commitment to the poor and a prophetic denunciation of the powerful:

> The disheartened world of field work, the laborers whose sweat waters their disheartened state as well, cannot wait any longer for their dignity to be recognized really and fully—a dignity no whit inferior to that of any other social sector. They have a right to be respected. They have a right not to be deprived of the little they have by maneuvers that sometimes amount to real plunder. They have a right not to be blocked in their desire to take part in their own advancement. . . .
>
> To you, responsible officials of the people, power-holding classes who sometimes keep your lands unproductive when they conceal the food that so many families are doing without, the human conscience, the conscience of the peoples, the cry of the destitute, and above all the voice of God and the Church join me in reiterating to you that it is not just, it is not human, it is not Christian to continue certain situations that are clearly unjust.[16]

At the same time, John Paul's view of radicalism and his insistence on integral liberation revealed his deep-seated fears of the direction of the Latin American church. He expressed these concerns in his opening address to the Puebla conference and helped to set the tone for this historic meeting. He also relied heavily on the concept of liberation set forth in *Evangelii Nuntiandi*. (In fact, the delegates to the conference received copies of the working drafts prepared by CELAM and copies of *Evangelii Nuntiandi* to help them in their deliberations.)

In his opening address Pope John Paul criticized the rereadings of the Gospel that are the product of theoretical speculations rather than of "authentic meditation on the Word of God and a genuine evangelical commitment."[17] What constituted a rereading? John Paul II argued that

[i]n some cases people are silent about Christ's divinity, or else they indulge in types of interpretation that are at variance with the Church's faith. Christ is alleged to be only a "prophet," a proclaimer of God's Kingdom and love, but not the true Son of God. Hence, he allegedly is not the center and object of the gospel message itself.

In other cases people purport to depict Jesus as a political activist, as a fighter against Roman domination and the authorities, and even as someone involved in the class struggle. This conception of Christ as a political figure, a revolutionary, as the subversive from Nazareth, does not tally with the Church's catechesis. . . .[18]

In language that would be mirrored in the final documents of Puebla the pope argued that Christ's message of conversion was open to all including the publicans of his day. For John Paul, evangelizing was not "an isolated, individual act; rather it is a profoundly ecclesial action, which stands in communion with the Church and its pastors."[19]

The interrelation between the concepts of church, evangelization, pastors, and integral liberation highlighted John Paul's concerns about the Latin American church and the growth of the grass-roots Christian communities: "In some instances an attitude of mistrust is fostered toward the 'institutional' or 'official' Church, which is described as alienating. Over against it is set another, people's Church, one which is 'born of the people' and is fleshed out in the poor. These positions could contain varying and not always easily measurable degrees of familiar ideological forms of conditioning."[20]

These statements foreshadowed the intraecclesial tensions that developed so rapidly in Nicaragua after the triumph of the revolution. They anticipated John Paul's own pronouncements in Nicaragua, made during his tour of Central America in March 1983. As will be shown in some detail in Chapter 9, by that date Rome had become deeply preoccupied over what it saw as the sectarian tendencies of

Christian communities in Nicaragua. Moreover, it saw an immediate danger that the sectarian impulse would be exploited by secular ideologies, such as that of the Sandinistas, in a way that would be harmful to the interests of the institutional church.

Clearly John Paul II thought it was the responsibility of the church to defend the rights of the poor and promote the dignity of the individual. Its activity was intended to be in the service of the human being within a Christian framework. But the church did not need to collaborate with other ideological systems in order to bring about total human liberation; through its own efforts a more just and equitable distribution of goods within nations and worldwide would eventually be achieved. In the pope's view the correct understanding of liberation was that set forth by his predecessor, Paul VI: Liberation "cannot be reduced simply to the restricted domain of economics, politics, society, or culture. . . . [It] can never be sacrificed to the requirements of some particular strategy, some short-term praxis or gain."[21]

It is hard to imagine that John Paul's address did not have a profound impact on the delegates to the conference, especially in light of their own first-hand experiences after having cast their lot with the poor of Latin America. The papal message offered to them was one of solace, of security to be found within the universal church and its traditional message of total liberation—a liberation that stood above mere political or economic understandings and that pertained to all Christians, rich or poor, taxpayers and publicans.

How then are we to understand the impact of the Puebla conference with its conflicting messages? To some, Puebla was a reaffirmation of Medellín; to others, it was the moment in which the church confronted liberation theology and reaffirmed the correct Catholic teaching of the church. The CEBs were still the hope of the church, but fears of a people's church were clearly expressed. The Christian must see Jesus as a liberating figure but not portray him as a political liberator. Evangelization must continue, but authentic evangelization must be done within the authentic church. In a church that ministered to all, the option for the poor remained preferential but not exclusive.

It seems evident that the sort of concerns that the Vatican and CELAM have today about church-state relations in Latin America were already visible at Puebla in 1979. The stage was set for the conflict that would divide the church in Nicaragua and increase church-state tensions after the revolution. The Nicaraguan Revolution was made with the broad participation of Christians, including many who took up arms against the Somoza regime. Thus, as the Puebla conference concluded, the church in Latin America was being thrust into a new stage. The doctrinal dilemmas that could be resolved on paper in a consensus final document were to be renewed in the immediate future on an empirical level. How should the church respond to a "revolutionary" government that Christians had helped to bring about, a government that was itself dedicated to a "preferential option for the poor"?

Latin America's Protestants Meet at Oaxtepec

As a result of the CELAM conference at Puebla, Mexico, the Catholic bishops could argue that despite their differences they had reached agreement upon an important series of final documents that would orient their church in future years. But for Latin America's Protestants, even a minimal level of consensus was elusive at their 1978 meeting in Oaxtepec, Mexico. In the course of these meetings several Pentecostal groups were on the verge of withdrawing their representatives, when at a late-night meeting they were guaranteed greater participation and were persuaded to stay. Yet within two years of the conclusion of this conference, two rival Latin American secretariats would be formed, reflecting a fundamental divergence of theological and pastoral viewpoints within the Protestant community. Let us examine that important meeting at Oaxtepec.

In September 1978 two hundred official delegates of 110 Evangelical churches and ten ecumenical organizations from nineteen Latin American countries gathered in Oaxtepec, Mexico. Their purpose was to seek "greater unity of the Christian people in order to be more faithful to the gospel in today's Latin America."[22] The recurring themes of this six-day conference included human rights, the national security doctrine, social change, cooperation between Catholics and Protestants, and most importantly, the search for unity.

Continuing the tradition initiated at Medellín (1968) where there were Protestant observers in attendance, Roman Catholics were present at Oaxtepec. Catholic Bishop Méndez Arceo of Cuernavaca, Mexico, in whose diocese Oaxtepec is located, made an appearance on the first day of the conference to welcome the participants. He also served as an impromptu commentator on one of the keynote speeches and celebrated a special mass to honor the contributions of Latin America's Protestants.[23]

The opening address at the conference was delivered by Carmelo Alvarez, president of the Latin American Biblical Seminary in San José, Costa Rica. His speech was important because it was representative of the profound changes that had taken place in Latin American Protestantism. The 1916 Congress of Panama had directed its appeals to the more privileged classes in Latin America; the 1978 Oaxtepec conference challenged the church to become a church of the poor. This direct challenge, which was captured in the Alvarez address, was quite controversial to some of the more traditional Protestants. Alvarez argued forcefully: "The history of Latin America testifies to a church handed over to the dominant classes, but it also shows the face of a church that opts for living from the underside of history. This is a church that wants to suffer with the beaten 'Christ of the Indies' to restore and transform this precarious, painful, critical history of ours. . . . This is a church which can affirm the horizon of hope so that we may see new days where justice dwells."[24]

Oaxtepec did not resolve intra-Protestant tensions; most of the papers that emanated from the various study groups were too controversial to be approved in plenary sessions. T. S. Montgomery has reasoned that to become a church that opted for radical change and defended the poorest of the continent was too "political" a position for many churches, although she was guardedly optimistic about the future of Protestant unity.[25] To carry the gospel to its ultimate (life-threatening) conclusions was a position that the conference as a whole could not endorse. What the conference did demonstrate was a continuing Protestant willingness to confront internal divisions and to continue the debate through the mechanism of CLAI, the Latin American Council of Churches (Consejo Latinoamericano de Iglesias).

The elusive dream of continental unity took a cautious step toward realization with the creation of CLAI. It was instituted as a "council in formation" at Oaxtepec, and all the powers and properties of UNELAM were passed on to the new steering committee of CLAI. The tentative establishment of CLAI, after four days of intense plenary debate, seemed to satisfy both progressives, who advocated its formation, and conservatives who were opposed to its commitment to social change.[26] But would CLAI, given its ambiguous, inconclusive origins, become another UNELAM? Worse yet, in the eyes of the conservatives, would it move quickly in radical directions?

The profound reorientation that shifted the focus of the church's definition and commitment to Latin American concerns was in part reaffirmed at Oaxtepec. Many Protestants hoped that CLAI would be an organism in the service of committing the churches to far-reaching changes in the economic and political structures of their continent. Closely integrated with this aspiration was the personal realization that their own internal renewal had to continue. For others there was apprehension about the formation of CLAI, but they were willing to at least give it a chance. But as CLAI defined itself more and more as a progressive and ecumenical organization that did in fact opt for the poor, more traditional Protestants began to organize their own council.

The tenuous unity of Oaxtepec was short-lived. In 1980 two conferences took place that in retrospect indicated the formalization of the emergent divisions within the Protestant world. The progressive World Council of Churches, under the direction of Emilio Castro, held an international meeting in Melbourne, Australia, while a subsequent conference, under more conservative sponsorship, took place in Pattaya, Thailand. Ironically, the subject of evangelization in the world was the dominant topic of both meetings—but during the conference in Pattaya a secret meeting was held to discuss the formation of a more traditional, "less-worldly" Latin American secretariat. Allegedly, the more progressive Evangelicals were excluded from this secret meeting.[27] Three years later, under the direction of Luis Palau and his associates, the Latin American Evangelical Confraternity (Confraternidad Evangélica, CONELA) was founded in Panama.[28] According to Alberto Barrientos, a Costa Rican pastor who was present at the founding of CONELA, "its clear objective was to counteract CLAI, which was itself in the process of formation."[29]

Conclusion

In this and the preceding chapter we have presented a discussion of the profound changes that occurred within Catholicism and Protestantism in less than two decades. Vatican II (1962–65) and CELA II (1961) occurred at the same point in time; both confronted the issue of internal renewal and mission within their respective churches. Medellín (1968) and CELA III (1969) witnessed the first exchange of Protestant and Catholic observers; both conferences decisively reoriented their churches toward a historical and realistic analysis of continental poverty. Oaxtepec (1978) and Puebla (1979) continued this ecumenical tradition and in large measure reaffirmed the churches'

transition from an exclusive to an inclusive mission. Against this back-
drop of historic conferences we must mention the work of individual
Protestants and Catholics who opened the channels of ecumenical
cooperation during the 1960s and 1970s in such organizations as ISAL
and the Theological Fraternity. Theologians such as José Míguez
Bonino, Richard Schaull, and Rubém Alves helped to create a common frame of reference for Latin American Christians who have opted
to work for the poor.

Yet by the end of the decade of the 1970s the implications of opting
for the poor were becoming more apparent and more threatening. The
Catholic commitment to Medellín was under severe stress at Puebla.
This contentious conference took place as the Nicaraguans were preparing for their final assault on the Somoza dictatorship. The final
documents of Puebla were issued before the July 1979 victory of the
Sandinistas, so that with the exception of Cuba there was no revolutionary regime in Central or South America for the churches to come
to terms with.

For the Protestants, who were never unified, the option for the poor
aggravated the internal divisions that had been apparent since the
arrival of North American missionaries. Within and across denominations one could identify progressive and fundamentalist factions;
CLAI and CONELA testify to the different paths taken by Latin
America's Protestants.

The Nicaraguan Revolution, which was coming to fruition when
Puebla and Oaxtepec took place, was a moment of truth for Latin
America's churches as well as for individual Christians. In a prophetic
action, one of the final acts of the Oaxtepec delegates was to condemn
the human rights violations of the Somoza regime and to send a letter of solidarity to the Nicaraguan people. The delegates also voted
unanimously to send a cable to Anastasio Somoza, calling on him to
resign.[30]

Seven

Religious Renewal and
Popular Mobilization

When Fidel Castro led the victorious 26th of July Movement triumphantly into Havana on January 1, 1959, the Roman Catholic and Evangelical churches were unseen and unheard on the stage of this great drama in Cuban history. They played no part in making the Cuban Revolution possible because promoting social change was no part of their theological reflection or their pastoral programs. The Catholic church adhered to a traditional, sacramentalist view of its role in society, while the Evangelical churches were preoccupied with "saving souls" but had little concern for improving people's daily lives. In these respects the Cuban religious scene was representative of the situation throughout Latin America, although the advance of secularism and a corresponding lack of religious vitality in Cuba may have been at the high end of the spectrum. In any event, the churches were not in any way prepared for the revolution. When the revolutionary government adopted a socialist model of development and began establishing a close alliance with the Soviet Union, the Cuban churches moved into opposition or exile.

Twenty years after the Cuban revolutionaries marched into Havana, another band of guerrilla fighters entered their nation's capital in triumph. This time the revolution was in Nicaragua—ironically, the country from which the ill-fated Bay of Pigs expedition, which was intended to overthrow the Castro government, had been launched. In the first days after the Sandinista forces entered Managua on July 19, 1979, one of the major public events to celebrate the popular triumph over the hated Somoza regime was a mass presided over by Archbishop Miguel Obando y Bravo, which was attended by thousands of joyous Christians welcoming the revolution. Dozens of other masses were simultaneously celebrated in parishes throughout the country. These religious celebrations only hinted at the vital role played by Nicaraguan churches, and by thousands of individual Christians, in the popular insurrection.

In the same year that the Second Vatican Council got under way, a report of the Catholic Press Association in the United States had offered a profile of the Nicaraguan Catholic church that highlighted its institutional and pastoral weaknesses. The report found priests to be few in number and "poorly formed," the hierarchy unable or unwilling to provide dynamic ecclesiastical leadership, and the institutional church virtually absent in the countryside where more than half of the population lived. It described the church as "living in the past," and saw its clergy as "blind about social problems," not to mention their being aligned with a government that was "hated by the people."[1] This was a church that openly criticized Fidel Castro but never ventured criticism of the Somoza regime. The Evangelical churches were scarcely different, although they tended to be apolitical rather than openly aligned with the government.

The first signs of change in the Nicaraguan Catholic church appeared in the late 1960s, stimulated by the historic Latin American Bishops' Conference at Medellín, in 1968. As we saw in the previous chapter, Medellín precipitated a dynamic process of reflection and experimentation within Catholicism, and indeed among Evangelicals as well. Above all, the emphasis on identifying the church with the poor led to the assumption of a more prophetic attitude toward society and politics.[2]

This process of change occurred all across Latin America. However, we will argue that the post-Medellín evolution of the churches in Nicaragua differed in significant ways from the experience of other Latin American countries, particularly the larger countries that had stronger institutional church structures. For example, in such countries as Argentina, Chile, Peru, and Colombia, which were much studied in the 1970s due to the appearance of religious radicalism, post-Medellín activism in the Catholic church took the form of organized clerical movements devoted to promoting structural changes in society.[3] In these instances a clerical elite, composed primarily of intellectuals, bore the burdens of religious and political protest almost entirely on their own shoulders, forming groups such as the Movement of Priests for the Third World in Argentina, and the Christians for Socialism in Chile. These clergy became strongly radicalized after 1968 in response to social injustice, as in Chile or Colombia, or to both social injustice and political oppression, as in Argentina and Peru. Their subsequent militancy brought them into bitter conflict with both church hierarchies and political authorities.

The long-term success of these radicalized priest movements was limited by the fact that they were opposed on two fronts. Their vulnerability to the pressures of church authorities and political regimes was accentuated by the absence of significant popular lay participation in the programs of protest and change that they advocated. Although as parish priests serving in marginal barrios these clergy had strong ties with the poor, generally speaking they did not choose to create autonomous structures of lay participation, nor to promote lay leadership within the communities of the poor. Such lay organization might well have enhanced the credibility of these movements in the wider religious and political arenas. A stronger, more self-sufficient grassroots base would certainly have been a practical asset in the drive to bring about societal change.

We can approach the Nicaraguan experience by contrasting it with the above examples. Although the Nicaraguan Catholic church was institutionally weak, and indeed remarkably so in comparison with the church in Argentina, Chile, or Colombia, post-Medellín developments in that country were so concentrated at the base of church and society that the advocates of change were significantly less vulnerable to pressures from either church authorities or the regime. This story is best told by focusing on four interrelated themes.

First, the emergence of a prophetic point of view in the Nicaraguan churches coincided with a dramatic growth in popular disillusionment with the Somoza regime, especially after the 1972 earthquake. At the same time, radicalization within the churches developed concurrently with a rapid growth in the strength and acceptance of the Sandinista Front as a legitimate political opposition.

Second, while many of its top leaders embraced Marxist principles, the FSLN was not antireligious. On the contrary, it accepted, and even encouraged, Christian participation in the unfolding political struggle. One of the most fascinating aspects of the Nicaraguan Revolution was the remarkable interaction of Sandinista guerrillas with a broad cross-section of Nicaraguan Christians. For a decade, beginning in the late 1960s, the FSLN struggled to build a viable political organization; in doing so, it frequently was instructed by Christians seeking to work out the prophetic implications of the Gospel. The FSLN developed a respect for these Christians and their religious beliefs that was highly unusual among revolutionary movements.

Third, the level of repression in Nicaragua increased sharply in the mid-seventies. Particularly in rural areas of the country, churches were the only source of refuge. By providing refuge, the churches came under attack, and so became a focal point of popular resistance.

After the assassination of Pedro Joaquín Chamorro in January 1978 this phenomenon spread to the cities, where churches frequently offered protection to participants in the anti-Somoza struggle, including armed combatants identified with the FSLN.

Finally, the Catholic church hierarchy became anti-Somocista, or at least was perceived that way by the populace. Acting as mediators between the FSLN and Somoza during such crises as the FSLN's seizure of the National Palace in August 1978, top Roman Catholic leaders gained credibility with the opposition, including the FSLN. Thus, during the popular insurrection that broke out in September 1978, the Catholic church was widely perceived as antiregime and therefore sympathetic to the revolution. Meanwhile, prominent Evangelical leaders, especially those associated with CEPAD, openly embraced the FSLN as the legitimate representative of the Nicaraguan people. Although these leaders were only a minority of the Evangelical clergy in Nicaragua, their visibility and outspokenness gave the impression of broadly based support within the Protestant community for armed resistance to the dictatorship.

The Origins of Church Radicalism

At Medellín, the Latin American bishops called on the church to "defend the rights of the oppressed," to foster grass-roots organizations, and to "denounce the unjust action of world powers that works against self-determination of weaker nations."[4] In Nicaragua, the Catholic church was not prepared to embrace this "option for the poor" and break its traditional alliance with the rich and powerful. However, there were fateful exceptions to this general picture. In 1965 the Nicaraguan priest Ernesto Cardenal founded a lay community on the Islas de Solentiname in Lake Nicaragua. At about the same time, a Spanish missionary, José de la Jara, set up a conscientization[5] team to work with families in the Managua barrio of 14 de Septiembre, developing CEBs that soon spread to other poor neighborhoods.[6] By the time of Medellín, the Jesuits, and Catholic students under their direction, were working in poor communities in the departments of Carazo, Masaya, and Masatepe. A Spanish Capuchin, Father Bonafacio, had begun three-day conscientization courses in Managua with the aim of enlisting students for a Church-sponsored radio school, broadcasting in the North, that provided a grade-school education.

The priests and religious who spearheaded these early efforts had in mind a socially conscious church that would concentrate its pastoral efforts on the poor and define its ministry in terms of their needs.[7] In the CEBs popular religiosity, which focused on the sacraments, was unconsciously but inevitably pushed aside in favor of Christian reflection groups that focused on social issues.[8]

The first indication that priests were beginning to take Vatican II seriously came in 1968 with the publication of a declaration signed by seven Nicaraguan clergy, who took great pains to avoid being political.[9] Citing conciliar documents, they called on the government to halt repression and torture and to free political prisoners. They also urged that the government commit itself to establishing a more just economic order. At the same time, the first in a series of national pastoral meetings was held to examine the country's religious and social situation in light of Medellín. Though it lacked focus and achieved few tangible results, this first pastoral meeting enabled the clergy to begin a dialogue on how to bring change to the Nicaraguan church. Finally, at about this time Managua's newly named Archbishop Miguel Obando y Bravo took a first step toward distancing himself from the regime by selling Somoza's gift of a new Mercedes-Benz and giving the money to the poor.

Between 1968 and 1970, Christian base communities took hold and grew. By the beginning of the new decade, only two of the original seven signers of the 1968 declaration were still actively working to implement the Medellín resolutions, but others in the church were moving in new directions. On returning from a 1971 Synod of Bishops in Rome, Monseñor Obando y Bravo was asked if he planned to register for the upcoming elections; his answer was no, he did not wish to dignify the electoral process. To underscore this attitude, the archbishop avoided both the inauguration of the Triumvirate in 1972 and Somoza's own inauguration in 1974 because each of these "elections" was seen by most Nicaraguans as fundamentally fraudulent and unconstitutional.

In 1971, a second national pastoral meeting was held. The priests who attended discovered that they were moving in a more concerted direction. They concluded that evangelization had to be aimed at "conscientization," although just what this meant still had to be worked out. The 1971 conference coincided with another development in the life of the church: the growing activism of Catholic high school and university students. The clergy working with these students were dubbed "the seven priests of Marx" by Somoza supporters, although at the time none identified himself as a Marxist.

Energized by the ideas of Medellín these priests began to push for change and experimentation at the grass-roots level. Their guiding initiative led to the establishment of the earliest CEBs in Managua, on the Atlantic Coast, in rural areas north of Estelí, and on the Islas de Solentiname. The "mother church" of the CEBs in Nicaragua, the community of San Pablo el Apóstol in Managua's 14 de Septiembre neighborhood, became a "pilot parish" under this initiative. It spurred base-level organization and set up programs to train lay leaders. Members of San Pablo organized retreats attended by priests and laity from other poor neighborhoods of Managua. A woman who joined the CEB in 1970 reported later, after the triumph, that the pastoral program helped greatly to strengthen family life in the parish: it brought husband and wife closer together, and helped individual parishioners to integrate the various aspects of their lives. Within the neighborhood, it led to a much stronger sense of community solidarity.[10]

Another current that fed the renovation of the church was the Catholic student movement. In 1970, students at the Jesuit Central American University attempted to challenge the "developmentalist" orientation of the curriculum and its tacit support of the Somoza dictatorship. When university officials refused to discuss student grievances, the students began to occupy local parish churches, staging what amounted to a Nicaraguan variant of the sit-in. Over the next year there were repeated occupations, one of which led some students and even several militants in the FSLN to be released from jail.

After repeated provocations of this kind, the government finally arrested more than one hundred students and expelled them from the university. In early 1971 eleven of these students approached the parish priest in Barrio Riguero, one of the poorest neighborhoods in Managua's so-called Zona Oriental, or Eastern Zone: they asked to be allowed to live in the barrio and, with the priest's help, to form a community for study and reflection. Their offer was accepted, and thus was formed, at lay initiative, the nucleus of the Revolutionary Christian Movement. During the decade of the seventies these idealistic young Catholic intellectuals, inspired by the post–Vatican II atmosphere of renewal, actively contributed tactical support to the growing revolutionary movement. Several of these young Christians later emerged as top leaders in the Sandinista Front.[11]

The Revolutionary Christian Movement was rooted in the emerging CEBs in Managua's eastern zones. Leaders of the movement settled in Barrio Riguero, entering into a period of sustained Bible study and reflection on the situation of their society under the tutelage of the parish priest. After 1973, Christian youth groups were formed in other CEBs, such as San Antonio Parish, and in a number of Catholic high schools. In these religious settings at the grass roots young Christian activists deepened their religious faith, established contact with the FSLN, and formed a commitment to the popular struggle to rid Nicaragua of the dictatorship.

In October and November 1970, and again in May 1971, Catholic students occupied the cathedral in Managua to protest human rights violations and the presence of the National Guard on campus. Occupation of the cathedral was accompanied by the occupation of five other churches around the country and was supported by twenty-two priests. A strong statement from the archbishop's office supported the students' demands while lamenting the involvement of the priests.[12] The protests attracted the attention of the FSLN, whose own leaders began making contact with these Christians to explore potential avenues of cooperation between the FSLN and the church. At the same time, between 1970 and 1972, Archbishop Obando y Bravo was drawn repeatedly into the political controversy created by the strikes at the universities and the student occupation of churches. In these conflicts, the public perceived that the Catholic church was beginning to take an antiregime stand. The very act of occupying the churches was a signal to many people that "priests and sisters were beginning to have some solidarity in opposition to Somoza."[13]

It is probably fair to say that in this early post-Medellín period, these activist Christians had little idea that their gropings toward a prophetic ministry would lead to intimate involvement in a popular revolution. As one participant later observed, however, they were beginning to "see Christ in an active, transforming charity, one that changes the world." And they were beginning to see that political action could be "a means of bringing about the redemptive action of God."[14]

The Emergence of Grass-Roots
Christian Communities in the Cities

The 1972 earthquake was a turning point in the country's political development and in the political role of the churches. The earthquake that struck Managua on the night of December 23, 1972, utterly destroyed the center of the city, creating a sense of confusion and panic, followed quickly by desperation and despair. Thousands of people were killed outright and tens of thousands were left homeless. Damage to industry and the disruption of normal commerce led to the immediate loss of thousands of jobs, setting industrial employment back to pre-1960 levels.[15] In the face of this devastation, Managua became entirely dependent on the emergency relief that now poured in from abroad. Both the Catholic church and Protestant agencies played important roles in facilitating the relief effort, much of which was provided by international church agencies. Although considerable tension had developed between the Catholic church and the government during the preceding two years, in the immediate crisis of the earthquake the church and the regime closed ranks momentarily. But this rapprochement lasted only a short while; within weeks, Somoza had arranged to channel all relief through the offices of the Liberal party, a party he dominated through an artful blend of intimidation and corruption. This openly political manipulation of humanitarian aid quickly alienated church officials, and soon not only the parish clergy but also the bishops began to criticize the government once again.

In the poorer neighborhoods of Managua the environment created by the earthquake enabled priests and religious to experience directly and vividly the connection between political structures and the suffering of the poor. The Sisters of the Assumption, for example, had lived and worked in one of the neighborhoods destroyed by the earthquake. They relocated in the barrio of San Judas, where they saw at first hand the consequences of official corruption: governmental intervention actually prevented relief supplies from reaching the suffering people of this barrio. Thus, the daily experience of life in San Judas moved the Sisters of the Assumption toward a prophetic interpretation of the gospel and into active sympathy with the growing popular resistance to the dictatorship.

The experience of the Maryknoll Missionaries in the barrio of OPEN 3 (now Ciudad Sandino) was similar. Prior to the earthquake OPEN 3 was a neighborhood of a few hundred people located several miles outside Managua. After the earthquake it grew rapidly due to the sharp influx of displaced persons. In this barrio the Catholic church at first mediated relief efforts through a Youth Club that had been formed by the Sisters of Maryknoll. But when the government took over the relief effort, the flow of supplies into OPEN 3 virtually ceased. The Maryknoll sisters and the Christian youth who worked with them were in a position to see the regime's indifference to the poor and its desire to profit at the expense of their misery. It was widely understood throughout OPEN 3 that Somoza and his officials were hoarding relief supplies and reselling them at inflated prices. As with the Sisters of the Assumption, these church people now took the first steps toward a prophetic interpretation of their religious mission as a direct consequence of living through the effects of systematic political corruption and oppression.

The Christian communities in Managua, particularly in the poorer eastern zone of the city, became a focal point of political protest following the earthquake. In these communities Catholics had to respond to the strictures of Medellín from a position of direct participation with the poor. In the prevailing conditions it was obvious that the government itself was responsible for the people's suffering. In Nicaragua the "structural sin" castigated by the Latin American bishops at Medellín had a concrete point of reference—*Somocismo*. Priests, religious, Catholic youth, and ordinary citizens in these communities began to organize their opposition to the regime. Among the youth particularly, there was an opening to the FSLN. From the ranks of the Revolutionary Christian Movement that had been founded two years earlier, a number of young Christians now joined the FSLN as combatants, while others helped establish a communications network.

In short, it was at the grass-roots level and through the actions of the laity that the Catholic church first became involved in Nicaragua's gathering revolutionary process and associated with the Sandinista Front. The political climate within which these developments took place became increasingly repressive over the next several years. As a result, the opposition activity of Christians was more and more clandestine, while the public protests of the pre-earthquake period, such as seizing churches, diminished.

The Delegados de la Palabra

In 1970 more than half of Nicaragua's population lived in the countryside, where they had limited contact with the institutional structures of the Catholic church. Under the stimulus of Vatican II and Medellín, however, the church began to reach out to rural people. In this regard two closely related programs, the Comité Evangélico de Promoción

Agraria (CEPA) and the Delegados de la Palabra, require detailed comment in the Nicaraguan setting.

The Jesuits created CEPA in 1969 with the support of the Nicaraguan Catholic hierarchy. The intent of the program was to train peasant leaders to organize politically in their local communities. Initially the training seminars were offered primarily in the coffee-growing regions of Carazo and Masaya, but CEPA later expanded into the north from León to Estelí. They attempted to "integrate biblical reflection and technical agricultural training," and they published a cartoonlike pamphlet entitled "Cristo Campesino" that suggested that such political demands as the right to land were sanctioned by the Christian gospel.[16]

Originally CEPA was created as a self-help program to enable peasants to meet their daily needs more effectively, but the program soon centered on strengthening campesino organization because it became clear to CEPA members that the peasants could not improve their conditions without organized, collective political action. When this awareness took hold, it raised the level of theological reflection among Catholics working at the grass roots. They saw the need to assist peasants in organizing to defend their interests in the context of the Somocista political system, which was deeply hostile to such interests. In this manner Christians working with CEPA became sharply politicized and militantly anti-Somocista. When the FSLN created the Asociación de Trabajadores Campesinos (ATC) in 1977, some key CEPA workers joined the ATC and became directors of the organization. Other CEPA workers were killed by the National Guard during this period of increasing radicalization.

As the radicalization progressed, the hierarchy became disenchanted and tried to restrict the activities of CEPA in order to prevent a closer association with the FSLN. Eventually these restrictions became too confining and CEPA cut its ties with the hierarchy. Now lacking official church sponsorship, CEPA continued to function as an independent Christian organization, working with campesinos while retaining its religious identity. Despite constant harassment by the National Guard, CEPA maintained a vigorous presence in the countryside. As Somocista repression of the peasantry heightened during the mid- and late seventies, CEPA workers identified more and more strongly with the cause of rebellion. By the outbreak of the insurrection in September 1978, CEPA was closely allied with the Sandinista Front.

Because of limited resources the Catholic church in Central America was never able to put many priests into the rural areas. A creative postconciliar response to this problem was to authorize lay persons, called Delegados de la Palabra, or Delegates of the Word, to perform many of the sacramental functions. The *delegados*, in turn, were closely associated with the emerging CEBs. If a more prophetic church was to consolidate its presence among the scattered population of the countryside, it had to entrust more responsibility to the laity by training grass-roots leaders who could themselves promote Bible study, teach catechesis, and help to organize CEBs. Thousands of Central American campesinos were prepared for the role of *delegado* during the 1970s.[17] As their numbers grew, at least three consequences became evident. First, the program fostered local leadership that had never existed before. Campesinos who could read the Bible, direct group discussion, and organize CEBs learned that they could also provide political organization and direction in their communities. Second, as *delegados* gained experience and as the CEBs were consolidated, the campesinos who took part in them drew closer together spiritually and also politically. Scattered families became communities bound together by a shared sense of identity and purpose. At this point CEBs were already contributing to the creation of peasant political organizations, while Delegates of the Word were emerging as leaders on that larger stage. This led to the third consequence: throughout Central America, *delegados* became targets of government repression.

Consider the testimony of Edgardo García, who became a *delegado* at the age of sixteen, soon after the Managua earthquake. Under the influence of progressive clergy, and through the auspices of CEPA, Edgardo trained to become a *delegado* and began organizing district juntas:

> In the District Juntas we were concerned with solving the problems of community services, safe drinking water, electricity, health centers, schools, learning some crafts, you see. . . . In order to strengthen this community struggle there had to be an element of faith. We had to foment a committed kind of religious practice. That was where I became a Delegate of the Word. . . . At first it was all a matter of learning how to use the Bible right, to get to know the Word of God, and then how to lead meetings, celebrations, religious ceremonies, to try to read a message where there were specific guidelines, or use studies that drew us into

the reality we were experiencing. We always made an effort to reinforce the overall aim of unifying the communities through organization. We had to find the causes of sin, of exploitation, of backwardness, and to support development projects.

When other kinds of organizations began to suffer repression, denunciation of the system was kept alive through the celebration of the Word of God. The Word of God shed light on and strengthened the whole struggle of the people in the countryside, the peasants, the rural workers. By their faith in God, they found reason to struggle for their rights.[18]

By 1977, after four years of work as a *delegado*, Edgardo was compelled "to go underground."[19] While maintaining close ties with other Delegates of the Word and with the Christian communities, he began to work with the ATC and to collaborate with the FSLN. In 1978 Edgardo García became general secretary of the ATC, and he has occupied important positions in the Nicaraguan government since the triumph of the revolution.

The Catholic church's experience in the state of Zelaya, which comprises much of Nicaragua's Atlantic zone, illustrates the role played by *delegados* in religious and political change. Zelaya was almost entirely rural and had traditionally been neglected by the government in Managua. Throughout the region, Catholic pastoral work was in the hands of the Capuchin Fathers. Following Medellín the Capuchins set up a program for the selection and training of *delegados* in conjunction with the establishment of CEBs. The training emphasized the promotion of Christian awareness among peasants, while providing instruction in literacy and community health. Religious services consisted of biblically based dialogues that focused on pressing needs in people's daily lives.[20] By early 1975 approximately nine hundred *delegados* were active among the dispersed population of Zelaya, providing the deepest religious presence the Catholic church had ever enjoyed in the region.

Although the intent of the Capuchin program was to give a voice to marginal groups in the spirit of Medellín, it was not consciously designed to have political impact. Nevertheless, the potential political repercussions of the *delegados* were soon apparent to the Somoza regime. Indeed, the National Guard viewed the religious activities of the *delegados* as subversive and began a campaign of harassment and intimidation. Peasants were soon "disappearing" or being murdered in areas where *delegados* had become prominent. When the Capuchins protested these assaults to Somoza through their bishop, a North American priest named Salvador Schlaefer, the president denied any National Guard role in the attacks. These deaths and disappearances forced the Capuchins to look more closely at the situation in their vast rural diocese.[21] They soon discovered that some *delegados* had in fact made a Christian option to work for the people by working against the regime. *Delegados* had taken the teachings of Medellín, which formed such an important part of their training, and developed those teachings in an explicitly political direction—without telling the clergy. After having repulsed the overtures of the Sandinistas a few years earlier because their Marxist arguments had little appeal, these Christians had now developed strong sympathies with the FSLN and were collaborating with the revolutionary movement. The Sandinistas, in turn, had confronted a new element in their own political education: the need to come to terms with distinctively Christian bases for political action. Meanwhile, the Capuchins now saw more clearly the structural basis of repression in the countryside and faced a decision as to what their own role would be in the emerging political crisis.

In June 1976 the Capuchins decided to make public their criticism of the regime. To avoid censorship, they published a letter outside Nicaragua in which they documented numerous killings and disappearances. Widely circulated, the Capuchin letter on human rights violations provoked international scrutiny of the Somoza regime at a time when pressure within the country was also mounting. The decision to publish the letter illustrates how important elements of the Catholic church came into the opposition to *Somocismo* and why that opposition took a pro-Sandinista course.

The Delegados de la Palabra also flourished in some parts of western Nicaragua, particularly in Carazo and Estelí. There *delegados* participated in CEPA training seminars and were radicalized by repression against themselves and the campesino communities they served. As repression intensified after the earthquake, many of these delegates became more clandestine in their political organization, which facilitated their collaboration with the FSLN; in the ensuing years the ties between the church and the Sandinista Front deepened through this connection. From these areas of the country too, and especially around Estelí where National Guard atrocities were common, *delegados* entered the ranks of the FSLN as armed combatants.

Finally, in the northern zone of Matagalpa, Jinotega, and Yalí, yet another story of Guard repression and Christian radicalization unfolded. When Father Miguel Vásquez took over the parish in Yalí in 1972, for example, he organized CEBs and courses in Christian conscientization. The formation of CEBs soon led to organized acts of peasant protest, which resulted in severe friction between the government and the CEBs. The local press labeled them "Communists." At one point the local National Guard commander accused Father Vásquez publicly of being the leader of a guerrilla unit. The "guerrilla unit" to which he referred was the Christian conscientization team of the parish.[22]

The parish of Yalí was 85 percent rural and depended heavily on the *delegados* for its pastoral work. In Yalí thirty-two CEBs were operating by 1974 under the direction of *delegado* leaders, most of whom were between the ages of twenty and thirty. When, by 1975, the Guard decided that these Christian communities were "subversive" and began to persecute the members, some of the CEBs began active collaboration with the FSLN. Over the next three years the estrangement of the people of Yalí from the government deepened. Churches were searched and sometimes occupied by the National Guard, while individuals were imprisoned, "disappeared," or were killed. Religious meetings were broken up or banned altogether. By 1978, most Christians not only opposed the Somoza regime but were collaborating in some way with the Sandinistas. In Yalí this was as true of Evangelicals as of Catholics. At least ten Protestant ministers joined the FSLN as combatants or worked full-time organizing their communities for the insurrection.

In January 1978 the Nicaraguan churches consisted of three identifiable groupings insofar as the coming rebellion was concerned. A small group remained loyal to Somoza. A larger, nonviolent opposition, exemplified by Archbishop Obando y Bravo, sought a peaceful transition of power. This group believed strongly that Somoza must yield power before his constitutional term of office expired in 1981, but was fearful of a military victory by the Sandinista Front. Because prominent clergymen like the archbishop were associated with this position and were visibly working to mediate Somoza's removal from office, their efforts furthered the isolation of the regime both at home and abroad, and helped to set the stage for the insurrection. The bishops' pastoral letter of January 1977 had described the atmosphere in the countryside as a "state of terror," pointing to the frequent instances in which greedy landowners associated with Somoza had forced peasants off of land they had cleared and brought under cultivation. The National Guard enforced these expulsions at gunpoint. Since the church had greatly increased its presence among these campesinos, it too suffered direct repression, "particularly the Delegates of the Word."[23]

The third group was the growing body of Christians at the grass roots who were by this time working to bring about a Sandinista victory. The threat that they represented was more and more evident to the Somoza government. In May 1977 Somoza's newspaper *Novedades* called on the archbishop to clarify the Catholic church's position with respect to the government and urged him to take a stand against subversive elements. In response the advisory council of the archdiocese defended Obando and, borrowing the language of Medellín, described the national scene as one of "institutionalized violence." In November the Guard burned the community at Solentiname, arresting some of its members and exiling others, and in December the Catholic Youth once again seized churches to protest Guard abuses and demand the freeing of political prisoners. A Spanish priest of the Sacred Heart, Gaspar García Laviana, announced his decision to join the FSLN and take up arms against the dictatorship.

The Radicalization of Nicaragua's Evangelicals

The earthquake was an even sharper turning point for the Evangelical churches than for the Catholic church in that the Protestants had not experienced the same degree of early ferment. Thus an important difference between the Catholic and Evangelical churches was that in the Nicaraguan Catholic church reflection preceded action; for the Protestants, that order of events was reversed.

Four days after the earthquake, a Protestant doctor, Gustavo Parajón, issued a call over the radio for a meeting of Evangelical leaders. Parajón, who was born in the parsonage of Managua's First Baptist Church and who is an ordained minister as well as a U.S.-trained medical doctor, called the meeting to propose the organization of a Protestant relief effort. Eight leaders responded the first day. Within three weeks, churches representing twenty denominations had expressed their desire to be involved in Parajón's initiative. The upshot was the creation of the Comité Evangélico por Ayuda a los Damnificados (CEPAD), which undertook five distinct relief programs. Because hunger was the most pressing problem, food kitchens were set up in Evangelical churches and schools throughout Managua; these were staffed by 800 volunteers and were soon serving breakfast to 30,000 people each day. In cooperation with PROVADENIC, an Evangelical health agency already in existence, three clinics were established immediately in the poor barrios of Managua. Refugee centers were set up around the country to provide shelter and to reunite families. Further, CEPAD started a housing program that led eventually to the construction of 500 homes. And finally, literacy classes were begun in conjunction with AFALIT, another existing Protestant agency; in short order there were about four hundred teachers employed in the program. Subsequently, however, CEPAD chose to withdraw from this project in order to concentrate its efforts on immediate relief needs.[24]

Three months after the earthquake, CEPAD changed the last word of its name from "Damnificados" (Destitute) to "Desarrollo" (Development). This decision reflected the important changes that were taking place in the organization's thinking about its mission. Its members had begun to consider the long-term situation of Nicaragua, while focusing more and more on the spiritual basis of social action. From the beginning, the guiding motive underlying CEPAD's work was service in meeting basic needs, rather than proselytism in winning new members for the church.

Gilberto Aguirre, director of programs for CEPAD, described a path leading directly from earthquake relief to the first of sixty pastoral meetings that were eventually held throughout the country between September 1974 and the end of 1980. At the first such pastoral meeting a week of study and reflection brought together 300 pastors from three dozen denominations. Such themes as "The Responsibility of the Christian in Latin America" and "The Keys of Liberation" were kept general to avoid Somoza's wrath. The emphasis throughout the retreat was "You're Christian; I'm Christian," which did much to break down traditional sectarian barriers. Substantively, the pastors began to wrestle with the same issues as the Catholic church: poverty, injustice, and human rights violations. According to Aguirre this conference generated "an explosion" within the Evangelical churches both spiritually and organizationally. Over the next five years twenty-three local CEPAD committees were established throughout Nicaragua, all initiated at the local level, and nine regional offices were opened to encourage a decentralized development program.[25] In time, Evangelical churches in more than two hundred communities contributed to the design and implementation of a range of rural community development projects. This experience of working, training, and organizing together, sometimes also in conjunction with Catholics, was formative to Evangelical participation in the insurrection.

Two years and twenty retreats after the first pastoral week in 1974, a group of fifty clergy and laity gathered for the first "Interdenominational Retreat of Evangelical Pastors" (Retiro Interdenominacional de Pastores Evangélicos de Nicaragua—RIPEN I) to reflect on the "social responsibility of the Church," church unity, human rights, and Christian ethics. Out of that meeting came a document that revealed a clear understanding of the growing political polarization within the country, the array of forces at work, and the social and economic causes of the problems. The document urged "joint action of the government, private enterprise, religious and cultural groups and the citizenry."[26] Although Nicaraguan Evangelicals associated with CEPAD were not prepared to embrace the FSLN in 1976–77, they were moving in a direction that would culminate less than two years later in strong support for the revolutionary process.[27]

The Churches Move toward Insurrection

On the first anniversary of the Managua earthquake, the Catholic church hierarchy held a commemorative mass in the city's central plaza. Somoza, who had intended to hold a government-sponsored event, decided instead to attend the church celebration. Meanwhile, the Christian communities of Managua, particularly from such parishes as San Pablo and Fátima, resolved to make their own presence felt at the celebration and to attend with the explicit purpose of expressing a theological position different from that of the bishops. The hierarchy conceived the event as a commemoration of the dead; the Christian communities wanted to focus on the needs of the living. As a former priest who provided live radio commentary said, "The people of God had one set of theological concerns and the bishops had another."[28]

With the assistance of their priests, parishioners made hundreds of hand-held placards and carried them secretly into the plaza. As the ceremony unfolded, Somoza and his officials were offended by the statements of the bishops, but especially angered by the display of antiregime slogans. Abruptly, President Somoza got up and walked out while National Guardsmen disconnected the loudspeakers carrying Archbishop Obando's speech to the audience. The episode revealed that, while the breach between regime and church was increasing at this time, the surface picture of regime-church conflict obscured a still deeper division within the church itself. On one side of that division stood a moderate hierarchy; on the other stood increasingly prophetic Christian communities at the grass roots.

Then, on December 27, 1974, Sandinista commandos raided a Christmas party in Managua, capturing several important Somocista officials who were then ransomed back to the regime. This event was important in the Catholic church's relation to the popular struggle because the hierarchy played a visible role in mediating this conflict between the government and the FSLN. Even more importantly, the hierarchy was perceived by many people to be "leaning" to the Sandinista Front, even though Archbishop Obando y Bravo presented himself as a neutral go-between. Intentionally or not, the church gained credibility with the FSLN during these negotiations.

Perhaps the most significant result as far as the church was concerned was the effect of the FSLN's success on the grass-roots Christian communities. The government acceded to Sandinista demands, including the broadcast and publication of a lengthy FSLN position paper, and a number of FSLN militants were freed from prison. Upon hearing this news over the radio the residents of OPEN 3 were "filled with jubilation." Said one Maryknoll sister, "it was like hearing our own salvation history" as they listened to FSLN leaders chronicle the record of regime injustice and the struggle of the popular opposition stretching back over twenty years.[29] With this success the Sandinista Front gained stature in barrios such as OPEN 3, Riguero, 14 de Septiembre, and San Judas, while Somoza "lost face" and ordinary people glimpsed the possibility that popular opposition could be effective against his dictatorship.

The next three years were a period of growing popular protest in the poor barrios of Nicaraguan cities. Repressive actions by the National Guard rose accordingly. The experience of OPEN 3 illustrates how elements of the churches moved to active collaboration with FSLN. University students from the Christian Youth Movement (founded by the Jesuit Fernando Cardenal, now Nicaragua's Minister of Education) came into OPEN 3 to work with the Maryknoll missionaries and their

Christian Youth Clubs. Their work was not explicitly evangelical. Based on the assumption that Christian faith was compatible with social action, these study and reflection groups focused on issues concerning the dignity of poor people and questioned the possibilities of achieving such dignity under a Somoza government. Many of these young people went from being anti-Somoza to being Christian revolutionaries.

Alongside this organized youth activity was a series of political struggles between the barrio and the government. During the summer of 1976, the barrio waged a campaign to reduce water prices, which the government had raised in poor neighborhoods but not in the wealthier sections of Managua. People were astonished to discover the degree of organization that had developed during the preceding two years. The Youth Clubs, the Christian community, the local workers' association, and a women's organization pooled their resources to carry out the struggle of the "water fight." Members of the local parish center became leaders in the struggle. The church used its mimeograph machine for announcements and its building for meetings. After nearly three months of struggle, OPEN 3 succeeded in getting a reduction in the price of water. The experience was an object lesson in political organizing; it helped to solidify the politically conscious members of the Christian communities and sharpened their confidence to act politically. For those in the Catholic church who were working at the grass roots, it was a lesson in how to "accompany" the people in a historic struggle for self-determination. As one Maryknoll missionary put it, participation in these struggles "carried our church into the stream of history."[30]

The assassination of Pedro Joaquín Chamorro on January 10, 1978, intruded powerfully upon this panorama of events. In the Christian communities, many people felt that they were now called upon to live out the values of the Gospel in a revolutionary situation. In the barrio of OPEN 3, the youth had occupied the Cruz Grande Church since December 14, but abandoned it on January 10 with the news of the assassination. Stunned, the people of OPEN 3 instinctively drew closer together. Church people in their community now concluded that "the church was the only place people could speak the truth in Nicaragua."[31] "Speaking the truth" thus became a political act that meant active opposition to *Somocismo*. For many, it also meant active collaboration with the FSLN. Churches and church schools now became focal points of organized resistance. From Managua to Masaya, and from Jinotega to Estelí, the Christian laity—above all, students and other young people—began to assume specific revolutionary tasks in preparation for the general uprising. They made bombs and stored arms; they accumulated supplies and taught courses in first aid. In Evangelical churches Christians cleaned baptismal fonts and filled them with drinking water. They published news and organized communications links for and with the Sandinistas.

On September 8, 1978, CEPAD held a meeting to discuss emergency measures in the event of an insurrection, during which one pastor commented, "I hope nothing happens tomorrow, because we aren't prepared yet." The next day, the September insurrection began. As a result of this meeting, however, some Protestant churches that had not already done so began to stockpile food and medicine in their buildings. During and after the September insurrection, CEPAD cooperated with CEPA and other Catholic agencies on relief efforts in Monimbó and Masaya, where the initial fighting was concentrated. In Monimbó the churches were supplying not only food and medical care but also "support to the combatants."[32]

Following the September insurrection, which was put down with brutal retaliation by the National Guard, CEPAD organized refugee centers around the country. Every pastor had a Red Cross flag to place outside his church or school. In eastern Managua, the Church of the Nazarene, like many others, painted huge red crosses on the outside walls; during the final insurrection that began in the spring of 1979, this church served as an important refugee center. The International Red Cross cooperated, advertising the fact that the flags would be in various locations and asking that they be respected. (As it turned out, the National Guard often ignored them.) By the end of 1978 CEPAD was working closely with Caritas, the Catholic relief agency, and their joint efforts were being closely coordinated through the Managua archdiocese of the Catholic church. In March 1979, CEPAD sponsored a national radio marathon that raised $20,000 for Masaya; the fund was administered by CRISOL, an ecumenical organization. During the final insurrection, the Evangelical churches supported the FSLN by providing medicines and, in a more limited way, food. This was especially true in the eastern barrios of Managua, and in Masaya and Carazo.

These actions were accompanied by exceedingly painful reflection on the meaning of religious principles and teachings. Christians were forced to ask, as one participant put it, "What do we do to live our faith now?" The prospect was frightening indeed, particularly in light of the violence it portended. Yet there was also a sense of a clear spiritual call to face this reality. They confronted "an enormous paradox of God's presence amidst terrible evil."[33] The experience brought the Christian community together in a powerful way. The centrality of prayer in their daily life was dramatically heightened. In September 1978, when the first uprising broke out, Christians throughout Nicaragua had accepted the need for revolution in their country. When the final insurrection began the following May, they were prepared to fight or to assist the combatants until victory.

In the midst of this process there was considerable speculation about the attitude of the Catholic bishops toward the revolution. On June, 2, 1978, the bishops issued a pastoral letter that seemed to endorse popular rebellion in the face of prolonged tyranny. Some Nicaraguans saw this declaration as evidence of the bishops' belated but authentic attempt to support armed revolution against *Somocismo*. Later on, however, there was growing doubt among those who supported the revolution that this had ever been the bishops' real intent. The bishops were clearly anti-Somoza, but they did not seem to want a Sandinista government either. After the triumph they were uncertain how the church could coexist with the revolution. Indeed, this question was uppermost in the minds of many Nicaraguan Christians. How could the church accompany the revolution? There was no precedent for the situation in which they found themselves.

The Latin American bishops had met in Puebla, Mexico, only a few months earlier. They had spoken of the "people of God" and had seemed to define this term in relation to the poor. In this sense, it was clear that the people of God, especially in the poorest barrios of Nicaragua's major cities, were with the revolution. What would happen now to the hierarchy's role in providing pastoral guidance and leadership? What impact would the revolution have on their authority with the faithful? What measure of control could they exercise over the participation of Catholics in the revolutionary process? These questions point to some of the key issues that would dominate both church-state relations and intrachurch turmoil in the early years of the Nicaraguan Revolution. As a concrete example, which will be discussed more fully later on, the government initially formed by the victorious Sandinista Front included several prominent Catholic priests who occupied important policy-making positions. The Catholic hierarchy was never comfortable with this arrangement and, in less than a year's time, tried to end it by requiring the priests to leave the government. Although there was some sympathy within the Vatican for the bishops' position, officials in Rome refused to intercede when the issue first arose in 1980; instead, they told the Nicaraguan bishops to resolve the problem themselves. Meanwhile, the priests in question indicated their intention to continue in the government as long as the revolution needed them. The issue continued to simmer over the next several years, occasionally breaking out in open conflict.

Another problem was that the government was taking the initiative in areas that were traditionally reserved for the Catholic church. In August 1980 the religious festival of Santo Domingo, one of Nicaragua's more important religious holidays, was vigorously publicized and endorsed by the government. The Sandinistas wanted to use it as an occasion to urge proper moral and social conduct in keeping with the principles of the revolution. The government urged that the festival be conducted with the utmost religious seriousness and that drinking not be part of the celebration as it traditionally was. By and large the public response was favorable, but rather than reassuring the bishops about the government's respect for religion, this event seemed to reinforce their fears of governmental interference in religious activities, and their own loss of influence among the people.

Perhaps the bishops' most profound fear was that there would be a gradual increase in atheism among the people as the government's influence reached into wider and wider areas of social life, and that at some point in the future, when it was no longer needed, the government would abandon the church. Archbishop Obando y Bravo stressed that the church must be vigilant not to lose its freedom to fulfill its mission in an independent way. From his point of view, one of the severest challenges facing the hierarchy was that of maintaining unity in the Catholic church. He spoke optimistically in this regard, but over the preceding decade the forces of pluralism had grown strong. In terms of the old, authoritarian model of church governance, this pluralism pointed toward a potential disunity in the church, especially between the hierarchy and the rank and file.

To a remarkable degree, such concerns were absent among the Evangelical leadership. Three months after the triumph, 500 pastors gathered for RIPEN II (recall that 50 had attended RIPEN I three years earlier). The meeting's theme was "Pastors in the Reconstruction." Following several days of study and reflection, these 500 pastors, who comprised about half the Protestant ministers in Nicaragua at the time, signed a declaration that began by giving "thanks to God our Father for the victory of the Nicaraguan people and their instrument of liberation, the Sandinista Front of National Liberation."[34] The letter then continued: "We are committed to offer cooperation in all the labors, projects, activities, and programs that the government develops for the real benefit of the people; understanding that our participation . . . is related to our fidelity to the Lord Jesus Christ." The pastors saluted the junta for "its program of government" and said they understood that the end of "this revolutionary process is the formation of the new person [and] of a just and fraternal society in which its inspiration is Jesus Christ." They called on all Christians to "participate in political actions that unite us in the common good; to study . . . the program of government [and] scientific methods of analysis in order to understand how our society works." This included an endorsement of participation in the Sandinista Defense Committees and service in programs such as "literacy, health and liberating education." Finally, they condemned "all counterrevolutionary intentions" against Nicaragua, together with the twenty-year-old U.S. economic blockade of Cuba, and urged Protestant churches in the United States to pressure their government to end the blockade.[35]

Clearly, this segment of the Evangelical community had moved toward well-defined positions concerning the revolutionary process over a span of three years. Unlike the Catholic bishops' pastoral letter, which appeared in November 1979 and carefully spelled out what kind of political system the church could live with, the RIPEN II declaration indicated the enthusiastic support of Evangelicals in CEPAD for the revolutionary government. The only specific appeal of the Evangelicals was for representation in the Council of the State and for greater attention and sensitivity on the part of the government to the special conditions of the Atlantic Coast, which has such a strong Evangelical presence.[36]

In sum, a number of centrifugal forces were at work in the Catholic church as the Nicaraguan Revolution got under way. At the base community level there were priests and lay leaders who wanted to promote a Marxist-Christian dialogue—particularly the Jesuit organization CEPA, which was so vigorous in promoting campesino development. Christian communities that were already well established at the time of the triumph continued to have vitality, although some of their members had begun to take part in Sandinista programs. Where the church's presence was weaker, the Sandinista movement had clearly begun to fill the empty spaces in community life. The fear among the hierarchy was that this would spread to the more vigorous Christian communities such as those in Estelí, where Sandinista influence was particularly strong. What is more, some of the most effective Delegates of the Word had left their lay ministries and gone into Sandinista organizations such as the ATC and other worker syndicates, or taken leadership positions in the Sandinista Defense Committees.

This loss of leadership at the base community level was seen as a clear threat to the institutional church by its highest officials. Grassroots leaders had relied on the church when they had had few other opportunities to experience creative social roles under Somoza. In that sense, the post-Medellín experience of the Nicaraguan Catholic church was that progressive theology and community organizing had greatly enriched the religious life of the church. Now the church seemed in danger of losing these same people, who were among its most valuable resources. Would they maintain their Christian orientation and retain their loyalty to the church? This was a question of great practical concern to the bishops. Their fears were valid, though there was room for disagreement as to what the church should do about the problem. For an important segment of Nicaraguan Catholics, above all the youth who had suffered such ruthless persecution by Somoza and who had participated in armed struggle alongside the FSLN, the answer could not be fear and mistrust; for them, only an active Christian presence in the process of national reconstruction could assure that the churches would not become marginal to the revolution. As we will see, the Catholic hierarchy adopted a much more cautious and pessimistic approach.

Part Three

Religion at the Center
of Revolutionary Struggle

The Christian church began as a sectarian movement in the ancient world. Although it spread rapidly throughout Roman territory in the first generations after Jesus' crucifixion, Christianity remained a persecuted minority religion. For a century or more, while the early Christians evangelized zealously, they saw no need to erect the corporate structures of a visible church because they were convinced that the end of human history was near. Thus, for many generations they remained a sect rather than becoming a church.

Gradually, however, as Christians began to accept that the Apocalypse was not immediately at hand, it became necessary for them to address the task of institutionalizing their religious faith. In the process of carrying out that task lay the metamorphosis of the sect into a church. During the third and fourth centuries Christians applied themselves to the work of creating a religious institution, and over time this institution exhibited more and more clearly defined structures of authority. Matters of religious doctrine were codified and became the authoritative teachings of the church. A clergy was established to convey those teachings and to administer the sacraments according to prescribed ritual. Christianity now found its expression in a church that would resist new sectarian tendencies of the sort from which it had itself developed.

There is no need here to review the institutional development of Roman Catholicism in a comprehensive way. Our concern is merely to remind the reader that the Roman Catholic church has been organized, for nearly two millennia, as a complex, vertical structure of authority. A church that embodies the hierarchical principle as pervasively as does Roman Catholicism will always be more comfortable with orthodoxy than with a plurality of religious expressions within its institutional boundaries. Indeed, authority will be exerted to establish and maintain uniformity, as was done so successfully throughout the Middle Ages. But one price the church paid for this achievement was a gradual loss of religious vitality. Form seemed to replace substance, and the hierarchy resisted any and all innovations from below. Eventually the cost of institutional inertia and authoritarianism was exacted in the Protestant Reformation, when the church generated a powerful new wave of sectarianism.

As we have demonstrated in earlier chapters of this book, the Catholic church in Central America had experienced a severe loss of vitality prior to Vatican II. In this respect it was, perhaps, only an extreme example of the condition of the church universal. In Nicaragua the church hierarchy had little contact with the mass of ordinary citizens. For the peasant majority, religious life found its chief expression in the rituals of a folk Catholicism that centered on the veneration of saints. Most Nicaraguans would have been described by sociologists of religion as nominal Catholics because their ties to the church were largely formal and often sterile.

The reforms introduced at Vatican II and at Medellín brought rapid and comprehensive changes to church life. The creation of Christian base communities and the emphasis on Bible study triggered a renewed interest in religious teachings and a new loyalty to the church. Stronger and more meaningful bonds were formed linking the campesinos to the institution. And this process was a two-way street, inasmuch as clergy and religious women found their own spiritual life energized by sharing in the life of the poor. In these respects Vatican II and Medellín were a great stimulus and boon to the church in Central America generally, and to the Nicaraguan church in particular.

Nevertheless, there were pitfalls that became obvious in Nicaragua only after the triumph of the revolution, even though they were present much earlier. Above all, there was the problem of the sectarian tendency latent in the CEB experiment. Nicaraguan society was sharply divided along class lines; the Somocista system utilized a combination of repression and cooptation, together with a considerable amount of neglect, to keep campesino and working-class groups from acquiring political influence or leverage. The CEBs helped to fill the political void in campesino life by providing space for group organizing and by justifying the struggle for justice. Even though their primary aims had been spiritual, because of their prophetic orientation the CEBs became identified with the interests of the poorest classes. Indeed, they embodied those interests. From the point of view of the church hierarchy they looked more and more "sectarian." Part 3 discusses why this sectarian aspect of the CEB experience in Nicaragua was seen by the hierarchy as so threatening to church unity. We also examine the steps taken to control or isolate the CEBs. In short, we ask how the powerful tensions between "sect" and "church" have been worked out in revolutionary Nicaragua.

Eight

The Churches in a
Revolutionary Society

The "Honeymoon Year"

Nearly all Nicaraguans would agree that July 19, 1979, began a new era in the nation's history—but not all would agree that Sandinista rule is fulfilling the promise evoked by the dawning of that new era. At the time of the triumph the country's most immediate task was the reconstruction of a devastated land, both materially and morally. In the final two months of the insurrection Somoza's struggle to retain power became indiscriminate. He authorized heavy bombing of key cities, where even the churches became targets for attack. The Sandinistas came to power determined to assert Nicaraguan sovereignty and effect a social revolution, but the political system they had conquered was in a state of near-total collapse: the old political institutions had lost legitimacy and the bureaucracy was in disarray. In short, the FSLN faced the task of nation-building in the broadest sense. As the Sandinistas saw it, their nation-building project hinged on two primary objectives: creating new political institutions responsive to the needs of the poor majority, and pursuing a nonaligned foreign policy.[1]

As Nicaragua set out on a revolutionary course in 1979, it contrasted sharply with Mexico in 1910, and Cuba in 1959. In those two earlier cases the Catholic church had set its face against the revolution. The leaders of the Mexican Revolution responded with a harsh anticlericalism, while the Fidelistas in Cuba paid little heed to the church as they embarked on a program of revolutionary change that was heavily inspired by Marxism. In neither case was the church expected, or encouraged, to play any significant role in the nation-building process launched by the revolution. In Nicaragua, on the other hand, it was evident that a large number of Christians proffered active support to the revolution and accepted the legitimacy of Sandinista leadership.

Their loyalty stemmed from the formative experience of grass-roots participation already examined in Chapter 7. At the same time, there were also Christians who approached the revolution apprehensively. Over the next few chapters, as we analyze nearly a decade of struggle and change, we will show that these different sets of expectations regarding the revolution have generated three broad types of conflict over the church's role in society.

By far the most publicized conflicts have been those between church and state, especially between highly visible members of the Catholic hierarchy and Sandinista leaders. However, this type of conflict represents only one aspect of church involvement in the revolution, and it is not necessarily the most important, either for the church's future or for the revolution's integrity. A second kind of conflict lies within the church itself, involving discord between elements of the hierarchy and the base over matters of theology, ecclesiology, and pastoral strategy—and its long-term importance to both the Catholic church and the revolution may be even greater than that of the first type of conflict. A great deal of tension surrounds the church at the community level where Christians have sought to retain their spiritual identity while supporting the revolution. An atmosphere of deepening polarization has made this more and more difficult. On one side, problems arise from the great demands made on these Christians by the many tasks of the revolution itself. These demands are exacerbated by the protracted Contra war, and are further compounded by resistance on the part of some bishops to any integration of Christians into the revolutionary process.

A third level of conflict involves the role of external actors who have tried to influence the course of religious and political developments in Nicaragua since 1979. In the following chapters we will discuss a variety of such external actors, including the Vatican, Pope John Paul II, representatives of CELAM, the United States Catholic Conference, and the White House, among others.

In the atmosphere of frenzied destruction that marked the final days of Somoza's rule the Nicaraguan bishops issued a pastoral letter affirming the right of an oppressed people to rebel against tyranny. Even though some Christians at the grass roots had yearned for words of support from their bishops much sooner in the struggle, this declaration of June 1979 was nevertheless a bold step for any episcopal conference to take. It was celebrated by Christians throughout the country as a sign of the bishops' solidarity with their struggle.

However, the pastoral letter against tyranny did not signify an embrace of the coming revolution. The bishops were not identified pastorally with the day-to-day struggle. Neither did they have strong links with the popular organizations, or with the FSLN. Just two days before the Sandinistas entered Managua, Archbishop Obando y Bravo was in Venezuela taking part in negotiations aimed at creating a moderate transition government that would, in effect, have prevented the Sandinistas from assuming power. In this respect the archbishop appeared to be identified with the efforts of the United States and some sectors of the Nicaraguan elite to deny the FSLN a definitive military victory, thereby undercutting their claim to leadership of any post-Somoza government.

Within two weeks of the triumph the bishops had already issued another pastoral letter. This one conveyed a more cautious tone and more skeptical sentiments: while acknowledging that "a new era in our history has begun," it also focused on "anxieties and fears" concerning the ideology and goals of the Sandinistas. Half the text was devoted to the future of religion in Nicaragua, warning the Sandinistas not to try to "impose something foreign" on the country.[2] In other words, at the very outset of the revolution, the Catholic hierarchy signaled that it had strong reservations, and that it approached the coming changes in Nicaragua from a greater emotional, experiential, and ideological distance than did Catholics at the grass roots.

Even so, the first year of the revolution was characterized by a general mood of euphoria. On the surface, church-state relations were correct and intrachurch relations were harmonious. Most Nicaraguans who remained in the country shared in the sense of liberation that came with the defeat of Somoza. Other countries, including the United States, pledged badly needed economic aid. The immediate tasks of reconstruction absorbed the abundant energies that had been released by the triumph. The initial governing junta included members of the middle class and private-sector groups that had joined the popular struggle after Pedro Joaquín Chamorro's assassination.[3] This was the honeymoon year of the revolution. External opposition was low, or at least not yet mobilized. Within Nicaragua, multiclass cooperation was relatively high. A number of the country's most prominent priests held important positions in the new government.

On November 17, 1979, the Nicaraguan bishops issued a remarkable pastoral letter entitled "Christian Commitment for a New Nicaragua." This letter marked the apogee of church-state relations and internal church solidarity. The bishops recognized the authentic Christian and pastoral character of the CEBs and seemed to invite dialogue between the hierarchy and the base. They acknowledged the depth of Christian participation in the revolutionary process and gave recognition to the FSLN as the nation's legitimate political leadership. They even embraced "the dramatic conversion of our church" and "the dynamic fact of class struggle that should lead to a just transformation of structures."[4] With such statements as these the bishops seemed to narrow the gap that had separated them from Catholics who supported the revolution, and to move toward accommodation with a government that was preparing a socialist transformation.

However, this pastoral letter also expressed reservations about the future, referring to the fears of many Nicaraguans concerning the likely direction of the revolutionary process. The bishops worried that some groups that had "contributed generously" to making the revolution possible would be excluded from shaping the nation's future, although they made no mention of which groups they had in mind.[5] In addition, the letter hinted at an issue that would later become a source of bitter and protracted conflict by suggesting that grass-roots elements of the church must be in communion with the hierarchy. Even at this early stage of the revolution some bishops apparently doubted whether revolution was in the best interests of the church: therefore, they were not well disposed toward popular participation in Sandinista programs or mass organizations. Nevertheless, "Christian Commitment for a New Nicaragua" is the strongest statement the Nicaraguan bishops have made in regard to Nicaragua's poor majority, and in defense of the nation's right to seek its own solution to the problems of development.[6]

Anticipating that some Nicaraguans might fear the socialist features of a reconstruction process led by the FSLN, the bishops distinguished between two types of socialism, one false and the other humanistic. False socialism denied people the right to express their religious beliefs, controlled the education of the young, and was sustained by the arbitrary power of the state. The bishops rejected the imposition of false socialism upon the Nicaraguan people but endorsed a humanistic socialism by saying: "If . . . socialism signifies, as it ought to signify, the preeminence of the interests of the majority of Nicaraguans and signifies a unified and progressively participatory model of national economic planning, we have no objections. . . . [I]f socialism means a social project where the quality of human life improves, that seems to us just."[7]

Scrutiny of the public declarations of the Catholic bishops during the first months after the triumph makes it clear that a major source of apprehension among the more conservative or traditional Catholics was the nature of Sandinista ideology. With its strong appeals to Nicaraguan nationalism, its uncompromising resistance to *Somocismo* and to U.S. interventionism, *Sandinismo* certainly had captured the imagination of many Nicaraguans. On an affective and symbolic level it appeared to have the power to challenge Christianity for a hold on people's loyalty, if it were put to that purpose. Apparently, some sectors of the church feared that it would be. They saw the future as a struggle for the hearts and minds of the faithful, in which Sandino might be made to replace Christ as liberator in the popular imagination.

These apprehensions were given credibility by the FSLN's enthusiastic and pervasive references to Sandino, often utilizing imagery that historically applied only to religious motifs in Nicaragua's Catholic culture. When the Sandinistas introduced the slogan "Sandino yesterday, Sandino today, Sandino always," for example, the Catholic hierarchy objected to this appropriation of a symbol from the sacred text (Hebrews 13:8).[8] In their eyes it signified an implicit substitution of Sandino for Christ. Conservative Catholics responded by proclaiming "Christ yesterday, Christ today, Christ always" in their religious and political meetings. Thus, a biblical passage that normally unites Christians began to acquire partisan significance, reflecting an emerging division within the Nicaraguan Christian community.

The hierarchy's fears were reinforced by a position paper that circulated within the Sandinista party during the fall of 1979. This paper, which was obtained and published by *La Prensa*, was prepared by a Sandinista militant named Julio López for discussion at a party conference. It assumed a dogmatic Marxist view of religion, arguing that spiritual faith was anachronistic in a revolutionary society. Consequently, organized religion should be discouraged, and gradually abolished. To that end, such prominent religious holidays as Christmas would be taken out of the hands of the churches and transformed into secular celebrations. Publication of this document in *La Prensa* gave the impression that it was soon to be Sandinista policy. This provoked an alarmed and angry response from Catholic church officials. Sandinista leaders responded, in turn, by explaining that the document was only a working paper and never had the approval of the FSLN. As we shall see, a year later they took a major step toward repudiating the document by publishing their own *Official Communique Concerning Religion*; that document will be discussed below.[9] At the time, Sandinista disclaimers did little to mollify the bishops and conservative Catholics who already distrusted the FSLN. To them the López position paper was readily interpreted as a signal that the FSLN intended to subordinate religion and eventually do away with the church as an institution.

In the same vein, the Catholic hierarchy also feared that Christian participation in government programs could eventually replace normal church activities. This concern had two primary focal points: the participation of Catholics in mass organizations and CEBs, and governmental usurpation of traditional Catholic customs or religious celebrations. In the Catholic church the long-standing tradition was for lay activity to be carried out under the tutelage of priests who were loyal to the bishops. In this respect both the CEBs and the mass organizations were a problem for the church. The mass organizations were entirely independent of the church; while the CEBs were theoretically under the supervision of the bishops, we have already seen that they grew up in Nicaragua in a condition of relative autonomy. Consequently, in practice the bishops exercised little direct control over Christian involvement in either type of popular organization. If such involvement were likely to lead to deepening commitments to the revolution, church officials were fearful that the government's authority would eventually supersede their own.

It is appropriate to take a moment here to compare Nicaragua's experience with that of other countries in Latin America. We will focus on Brazil because of the importance of CEBs in Brazilian church life, and because a number of excellent studies have shed a great deal of light on the role of the popular church in that country. The first point to stress is that the Brazilian hierarchy made a major commitment to developing CEBs, so that by the late 1970s tens of thousands had been successfully established throughout the country. While not all bishops were enthusiastic about CEBs, particularly when it became clear that they were associated with popular political struggle, on the whole it can be said that the hierarchy actively promoted CEB development.[10]

A second point concerns the setting in which CEB development took place. The years of dynamic CEB growth in Brazil coincided with a period of extremely repressive political rule in which an authoritarian military regime severely limited the channels of political expression. In this setting, as in Nicaragua during the late 1970s, CEBs were one of the few surviving societal mechanisms through which popular dissent could be articulated. However, an important difference distinguished Nicaragua and Brazil. On the one hand, Brazil is a much larger and more complex society with far more complex linkages between local and national levels; in terms of national politics, CEBs represented only one factor, albeit a significant one, among many that shaped political developments. In the much smaller scale of the Nicaraguan political arena, on the other hand, crises at the local level could have immediate repercussions at the national level, and CEBs had an exaggerated impact far out of proportion to the relative size and sophistication of the CEB experiment as compared to that of Brazil.

A third point has to do with the differing political outcomes in Nicaragua and Brazil. In the latter country the military initiated the transition to democratic rule: by gradually restoring electoral mechanisms, it placed a premium on redemocratizing Brazil through party competition. In Nicaragua the democratic opening came precipitously through the popular insurrection and brought a revolutionary movement to power; political party competition then had to be reestablished in the context of a revolution dominated by the FSLN. With respect to CEBs, the effect of these differences was as follows: in Brazil the gradual democratic transition greatly diffused the political options available and diluted the impact of popular movements; in Nicaragua the revolution sharpened the political options and heightened the impact of the popular organizations, including the CEBs.[11]

To return to the early events of the Nicaraguan Revolution, we have indicated that the Catholic hierarchy was beginning to fear that its influence in society would be eroded by the Sandinista Front. These embryonic fears seemed to crystallize over the celebration of the *Jornada Navideña,* or Christmas Day, of 1980. Ordinarily, Christmas celebrations were organized either by individual families or by the local parish church, according to the customs of Nicaraguan folk Catholicism. The central custom, which had developed over a long period of time, was *la Purísima.* But actions undertaken by the Sandinista government with the approach of the Christmas season gave the impression among more traditional Catholics that the government intended to preempt *la Purísima.*[12]

At the end of November the minister of social welfare, Father

Edgard Parrales, announced the introduction of the *Jornada Navideña*
to the Nicaraguan public. The Social Welfare Ministry would take part
in Christmas celebrations by seeing to it that every Nicaraguan child
received some sort of gift, a game or a toy.[13] Father Parrales explained
this gesture against the background of a past in which some Nicaraguan children received many gifts at Christmas while others received
none. Under the revolution no child would be deprived of the happi-
ness of Christmas; each would receive at least one gift. The ministry
called upon the Sandinista Defense Committees (Comites de Defensa
Sandinista, CDS) to help in the distribution of the gifts. This practice
has been carried on by the revolutionary government since 1980.[14]

The Nicaraguan episcopate countered the government's initiative
by calling for a week-long festival of the *Purísima*, to be held in the city
of Masaya. The celebration would be inaugurated with a traditional
procession in honor of Mary known as the *gritería*. It would include a
large outdoor mass, and would close with a public celebration of first
communion for the children of Masaya.[15] At the same time, *La Prensa*,
which was now giving increasing play to the activities of the more
traditional sectors of the church and also devoting more and more
attention to the views of Archbishop Obando y Bravo, printed an
article sharply criticizing the "Sandinista Christmas holiday." The government was taken to task for failing to consult with the bishops
before announcing the *Jornada Navideña*, which the newspaper said
had "converted [Christmas] into a popular political theater."[16] These
events suggested a latent, but now emerging, tension between church
and state, a tension that would more and more take the form of a
competition for the allegiance of Nicaragua's poor majority.

Christians Mobilize for Change at the Grass Roots

The search for appropriate Christian roles in the Nicaraguan Revolution began almost immediately after the triumph. In September 1979 a
group of Catholic clergy organized a week-long seminar for church
people and members of the FSLN in order to discuss ways the church
could accompany the revolution. The seminar was held at the Jesuit
Central American University (Universidad Centroamericana, UCA)
and included members of the junta, Catholic priests, Evangelical ministers, and leaders of Christian communities. Its major thrust was to
encourage the critical but sympathetic and active support of Chris-

tians for the revolution. The organizer of the conference, Father Álvaro Argüello, S.J., director of the Instituto Histórico Centroamericano (Historical Institute) at UCA and a strong supporter of the
revolution, was later elected by the Association of Nicaraguan Clergy
to a seat on the Council of State, a broadly representative advisory
body to the junta.

Even before the UCA seminar, during the month of August, another group of Catholic priests and Protestant pastors who were
closely identified with the popular sectors and sympathetic to the
aims of the revolution established the Centro Antonio Valdivieso
(CAV). This ecumenical religious center was designed to promote
dialogue between churches and the government, and to encourage
the participation of Christians in the revolution. Through such measures as the sponsorship of conferences and workshops, the publication of a wide assortment of theological and pastoral materials, and
the training of pastoral leaders for the local level, the CAV rapidly
acquired a high profile as a prorevolutionary Christian organization.[17]
Its work was complemented by that of the Central American Historical
Institute, based at UCA, and by CEPA, which continued to nurture
peasant skills in agriculture, community development, and leadership
in religious celebrations.[18] Seen in their entirety, these organizations
linked together a prorevolutionary intellectual leadership within the
church and the mass-based Christian organizations, rendering mutual support and encouragement. They also gave these elements of
the church strong contacts with Christians outside Nicaragua.

The Catholic hierarchy followed a divergent path. In January 1980
the bishops met with leaders of CELAM in San José, Costa Rica. At
this meeting the CELAM officials offered "fraternal assistance" to the
Nicaraguan church, pledging to distribute Bibles and CELAM publica-
tions, to help develop courses in catechesis, and to devise an overall
pastoral plan for the country. They noted the serious illiteracy problem in Nicaragua and offered more than $300,000 to support church
efforts in combating it. While some bishops seemed enthusiastic,
Catholics at the local level were upset by the initiative. This episode
was essentially the inverse of the *Jornada Navideña*, except that criticism came from the popular sectors of the church, not from the
Sandinista government. The cause of this disagreement between base
and hierarchy marked a major fault line of conflict in the ensuing
years: Christians at the base pointed out that those who were clos-
est to the reality of Nicaragua's poor were not consulted about the

church's pastoral needs. Nor had church officials taken proper account of the Literacy Campaign, which was just then being mobilized by the government, and which was to be directed by a prominent Nicaraguan Jesuit, Fernando Cardenal. In the view of these Catholics, their bishops and the CELAM leaders were approaching evangelization in revolutionary Nicaragua with a "missionary mentality." Such an approach was anachronistic. Instead, pastoral work in the new Nicaragua should reflect the people's own historical experience.[19]

On March 20, 1980, a large ecumenical group of activist Christians published a pamphlet containing the bishops' pastoral letter of November 17, 1979, along with a brief discussion of the views of pro- and antirevolutionary Christians. Members of most of the religious orders in Nicaragua, representatives of CEBs, members of CEPA, faculty from UCA and the Catholic high schools, communities of religious women, and some Evangelical pastors signed the document. The pamphlet criticized those who feared the government and refused to work actively in support of it. It pointed out that top Sandinista leaders themselves had insisted religion would not decline in Nicaragua "because the Nicaraguan people are religious and Christian." Junta leader Daniel Ortega, it added, had stated publicly that Christian arguments were the best arguments the Sandinistas had in urging the people to take up revolutionary struggle.[20] Therefore, the churches should make themselves fully and forcefully felt in the work of transforming society and building a new nation. In this connection, what role would the CEBs play? They had been a catalyst in the insurrection. Could they have a similar influence in the phase of national reconstruction, particularly if the Catholic hierarchy grew disillusioned with the revolution?

At this point it may be helpful to elaborate on the nature of CEBs in Nicaragua. In the first place, they are typically small groups of perhaps twenty or thirty persons from the same neighborhood and social class. They meet often, usually more than once a week, to pray, read Scripture, share experiences and ideas, and provide mutual support. Eventually they begin to work together to achieve common goals. The Bible is central to their outlook and to the day-to-day functioning of the CEB. Secondly, the members of CEBs see themselves as working to achieve a spiritual bonding with one another, and as doing so within the institutional framework of the church. Ordinarily it is priests or religious who have taken the initiative to form the community. In at least two dioceses, Estelí and Zelaya, they initially had the close collaboration of the bishop—but this was not always the case, as will become clear later on. The important point here is that within the setting of the Nicaraguan Revolution CEBs have always thought of themselves as being an authentic part of the Catholic church.

By its very nature, CEB activity tends to reorient the thinking of church members, opening up the possibility of redefining the church's mission in concrete ways. The stress on Bible reading and critical discussion leads to the cultivation of new, more critical attitudes toward life. Institutional structures and existing systems of authority come under scrutiny. Not only does this tend to release the latent social and political criticism that exists at the grass roots, it can also lead to criticism of the church itself, particularly where it has been slow to combat injustice. It is in this respect in particular that the CEB experience in Nicaragua has called to mind so vividly the Puritan churches of England and America during an earlier period of religious and political change. In other words, CEBs are likely to put pressure on the church to take sides in social conflict, thereby highlighting the class nature of society. Since the CEB exists in part to encourage each member to express her or his voice, it can serve as a local-level training center for societal participation, including political participation. In this way the growth of CEBs could signify a broadening of the locus of authority in a society where authority has traditionally been concentrated in vertical structures.

The CEB concept typifies the post–Vatican II emphasis on being a church of the poor. It has been endorsed by Popes Paul VI and John Paul II, and by the Latin American bishops at both Medellín and Puebla. At Puebla, although the bishops were cautious at times and sought to stress the evangelical nature of the CEBs, they also showered favorable attention on them as "an expression of the church's preferential love for the poor."[21] However, there is a great diversity of CEBs throughout Latin America, which can be traced in part to widely differing social contexts and political histories. It is necessary to clarify the context in which CEBs arose in Nicaragua in order to understand why they have been viewed with suspicion by some bishops, especially in the highly charged atmosphere that developed after the initial honeymoon year.

In some countries, such as Brazil and Chile, the church hierarchy initiated and encouraged the development of CEBs, as was suggested earlier in this chapter. In others, including Nicaragua, CEBs originally developed independently of the hierarchy. This fact was a source of potential conflict within the church. The conditions of uncertainty and change that marked the early days of the revolution could only exacerbate the latent tensions. Phillip Berryman has suggested a fourfold typology for illustrating CEB development in varying Latin American contexts. First, he identifies those countries "in which the power structure does not need to employ widespread and extreme repression, even though most of the people are poor and the economic structure works against them"; examples are Mexico, Venezuela, and Costa Rica. Second, there are those countries in which significant repression exists and no opposition favoring the poor is tolerated; all the countries of the southern cone were of this type at the time of the Nicaraguan Revolution, including Brazil, Argentina, and Chile, although Brazil was beginning the process of liberalization that eventually restored an elected civilian government to power. A third type of country is one in which "serious revolutionaries are struggling to take power," as illustrated by the case of El Salvador. The fourth type is a country that already is in revolution, Cuba and Nicaragua being examples.[22]

During the 1970s Nicaragua increasingly resembled the second type of situation, that of extreme repression, even if it never reached the desperate proportions of Argentina, Chile, or neighboring El Salvador. Although Somoza tried to avoid conflict with the church hierarchy, the National Guard directed a growing physical violence at the poor, including Delegates of the Word and other CEB activists, as was shown in Chapter 7. Emerging in this repressive environment, Nicaraguan CEBs became an important resource of the Sandinista Revolution, but they did so independently of hierarchical direction. As a result, many CEBs were strongly committed to the revolution in 1979 and 1980, even though the bishops were uncertain and tentative.

If we look at the Nicaraguan church as a whole during the first year of the revolution we find a complex picture of innovation at the grass roots, with differing sets of relationships between base and hierarchy, and between church and government, from one diocese to the next. This can be illustrated by contrasting the Atlantic Coast region and the northern diocese of Estelí with the Managua archdiocese. Zelaya, the easternmost province of Nicaragua, which includes the Atlantic Coast, has long been relatively isolated and neglected in national affairs. At the time of the triumph CEBs had been well established in the Atlantic Coast area for a decade, and the role of lay leaders was familiar and accepted. A typical CEB enrolled between sixty and one hundred families and *delegados* provided most of the pastoral leadership. The bishop of the diocese strongly endorsed the program as the only way to provide a church presence where there were so few priests. In short, CEBs were an integral part of the pastoral plan of the diocese. A similar situation prevailed in Estelí, but for different reasons. There Bishop Rubén López Ardón supported a vigorous network of CEBs prior to the triumph even though they were not created at his initiative. The bishop was content to give free rein to a number of dynamic clergy and lay leaders who demonstrated great skill at organizing CEBs. They worked with his approval, but not under his direct supervision. The prophetic thrust of the CEBs in the diocese of Estelí was particularly strong. Prior to the insurrection, Christians in Estelí stored food and weapons—as one leader put it, "not to kill, but to defend ourselves and to prevent the National Guard from taking our young people away."[23] These Christians organized Civil Defense Committees (which became Sandinista Defense Committees after the triumph) apart from any direct structural links with the FSLN. Since Estelí was a strategic city during the insurrection, it is not surprising that the CEBs there played a vital role in the popular struggle, or that their members were strongly supportive of the Sandinista Revolution.

However, it does not necessarily follow that where CEBs were well established they always worked easily in concert with the revolution. What was true in the diocese of Estelí and, as we shall see, in the archdiocese of Managua, was much less the case in Zelaya, where CEBs came into conflict with the Sandinistas during that first year. Ironically, this occurred in part because the Sandinistas took such a keen interest in the Atlantic Coast. They sent agricultural experts and literacy *brigadistas* to the region in significant numbers; but however well intentioned they may have been, these "experts" from Managua were inexperienced in dealing with Costeños and sometimes insensitive to the needs of the Atlantic Coast as the people themselves saw them. Sandinista policy created friction with the church because the CEBs had already established agricultural programs, literacy training, and health care. Sandinista efforts came across as intrusive and heavy-handed when they either ignored or discounted the effectiveness of these church programs.[24]

In some dioceses, then, the democratization of the church had advanced a considerable distance at the time of the triumph, and had done so with the tacit approval or even the active collaboration of the bishop. In these dioceses the CEBs functioned without any perceived threat to the integrity of the church. This was not the case in the archdiocese of Managua, however, where the issue of a "parallel church" soon generated a conflict of growing proportions and intensity. While in some respects this conflict appears to be peculiar to Managua, it has been treated by many as a microcosm of the church in the Nicaraguan Revolution. Such a view overgeneralizes, even though intrachurch conflict in Managua certainly is of great importance for long-term church-state relations in Nicaragua.

Beginning with the uprising in Monimbó in September 1978, the struggle against the Somoza dictatorship involved the CEBs of Managua in intensive political activity that deepened their ties to the FSLN. The FSLN's military success in such key areas as Masaya, the eastern barrios of Managua, and OPEN 3 was greatly facilitated by the cooperation of CEBs, which provided intelligence, communications links, food, safe houses, medical aid, and combatants. It is important to appreciate that many of the combatants, including a significant number of the *muchachos* martyred in the fighting, were young Christians who joined the struggle out of a deep identification with the FSLN. The actions in some of the cities were not even initiated by the Sandinista Front, but were carried out by the residents of the communities themselves. Their strong identification with the revolution stood in sharp contrast to the cautious posture of the hierarchy.

What, then, was the proper role of the CEBs in revolutionary Nicaragua? Insofar as they were geared to concrete support of the revolution, what danger, if any, did CEB activities pose for the church? These questions suggest a comparison of the sense given to the phrase "popular church" in Nicaragua, on the one hand, and in neighboring El Salvador on the other. In El Salvador during this period the term was proudly and positively applied by church people to the CEBs because opposition to a repressive and unpopular regime was seen as part and parcel of an authentic spiritual role. To the degree that Salvadoran bishops did not support such opposition they were seen as reactionary.[25] In Nicaragua after the triumph, however, CEBs avoided using the term to describe themselves so as not to aggravate tensions within the church and to avoid the charge of playing a political rather than a religious role in society. In other words, the term "popular church" implied a denial of religious authenticity in Nicaragua, while it affirmed that same authenticity in El Salvador. This divergence points to a profound difference between the pre- and posttriumph stages of the revolutionary process. Reflecting on the use of the term "popular church" to discredit Christian activists at the grass roots in Nicaragua, one CEB leader in Estelí asked: "Why do they call us the 'popular church' in a way that implies they represent the 'unpopular church'?"[26]

The Latin American bishops at Puebla did not endorse a "popular church" model for Latin America. Yet they did endorse the CEB as an appropriate pastoral option to carry out the church's preferential option for the poor. How can the CEB respond to the needs of the poor while remaining aloof from partisan political action? In a recent essay Alexander Wilde suggested that it was not possible for the CEBs to do so in the context of authoritarian societies.[27] The Nicaraguan case confirms this suggestion, for it is clear that by virtue of their birth in Somocista Nicaragua, CEBs were strongly politicized as a result of government repression. Indeed, the process of creating and activating CEBs helped politicize the entire church. But politics is not a one-way street, and the point holds just as true in a revolutionary setting. The openness of the Nicaraguan Revolution has invited the "repoliticization" of religion in the struggle over the fate of the Sandinista Revolution. CEBs born in the revolutionary process saw pastoral work as authentic only if it supported efforts to transform Nicaraguan society. However, high church officials were inclined to see this as unwarranted partisanship. They also saw a potential challenge to hierarchical authority and a rupture in church unity.[28]

The conflict is captured neatly in a model put forward by Daniel Levine, who writes of two contrasting models of the church. The bishops' model, as in Nicaragua, stresses control from above, obedience to hierarchical authority, the transmittal of truth and hope from the church to the world, and an overall emphasis on the re-Christianization of society. Each of these points represents a highly sensitive issue in revolutionary Nicaragua because the Christian base communities by and large embrace a second model, that of the church as a "historical community of believers." In this view a solidarity among bishops, priests, and laity replaces a centralized chain of command from top to bottom; dialogue and shared experience replace strict obedience to hierarchical dicta. The church is viewed as a pluralistic body encompassing a broad distribution of authority and power that accords a significant pastoral role to the laity. This model seeks to change society rather than to impose a new version of Christendom.[29] The creation and evolution of CEBs in Nicaragua strikingly illustrates the emergence of this second model. Viewing the "popular church" through this model helps to explain why conflict both within and about the church in the Nicaraguan Revolution is so intense in the present stage.

The potential for conflict that grows out of these two models is obviously more than a clash of wills—it is a clash of theologies and pastoral strategies, and it has brought unexpected pressure to bear on traditional church authority. Its roots lie in the democratizing experience of the popular struggle that gave diverse groups within the church great latitude to develop their own pastoral options. Clerical involvement in the struggle nurtured a strong identification with the FSLN and helped to authenticate a pastoral option for the poor. In the posttriumph period, the government has had frequent occasion to recall and to laud the Christian presence in the insurrection. But to those in the church who fear the drift of Sandinista policy, such testimonials seem to be efforts to coopt groups within the church and therefore are taken as a challenge to church unity and hierarchical authority.

The Catholic Church in a Changing Society

If the experience of the insurrection led Christians at the grass roots to see popular rebellion as compatible with Christian faith, what concrete expectations about the shape of a new political order did that experience carry with it? The key, no doubt, lay in the participatory nature of that experience. The participants understood themselves to be struggling, in some sense, for a more democratic Nicaragua. To members of Christian base communities or such organizations as CEPA, any effort to democratize Nicaragua would need to institutionalize the participation to which popular groups had become accustomed through the insurrection. This pointed to a much broader representation of political interests in Nicaragua than had ever been the case before. The broadening of representation, in turn, implied sweeping changes in Nicaraguan society.

Underlying these changes was a new self-awareness among poor Nicaraguans, including many Christians, who had taken part actively in the insurrection and were aware of the importance of their contribution. Their critical, determined participation in both the religious and the political life of posttriumph Nicaragua is an important element of the revolutionary process. We can illustrate this point best by sharing with the reader the comments of CEB members themselves as they were made at a gathering in the summer of 1982.[30] What follows is a description of the event and the setting in which it took place, and then the reflections of some of the participants.

On the third anniversary of the Nicaraguan Revolution a Christian conference and celebration, organized by the National Coordinating Committee of Christian Communities of Nicaragua, was held in Masaya. In attendance were groups from Chontales, Masaya, León, Managua, Chinandega, Darío, Granada, and the Atlantic Coast, together with a delegation from Guatemala. The morning plenary session opened with a speaker from each participating community introducing his or her fellow members. These introductions were followed by music and a presentation by Father Uriel Molina, who spoke on the book of Exodus, chapter 15.

All the bishops had been invited to participate, with a special effort to secure Monseñor Obando's attendance. However, no bishop showed up. When asked why, a member of the Coordinating Committee of CEBs for Managua speculated that when the archbishop saw Father Molina's name on the program he decided not to come. The committee member spoke of "campos bien definidos," or well-defined positions within the church, implying that there were strong theological or ideological positions separating the archbishop from the priests and CEB members. He went on to say that CEB participants had not given up hope that the differences would be reconciled and added, "We do not want a parallel church."

Consignas, or slogans, were shouted spontaneously from the group throughout the program, the most frequently voiced being "somos una iglesia" (we are one church) and "El Salvador vencerá" (El Salvador will overcome). There was an air of festivity and joy about the entire meeting. Musicians from Jalapa and Ciudad Sandino performed.

After Father Molina's talk and a short break, the conference divided into small discussion groups of from five to eight members, chosen randomly. Each group had a lay leader to facilitate the discussion, which centered around a common set of questions. One of the authors took part in a group discussion that lasted for almost two hours. The following dialogue took place among the seven Nicaraguans—three men who described themselves as "pequeños agricultores" (small farmers) and who worked for UNAG (Unión Nacional de Agricultores y Ganaderos), one construction worker, two women who worked in a local CEB (one of whom also worked with the CDS in her neighbor-hood), and one nun. The group discussion leader was a woman.

(A dash in front of a response indicates that a different person in the group is responding.)

Question No. 1: What kind of faith did we have in the time of Somoza?
Responses:
—We lived under oppression.
—We had a traditional faith, and then the repression came later.
—The repression did not allow us to live freely.
—How could Somoza have been called the First Prince of the Church? This confused many people.
—We were trembling in the night. . . . We did not know if the Guardia would come to take us away.
—The church was a church of pure luxury, but they never were churches.
—We had a Christianity without faith, a sleeping faith.
[One of the women spoke of communion:]
—I remember what communion used to be like. I remember when my child was 12 years old she could not have her commu-nion because she did not have a dress and crown. [Reflecting on this past event for a moment, she said] Wasn't it silly of us to think that the white dress mattered to our Lord? [Speaking of that old church of fancy communions, she said] It was a church of individuals.

Question No. 2: Are we working in the revolutionary process now? How has working in the revolutionary process helped us to live as Christians in our communities?
Responses:
[The women responded first:]
—My community [CEB] has helped me a great deal. I almost went crazy when my son died in the war. The CEB helped me, encour-aged me to join a CDS where I worked responsibly. There was work for me to do—the work of the revolution integrated into Christian life. I began to work with other mothers. My dead son was a *catequista* who had traveled all around the country. Now I have another son who is also a *catequista* and is learning to be an engineer.
—We earn our living as agricultural workers in a cooperative of UNAG.

—I am a construction worker, working with a union. The union is helping us to share our profits and reinvest. Before you just earned a set salary that someone paid you. This is not just revolutionary but it is a Christian act. [He spoke of the New Man[31] and this was discussed for a while.]

[One of the UNAG workers brought up the health campaigns, vaccinations, and the literacy crusade.]

—This was eminently Christian work.

[At this point the facilitator tried to get people to talk of their experiences.]

—I remember the campesinos dancing after the revolution.

—When?

—At a simple wedding at which everyone was happy. Two of the campesinos were married in a house that used to belong to a Somocista. The lands used to belong to him also. We worked the fields and never saw the inside of the house. When the landowner fled and the government was deciding what to do with the property one of the field hands asked the priest if he would marry him in the large foyer of the house. The priest said yes and the government gave its permission. We were dancing all night.

Question No. 3: What commitment do Christians need to work in the reconstruction?

Responses:

—It is not easy.

—We work to defend what we have against the counterrevolution.

—Christians in the revolution have to fight with their faith and we are going to win.

—Remember the text of Exodus. . . .

—We have to set the example of sharing.

Question No. 4: What kind of commitment can each one of you personally make?

Responses:

—Work to change people's values. To make them less individualistic.

—Work to get more riches to rebuild their society.

—Stop decapitalization. . . .

—Organize ourselves more.

—Volunteer for *vigilancia* [a sort of neighborhood crimewatch].

—Help in hospitals.

—See that medicines stay there and are not taken illegally.

—We must fight U.S. policy toward Nicaragua. We must fight the boycott of the Nicaraguan Revolution with a Christian boycott.

—We must not let them do to us what has been done to Cuba economically or to Chile militarily.

—The challenge that we have is to change some bourgeois Christians.

—They are the majority.

—No. I do not think they are a majority.

—They are a majority in influence.

—They can be influential in the counterrevolution.

—They do not like the revolution because it was not made for them.

[At this point the author present interjected a question:]
What can you do to help the middle-class people in your barrios who are confused or are not with the revolution?
Responses:
—I invited some of them to church with me [in the barrio of Monseñor Lezcano, the parish church of Father Manuel Batalla, which will be discussed below].

—I had some success but some were afraid to listen to me.

—Fight their ignorance and rumors. These people do not know about life in other countries. We believe that it is better here. They [the wealthy] say that they have had brown and white sugar in Mexico for years. [The reader should note that white sugar was one of the first items rationed in Nicaragua in 1981, to four pounds a month. This prompted opposition within the middle class, who believed that white sugar was better.] Moreover, before the revolution they were never limited in the amounts they could purchase.

—There are poor and rich who do not like to work. The charismatics make inroads into them, offer them things. Maybe we could use this method?

—We should make house-to-house visits and talk to them.

—We must make them see that the revolution will benefit them.

The groups broke for a late lunch, after which they met again to share and combine statements. Then they put on a series of skits and sang songs or read poetry. The meeting broke up at 4:15 and the conference concluded with a march through Masaya. The participants were asked to march with decorum. They were also asked to shout only Christian *consignas*—out of tact and respect for others.

This dialogue demonstrates vividly the effects of religious innovation in a time of intense and violent political change. These humble people have a keen awareness of the society around them and a coherent sense of competing group and class interests. They have a strong vision of a better society and are prepared to make great sacrifices to achieve it. Gone is the traditional fatalism of the peasant; in its place is a determination to organize, which is seen as "eminently Christian work." Gone is the "sleeping faith" of the past; in its place are Christians willing "to fight with their faith" for a better life within the Nicaraguan Revolution.

Church-State Relations

Through the commitments undertaken at Medellín and Puebla, the Catholic church had appeared to endorse and legitimate the activist outlook articulated by these Nicaraguan campesinos. However, when confronted with the fact of revolution, Nicaragua's Catholic hierarchy found it difficult to embrace this outlook fully. For one thing, they preferred to maintain a traditional European distinction between the proper "nonpartisan" role of the institutional church, and the political activism that any individual Christian might derive from the teachings of the church. They could not accept the political advocacy implied in the Medellín documents because these implications did not fit within the framework of traditional European Catholic teachings. As a result, they faced a dilemma. Their commitment to the separation of church and state, a key element of the liberal European tradition, seemed to mean that the church, as an institution, could not participate in the political programs of the revolution. And yet the social teachings of Medellín called on the church to lend its weight to the task of building a more just society.

As the Sandinistas proceeded to consolidate their power in the early months of the revolution a nexus of opposition began to coalesce around the traditional wing of the Catholic hierarchy. This anti-Sandinista opposition incorporated the more privileged sectors of Nicaraguan society, including the private sector and the editors of *La Prensa*. These groups aspired to create the institutions of a liberal democracy in Nicaragua, while the Sandinistas and their supporters envisioned a democracy rooted in popular participation through the mass organizations. The conflict between these two democratic visions crystallized in the formation of the Council of State in May 1980. At that time the relationship between the private sector and the Sandinistas was tenuous but still cordial. The program of a mixed economy, a just agrarian reform, and a governing junta drawn from the private sector and the Sandinista Front was momentarily acceptable to both the elite and the popular classes. Yet the events surrounding the formation of the colegislative body proved to be a turning point in which the temporary accommodation between the Sandinistas and their opponents was abruptly shattered.

As the elites in the private sector saw it, the Council of State was intended to be a colegislative body that would share power with the ruling junta until elections could be held. They envisioned an organization similar to a parliament, where political parties, and those who had the skills to advance within political parties, could press their demands. In effect, the Council of State would be a counterweight to the ruling junta, which the middle-class opposition saw as controlled by the National Directorate of the FSLN. The Sandinista Front, on the other hand, was initially uncertain as to how it wished to see the Council of State composed, and therefore it delayed the opening of that body. Some members of the National Directorate were hesitant to permit conditions that would allow the politically skilled bourgeoisie to dominate the colegislative branch of government and overpower the popular classes, who at this point did not possess the organizational or rhetorical skills of the upper middle classes.

When the Council of State was finally inaugurated in May 1980 it did not take the shape of the parliament that the private-sector elite had desired: it resembled a corporatist body, organized along sectoral lines, rather than a parliament based upon geographic representation. The position that finally prevailed was the one adopted by the National Directorate, who contended that groups and elements within Nicaraguan society should have representation in accordance with the level of their participation in the insurrection. Originally the Council was to include thirty-three members; however, as a result of this decision the final number was fifty-one, with the increase coming in popular representation. As a pro-Sandinista source explained the decision: "The mass organizations were assured their representation in the popular parliament and for the first time in the history of Nicaragua they began to act on the national level. With this participation the Council of State was converted into a model of democratic excellence, accurately reproducing the struggle of different social classes in the nation."[32] Thus, the mass organizations were awarded more voting power in the Council of State than the traditional political parties or such private-sector groups as Consejo Superior de la Empresa Privada (COSEP). These groups had to settle for a corporatist parliament in which their strength was diluted.

To the private sector, which was losing power in the junta, this corporatist structuring of the Council of State was a betrayal. As the Sandinistas assumed control of cabinet ministries and expanded the Sandinista army, the upper middle class saw its sphere of influence contracting sharply. Both private-sector representatives in the junta, Alfonso Robelo and Violeta Chamorro, resigned the month before the opening of the Council of State, once the final configuration of representation became clear. Robelo charged the government with leading the nation to "totalitarianism." The subsequent appointment of Rafael Córdoba Rivas, a member of the Conservative party, as his replacement on the governing junta did not placate the bourgeoisie. To the contrary, Córdoba Rivas's acceptance almost caused a split in the Conservative party. Only his public declaration that he was a member of the junta, but not a Sandinista, prevented a division within party ranks.[33] The Democratic National Movement (Movimiento Democrático Nacional, MDN), led by Alfonso Robelo, accepted its limited representation in the Council of State but withdrew by 1981. And COSEP accepted its representation of six seats but resigned and returned several times during 1981–82.

On May 13, 1980, in the midst of this political turmoil, the Catholic hierarchy suddenly called for the resignation of the priests who held cabinet positions: Miguel D'Escoto, minister of foreign relations; Ernesto Cardenal, minister of culture; Fernando Cardenal, S.J., director of Sandinista Youth; and Father Parrales, minister of social welfare.[34] The presence of these priests in key ministries was of great practical importance to the Sandinista government. Each brought a high level of training to his position and the new government desperately needed this expertise. Moreover, each brought a measure of prestige or other intangible qualities to his job that seemed to make him peculiarly well suited to it. For example, D'Escoto was fluent in English and knew the United States well. Ernesto Cardenal's reputation as a poet and his association with the founding of the artistic community of

Solentiname made him a particularly appropriate figure to head the Ministry of Culture. But their presence was also important symbolically, for it demonstrated an explicit link between the Catholic church and the revolutionary government. The fact of priests serving in high public office made it difficult to assume that the government was antireligious.

In this regard the struggle that now developed over whether the priests would continue in office highlighted the competing views of authority and participation that separated five key actors on the Nicaraguan scene. The present discussion examines these five actors as follows: Archbishop Obando y Bravo and the conservative faction within the hierarchy; the priests themselves, who were in effect asked to choose sides; the Nicaraguan government, which needed the priests' expertise and argued strongly to retain their services; the organized laity at the grass roots, who vigorously supported the presence of the priests in government; and the Vatican, which played an important but ambiguous role.

Within a week of the bishops' call for their resignation, the affected clergy responded by urging dialogue with the bishops. In effect, they refused to resign. An impasse was created, and tension mounted as the conflict went unresolved. The government entered into the conflict by designating Roberto Argüello, the president of the Supreme Court, to head a special mission to Rome to obtain a judgment from the Vatican. In October, he reported that, in the Vatican's view, "it is the bishops who have to resolve the situation."[35] In January 1981 the priests asked the bishops for a face-to-face dialogue, but they were informed instead that they no longer had the episcopacy's approval to participate in the government. In May, Archbishop Obando told an interviewer that the Nicaraguan hierarchy had done all it could and had sent details to the Vatican for a final resolution, which only the pope could provide.

Then, on June 1, 1981, the bishops issued another pastoral letter. Stating that they had "total backing and authorization to proceed" from the Holy See, they insisted that the priests leave their government posts forthwith: "We declare that if the priests who are occupying political office and exercising partisan functions do not leave those responsibilities as soon as possible, . . . we will consider them in an attitude of open rebellion and formal disobedience to legitimate ecclesiastical authority and subject to the sanctions provided by the laws of the church."[36] With this declaration the level of conflict rose sharply.

Although issued in the name of unity, the statement simply triggered off a new round of intense public controversy. The bishops not only demanded resignations, they also went out of their way to declare that CEPA, the CAV, and the Historical Institute were not official church organizations and had "neither the approval nor the recommendation of the Episcopal Conference." Again, the priests refused to resign under these pressures, insisting on "our unbreakable commitment to the Sandinista popular revolution, in faithfulness to our people, which is to say, in faithfulness to the will of God."[37]

For conservatives in the Catholic hierarchy, the presence of priests in the government was a continual reminder that the church had not maintained a separate identity from a revolution that they distrusted. The priests' presence also gave credence to the government's stated position of religious tolerance. Now, had these men been lay Catholics, their participation might have been more palatable to the hierarchy and more consistent with the teachings of Puebla and the 1971 Synod of Bishops. According to those teachings, priests were entrusted with greater responsibility than lay persons because of their divine calling and their ministry of the sacraments. As priests they were also in the line of succession to become bishops and cardinals. Thus, they constituted the future magisterium of the church, which in the Catholic tradition must uphold the universal teachings of the church. It is important to note that these teachings also allowed for "exceptional circumstances" in which priests could assume partisan responsibilities. However, in the view of the conservatives in the hierarchy, by 1980 any exceptional circumstances had ended.

The response of the priests to these calls for their resignation was also disturbing to the conservative faction of the hierarchy. While the priests were respectful of the bishops, they were also firm in refusing to accede to their demands. The episode seemed to confirm the hierarchy's worst suspicions of their loss of authority in a changing church. The priests responded insistently that, in their judgment, the exceptional circumstances were not over. Moreover, they saw no contradiction between "faithfulness to the church and faithfulness to the poor."[38]

It is testimony to the importance given to this issue that it was addressed at length by the Sandinistas in their *Official Communique Concerning Religion*, which was published in the party newspaper, *Barricada*, on October 7, 1980. The *Official Communique* went out of its way to praise the church for its role in the liberation of Nicaragua. It also committed the government to guaranteeing religious freedom, which was described as an "inalienable human right."[39] At the same time, it promised to assure conditions under which all manner of religious celebrations could be carried out and urged that they be kept free from the taint of politics. This assertion belied a concern on the part of the FSLN that religious belief and institutions might be used to attack the revolution.

The *Communique* also guaranteed the right of all Nicaraguan citizens, regardless of their civil status, to participate in the political affairs of the nation. With regard to clerical participation in government, the FSLN argued as follows:

> The priests who hold office in the government, heeding the call of the FSLN and their civic obligation, have done an extraordinary job so far. Confronted as it is by large and difficult problems, our country needs the cooperation of all its patriots, especially those who had the possibility to receive a higher education, which was denied to the majority of our people. That is why the FSLN will continue demanding the participation in revolutionary works of all those religious and lay citizens whose experience or qualifications are necessary for our process. If any one of these religious persons decides to give up governmental responsibilities due to personal reasons, that, too, is their right. To exercise the right of participation and to fulfill patriotic obligation is a matter of personal conscience.[40]

The bishops' swift reply to the FSLN communique was combative in attitude and argumentative in style. The overall effect was to impute totalitarian tendencies to the government and to imply a latent hostility toward religion. The reply criticized totalitarians because they orchestrate a false participation that merely manipulates social groups. Against this tendency the bishops declared that Nicaraguans "must demand a *conscious and deliberate participation*, as free men, not as slaves" (emphasis in the original).[41] The reply went on to talk in general terms of "an ideology" that rejects religious values and undermines religious belief. It implied that the priests serving in the government had been lured into service with "flattery and sinecures," and suggested that the government they served was "extremist."[42] In short, the bishops' reaction made it clear that they distrusted the motives of the FSLN and expected the church to suffer under the Sandinista government. The Catholic hierarchy thus approached the revolution in a resistant frame of mind. This approach was based on generic concerns and prior assumptions about the nature of Marxism, revolution, and mass mobilization, rather than on specific actions the government had taken against the church—as we have seen, at this juncture the FSLN had adopted a solicitous and conciliatory approach toward the church.

Against this background it is not surprising that Archbishop Obando y Bravo made several trips to the Vatican during this period. Two of these trips immediately preceded the issuance of calls for the priests' resignations—the first in April 1980, and the second in May 1981. In the aftermath of this second request and the priests' opposition, Obando returned to Rome to plead his case at the same time (June 8–12, 1981) that a high-level delegation from CELAM, headed by then-Bishop Alfonso López Trujillo, traveled to the Vatican to discuss Central America. López Trujillo reported that he was pleased with the results of these meetings in which the CELAM delegates talked with Cardinal Baggio of the Pontifical Commission for Latin America. According to López, the consensus of their meeting was that the Nicaraguan priests should resign from government.[43]

The Nicaraguan government's high-level delegation—consisting of Miguel Ernesto Vigil, minister of housing; Roberto Argüello, president of the Supreme Court; and Emilio Baltodano, of the FSLN— visited Rome in August 1980 and again in June 1981, immediately following the visit of the CELAM delegation. On both occasions, they met with Cardinal Agostino Casaroli, Vatican secretary of state, and on both occasions they reported, as has already been suggested, that the issue must be resolved within Nicaragua.

Realizing that the Vatican would not resolve this dispute for them, the episcopal conference and the priests finally reached a temporary accommodation on July 15, 1981. According to the statement of the bishops, the priests were to maintain their faith "in communion with the hierarchy," and a state of temporal exception would be conceded under the following conditions: "That while they exercise their public offices and performance as party functionaries they will abstain from all performance of priestly duties, in public or in private, within the nation or internationally."[44]

Predictably, the Christians who worked in the CEBs were extremely supportive of the priests' government service. If one can measure public opinion by the editorials and letters published in Nicaragua's three daily newspapers over the course of two years, the majority of

responses in *El Nuevo Diario* and *Barricada* were in favor of the continued service of the priests. Christians at the grass roots defended the
priests because they remembered their active participation during the
revolution. They also felt that the removal of these priests from office
could severely weaken the commitment of the Nicaraguan church to
the poor.

As a result of this accord, the government initiated a regular forum
for dialogue with the bishops called the Permanent Commission for
Dialogue. The Sandinistas were intent on keeping open the channels
of communication and preventing further conflicts between themselves and the hierarchy. The government representatives on the commission were junta members Daniel Ortega, Sergio Ramírez, and Rafael Córdoba Rivas, together with René Nuñez of the FSLN. They
were joined by Bishops Julián Barni, López Ardón, and Leovigildo
López Fitoria.

The dialogue was suspended in February 1982 following the release
of an episcopal letter that severely criticized the government for its
handling of the Miskito Indians. However, contacts between the
church and the government were revived subsequently, and despite
frequent strain they continued throughout the early years of the
revolution.

Divisions in the Hierarchy and in the Body of Christ

While division between the Catholic hierarchy and the Sandinista
government was impossible to conceal, divisions within the episcopal
conference itself were less apparent. But despite the public appearance of unity in the years following the triumph, significant differences of attitude and style underlay the bishops' letters and public
statements. The two important letters issued by the episcopal conference in October 1980 illustrate the point. The bishops' response to
the FSLN *Communique Concerning Religion* was defensive in tone and
served better to express fears of the revolution than to address the
issues raised in the communique. Dated October 17, 1980, it warned of
"ideological control of the revolution" and of a tendency to adopt the
"dogmatic rigidity of other previously known models." It implied that
the government encouraged atheism and intentionally provoked divisions within the church.[45] Yet the very next week the bishops released
another document, entitled "Jesus Christ and the Unity of His Church
in Nicaragua." Although it reiterated some of the criticisms men-

tioned in the reply to the FSLN communique, this statement also exhibited a measure of self-exploration and attempted to analyze the unique role of Christ in Nicaragua. At one point the bishops wrote: "We are aware of the novelty of the historical experience that we are living, we find ourselves at the beginning of a new era in the life of Nicaragua. We believe that this moment gives us the possibility and responsibility to remake our nation from its foundations."[46]

The notable differences of tone and orientation between two letters that were issued so close together in time suggests a lack of agreement within the episcopal conference on key issues of the revolution. In fact, on several controversial issues the bishops took different positions publicly. The ultimatum demanding the resignation of the priest-ministers in June 1981 was signed in the name of the episcopal conference, yet Bishop López Ardón later asserted that he was not aware of the letter before its release.[47] Several other bishops, while agreeing with the general intent of the directive, were more willing than the archbishop to work for compromise. Before he was named Bishop of León, Monseñor Barni spoke with the priests and offered his services to obtain an extension from the pope. Bishop Schlaefer of Bluefields said that it would be consistent with the Puebla documents for the pope to grant an extension of the exceptional circumstances. As far as the Catholic church was concerned, then, what can we say was happening in these first two years of the revolution?

Under the aggressive leadership of Archbishop Obando y Bravo, the episcopal conference undertook to promote its own pastoral agenda for Nicaragua. The nation's seminary was reopened and Mexican priests were brought in to provide instruction. The church revived and promoted two religious movements associated with a highly spiritualist, other-worldly, and socially conservative form of worship: the "charismatics" and the "cursillos de cristiandad." A Catholic parents' association was established. In the archdiocese of Managua, a Diocesan Lay Commission was set up to link each parish to the Curia and to the bishop; the Lay Commission then served as an instrument for implementing diocesan plans at the parish level. Structurally, it represented an effort to recentralize control within the institutional church. To parish priests and lay Christians attempting to work in harmony with the revolution, it seemed an effort to preempt local initiatives and impose on each parish the pastoral strategy of the bishops, to the exclusion of any other strategy. This approach seemed aimed at discouraging grass-roots Christians from participating in FSLN programs and projects.[48]

In mid-1981 a CELAM team, consisting of five Latin American bishops, visited Nicaragua as part of a fact-finding mission in Central America. The team interviewed the Nicaraguan bishops at length and also met with government leaders. Its subsequent report portrayed the Nicaraguan church as divided, in the following terms: "Those faithful to the [revolutionary] process and critical of the church, on one side; and those faithful to the church and critical of the process on the other."[49] The report asserted that the institutional church was beginning to be held hostage by small groups within its midst, assisted by the government; at the same time, it claimed, a majority in the church disagreed with this radical minority, preferring that the church situate itself "above" the revolutionary process and exercise a critical role vis-à-vis government programs. It is impossible to determine the extent to which this view portrayed the thinking of all the bishops in the Nicaraguan episcopate, but there is no doubt that it was accurate in regard to the assessment of Archbishop Obando. Concrete actions taken by Obando in the second half of 1981 and in 1982 reflected vividly the attitude presented in the CELAM report. In the name of church unity he began to move against priests and religious whose pastoral work he deemed divisive. These moves, which often were made without consulting those affected, were sometimes accompanied by conflict that exacerbated division rather than increasing unity. Some examples will illustrate.

The parish priest of San Judas, a poor barrio in Managua, was removed in this way, and the Sisters of the Assumption were ordered to move out of the parish house. In August 1981 a bitter controversy raged for weeks over Archbishop Obando's removal of Father Manuel Batalla from the parish of the Sacred Heart in the barrio of Monseñor Lezcano: the superior of the Dominican Order traveled to Nicaragua to urge dialogue in the matter; meanwhile, parishioners occupied the parish church demanding the priest's reinstatement, and Curia spokesmen insisted on the bishop's right and duty to remove him for the sake of parish unity.[50] There have been numerous other cases of such interventions to remove priests or religious considered disruptive to diocesan pastoral programs. Often these actions have affected foreign clergy and religious, as in each of the above cases. Similarly affected in 1981 were Jesuit priests Luis Medrano and Otilio Miranda, who also worked in poor barrios of Managua. Father Pedro Belzúnegui, who worked in Tipitapa, a poor Managua suburb, was replaced by the archbishop while he was out of the country.[51] In July 1982

Obando removed from the poor barrio of Santa Rosa Father José Arias Caldera, who had been parish priest there since 1974. Father Arias was known for his frequent protection of young combatants during the popular insurrection and was quite popular in his parish. Upon receiving notice of his removal, parishioners gathered at the church to hold a prayer vigil. While they were assembled Monseñor Bosco Vivas, the auxiliary bishop of the archdiocese, arrived, announcing that he had come not to initiate a dialogue, which the parishioners had requested, but to remove the ciborium; his efforts to do so led to a scuffle in which he was pushed and fell. Father Arias accepted the transfer imposed upon him, but the indignant parishioners demanded that the hierarchy take them into account in its decisions. The archbishop's answer was to excommunicate all those involved in the incident with Monseñor Vivas and to place the parish church under interdict so that religious services could not be held there.[52]

By the end of 1981 both church and state were inevitably caught in the polarizations of Nicaraguan society: between rich and poor, Sandinista and non-Sandinista, hierarchy and base. The fragile accord of the early years of the revolution was increasingly tenuous and would face even greater challenges as external actors began to play more decisive roles.

Nine

The Churches and the
Emerging Contra War

The Presidential Finding on Nicaragua

During Ronald Reagan's first year in office his administration placed the Nicaraguan Revolution near the top of its agenda as a foreign policy challenge. But how would the administration respond to that revolution? Would it follow its predecessor's lead and try to achieve influence in Managua by offering aid conditioned on acceptable Sandinista behavior? This approach was rejected almost immediately through the suspension of Carter administration funds that had not yet been released. But the Reagan administration's alternative did not become clear for some time.

However, by the spring of 1982 U.S. journalists had begun to discern the shape of a policy. Articles appeared suggesting that some sort of covert actions, possibly aimed at destabilizing Nicaragua, had been approved by President Reagan. When pressed to clarify the matter, the administration refused. Typical is the comment reported in the *New York Times* on March 17: "The White House refused today to confirm or deny the Nicaraguan accusation of CIA involvement in guerrilla attacks. According to White House counselor, Edwin Meese III, 'the U.S. is not in the habit of engaging in sinister plots. Beyond that, however, it is our policy not to either confirm or deny such statements as that.'"[1] It was, indeed, another six months before the extent of the administration's commitment to destabilizing Nicaragua through the training and support of counterrevolutionary guerrillas was fully reported in the U.S. media.[2] By then, the gathering Contra war had been under way for nearly a year and a half.

On March 9, 1981, Ronald Reagan signed a Presidential Finding that authorized the CIA to provide financial assistance to individuals and groups in Nicaragua who opposed the Sandinista government. In addition, the president agreed to expand the scope of U.S. intelligence-gathering in Central America and the Caribbean. Each of these programs had been initiated during the last year of the Carter administration, but the Reagan team added a new dimension: covert military action to interdict supplies said to be flowing from Nicaragua to guerrillas fighting in El Salvador. The projected cost of these operations was $19.5 million.[3]

In November 1981 President Reagan again met extensively with his National Security Council advisors to consider further policy options regarding Nicaragua. As a result of these meetings the president approved an extension of the programs he had authorized in March, including covert financial assistance to internal opponents of the Sandinistas, and the expansion of the U.S. intelligence network in the region. At the same time, a debate developed among Reagan's advisors concerning the funding, the training, and especially the overall goals of the recently established paramilitary force. One option was to create a 500-man commando force made up of Cuban exiles whose objective would be to disrupt the Nicaraguan economy. Another possibility was to provide the financial and logistical support for a 1,000-man force of Nicaraguan exiles, the training of which had been initiated by the Argentinian military. Some of the president's advisors argued that the goal of the covert operation should be the overthrow of the Nicaraguan government, while others argued for the more limited objective of interdicting arms destined for the Salvadoran guerrillas. This latter group, which included officials from the departments of State and Defense, argued against the risk of associating with former Somocista National Guardsmen, and also voiced concern about the danger of escalation into a regional war.[4]

Eventually President Reagan signed another Finding, dated December 2, 1981, which gave the CIA broad authority to conduct covert political and paramilitary operations against alleged Cuban supply lines in Nicaragua and throughout Central America, and to work with such governments as Honduras and Argentina to achieve these objectives.[5] While the authority given to the CIA was broad in scope, the declared objective of this policy toward Nicaragua was limited to the interdiction of arms flows. When notified of this Presidential Finding, the intelligence committees in Congress also insisted on the pursuit of limited objectives. They approved the training of the 1,000-man force to interdict supplies, but not the 500-man commando unit. They also acquiesced to supervision by Argentinian and Honduran military officers in the training program. However, the Argentinian and Honduran trainers were explicit in their desire to see the overthrow of the Sandinista government. They did not hesitate to employ former National Guardsmen, many of whom were readily available because they had fled to Honduras after the collapse of the Somoza regime.

In retrospect, the contradictions inherent in this policy are evident. On the one hand, the United States was officially pursuing limited goals that in no way implied an intention to overthrow the Nicaraguan government. On the other hand, some of the president's advisors certainly harbored stronger ambitions than merely halting the flow of arms, while the assets being utilized by the CIA openly sought the overthrow of the Sandinistas.

In the spring of 1982 a brief war broke out between Argentina and Great Britain over control of the Islas Malvinas (Falkland Islands). The United States initially tried to mediate the conflict, but eventually threw its support to Great Britain. In retaliation, Argentina abruptly terminated its role in building up the paramilitary force of Nicaraguan exiles. These developments meant that the United States now had to assume a larger role in training the counterrevolutionary forces. While officially pursuing an arms interdiction policy, the Reagan administration was in fact facilitating the efforts of a guerrilla army that was rapidly escalating its attacks on economic and strategic targets. As 1982 wore on, this exile force staged commando raids on a growing number of villages and rural settlements, especially agricultural cooperatives, with a growing loss of life in the Nicaraguan countryside.

This strategy of covert war aimed at rolling back the Nicaraguan Revolution flowed logically out of the assumptions that President Reagan brought with him to office. During the presidential campaign of 1980, the Committee of Santa Fe had prepared a document entitled "A New Inter-American Policy for the Eighties," which became the foundation for the Reagan administration's policy in Central America.[6] According to the report, the United States had entered a period of military and moral decline and needed to take strong initiatives to recover its former greatness. The decline was traced to the U.S. failure at the Bay of Pigs to prevent the establishment of a Communist beachhead in the western hemisphere. America's strength was then further eroded by the human rights policy of the Carter administration under which such allies as Anastasio Somoza in Nicaragua were punished, while our enemies grew stronger. In the 1980s, the committee warned, the United States would have to demonstrate the will to meet the threat of Soviet expansion through surrogate powers such as Cuba and Nicaragua.[7] Such was the world view that underlay the policy of covert war against Nicaragua.

Under U.S. sponsorship the 1,000-man force that had been recommended in December 1981 grew to 4,500 by the following July. It now called itself the Nicaraguan Democratic Force (Fuerza Democrática Nicaragüense, FDN). Its weaponry improved significantly and the number of attacks increased, especially in the Atlantic Coast region where most of Nicaragua's indigenous population resides. An attack on the city of Waspam in December 1981 prompted the Nicaraguan government to relocate eight to ten thousand Miskito Indians from the Río Coco border area. This enforced relocation dramatically raised tensions between the FSLN and the Miskitos, ultimately leading to armed confrontations between disaffected Miskito fighters and the Ejército Popular Sandinista (EPS). Both the Catholic and Protestant churches were rapidly brought into this conflict.

The Counterrevolution, the Miskitos, and the Church

Even without the counterrevolutionary war, relations would have been difficult between the Sandinista government and the indigenous population of Zelaya. During the years when it was building its political base in the more populous western zones of the country, the FSLN had done little organizational work in the coastal region. By and large, the indigenous peoples had stayed aloof from the insurrection—thus, they did not have the sense of participation in the revolution that was so widely shared among the ladino (people of mixed Spanish and Indian descent) majority. This divergent experiential base merely compounded the significant historical, cultural, and regional differences that already separated the peoples of the Atlantic Coast from the rest of Nicaragua. When the government did begin to organize in the Miskito areas, and to implement its programs, it met with some hostility and resistance. The situation was severely exacerbated by U.S. policy through the "Red Christmas" military campaign of November–December 1981.[8]

Miskito fighters were being actively recruited to the counterrevolutionary cause at this time with the help of Steadman Fagoth, a German national who had married a Miskito woman. Fagoth established MISURA (Unidad de los Miskitu, Sumu, y Rama), a Miskito organization, and helped integrate it into the FDN. It was MISURA, using U.S.

funds, that organized the Red Christmas campaign. This major military offensive was initiated in November 1981 with attacks on Indian villages and the destruction of bridges located on the borders of the Río Coco. The proposed objective was to take control of a portion of northern Nicaraguan territory and to declare a government in exile. Although the plan failed, in less than two months more than sixty civilians and Sandinista soldiers were killed.

The forced relocation already mentioned was undertaken in direct response to this campaign. In January 1982 the government moved the Indians from the Río Coco to a resettlement area named Tasba Pri, located further toward the interior of the country. When the Indians resisted, the Sandinista forces burned their crops and livestock to force them to move. While the relocation was under way, then-Secretary of State Alexander Haig held a press conference at which he waved a photograph of bodies being burned and claimed to have proof of a Sandinista massacre of Miskito Indians. It was soon revealed that the photograph had been taken several years earlier and that no massacre had in fact taken place.[9] However, a long-standing mistrust between Nicaragua's ladino and Indian populations deepened into estrangement in these early years of the revolution, largely, although not exclusively, as a result of this relocation. Anthropologist Philippe Bourgois has noted that at this time the Sandinistas were responding to three military exigencies: "to defend the civilian population supportive of the Revolution from contra reprisals; to prevent the Somozist-MISURA alliance from establishing a civilian base of support along the Coco River; and to prevent civilians from being caught in government-contra crossfire."[10] However necessary the relocation may have been from the government's point of view, it created a deep reservoir of resentment that later proved difficult to overcome.

In the midst of this profound escalation of conflict between the Sandinista government, the Contras, and the Miskito population, the Nicaraguan bishops' conference issued a statement severely criticizing the government for its actions in undertaking the relocation effort. While recognizing the government's duty to defend the territorial integrity of the nation, the bishops' statement condemned the government for violating individual rights: "We wish to remind everyone that there are inalienable rights that may not be violated under any circumstances and we state with sad surprise that in some concrete cases there have been serious violations of the human rights of indi-

viduals, families, and even entire villages."[11] Stung by these criticisms, the government quickly rejected the allegations of serious violations of human rights in the Miskito resettlement.[12] Sandinista
leaders pointed out that the bishops had been invited to visit the
resettlement areas but had ignored the invitation—hence, they lacked
firsthand information on which to base their judgment. The government also criticized the bishops for failing to mention the documented
participation of some Catholic deacons and Moravian pastors in the
Contra activities. In the government's view the bishops' harsh public
criticism was precipitous and confrontational. The Catholic hierarchy
had disregarded the Permanent Commission for Dialogue and had
spoken out without first obtaining the full facts of the situation.

On what basis had the episcopal hierarchy made its accusations of
severe violations of human rights? Archbishop Obando insisted that
the hierarchy had evidence, which he claimed had been provided by
North American priests and channeled to the episcopal conference
through Bishop Salvador Schlaefer (whose diocese of Bluefields includes much of the Miskito lands).[13] The Sandinista government did
in fact question Bishop Schlaefer closely about the bishops' allegations
in order to discover what evidence was used to verify them. At the
time, La Prensa reported that Schlaefer had been imprisoned during
the time this questioning took place; in a later interview, Archbishop
Obando asserted that the bishop of Bluefields had been "sequestered
by the government."[14] Bishop Schlaefer himself later issued a statement saying that he had never been imprisoned, either in Nicaragua
or anywhere else.[15] Whatever the merits of the hierarchy's accusations, or the validity of the government's denials, this episode vividly
illustrated a pattern that was to harden over the ensuing years. The
Catholic bishops, especially Archbishop Obando, were strongly disposed to see threats and intended abuses in Sandinista actions and
policies. For its part, the government became increasingly suspicious
of the hierarchy's motives, leading to a growing friction between
church and state that diverted and sapped some of the energies of the
revolution.

With the Contra army now launching serious attacks in several
parts of the country, the Nicaraguan government declared a state of
emergency in March 1982. Under its provisions the government could
control the flow of information in two specific areas: the status of
military operations, and the status of the economy, especially as it
pertained to food distribution. Although it was first presented as a

temporary measure, as the Contra war accelerated, the state of emergency was renewed continually over the following years. The Sandinistas interpreted its mandate broadly to include censorship of newspaper articles and radio broadcasts. The dominant opposition newspaper, *La Prensa*, was repeatedly censored before being closed in June 1986 (events that will be discussed more fully in Chapter 10). The Catholic radio station of the Archdiocese of Managua was also censored until it was closed in January 1985. What was not censored by the government was the weekly newssheet of the Archdiocese of Managua, *La Hoja Dominical*, which frequently disseminated news and commentary critical of the government.[16]

In April 1982 the government sent another special mission to the Vatican to discuss the problem of church-state relations. Continuity with previous delegations was maintained by the selection of Roberto Argüello and Miguel Ernesto Vigil, who were joined by Minister of Education Carlos Tunnerman, one of the best-known lay Catholics in Nicaragua. Again, the Nicaraguan delegation met with Vatican Secretary of State Cardinal Agostino Casaroli, who played a positive role in ameliorating the tensions. While trying to mediate the personal and doctrinal differences between Sandinista leaders and certain members of the Catholic hierarchy, he made it clear that he did not question the legitimacy of the Nicaraguan government. For the moment, Cardinal Casaroli's intervention preserved a facade of civility in church-state relations, while bolstering elements of the church that wished to work within the revolution. He facilitated the continued service of priests in the government. He was also instrumental in the June 1982 appointment of Monseñor Carlos Santi as bishop of Matagalpa. (Bishop Julián Barni, who had held this appointment, was simultaneously named Bishop of León.) Bishop Santi came from the parish of Darío, where CEBs had flourished, while Bishop Barni was a constructive critic of the government whose honesty was respected. In the same month Pope John Paul II named another moderate, Pedro Vílchez, as the prelate of Jinotega.[17] These new figures in the Nicaraguan Catholic hierarchy showed themselves more amenable to dialogue with the government than was Archbishop Obando at this time. Indeed, Monseñor Santi distanced himself from the more reactionary position in the hierarchy by declaring, in his first homily as bishop: "Anyone who says there is no religious freedom in this nation is a liar."[18]

Before turning our attention to Pope John Paul's historic visit to Central America in the early spring of 1983, we would remind the reader that the scale of Nicaraguan society has an important bearing on the process of the revolution. In Nicaragua the political elite, both before and after the triumph of the revolution, is by U.S. standards an astoundingly small circle of people. Everyone knows everyone else. In the setting of this face-to-face society the passions that are associated with political positions run high and take on a particularly personal tone. Certainly this has been true in the field of religion and politics, as the following example illustrates.

On the heels of the church-state clash over the bishops' Miskito letter, a Holy Week sermon by Archbishop Obando y Bravo provoked fresh tensions between himself and Sandinista leaders. In this sermon the archbishop drew attention to the figure of Judas Iscariot. He said that Jesus did not call Judas "brother" as he did the other disciples; instead, he called him "compañero," which the archbishop said meant "traitor."[19] Now, *compañero* is a special word in the Sandinista lexicon because it expresses not only friendship between persons but also solidarity with the revolution. At the same time, it cannot accurately be translated as "traitor," nor did it ever have that meaning in the Bible. The FSLN saw Obando's interpretation as gratuitous, and therefore as a deliberate insult intended to depreciate *Sandinismo*. As such it was an explicit use of theology for political purposes.

Interior Minister Tomás Borge responded to the archbishop's thrust with a personal attack of his own, delivered at the Second Congress of the World Christian Conference for Peace in Central America and the Caribbean in late May. In a speech entitled "The Revolution Fights against the Theology of Death," Borge remarked on the archbishop's interpretation of the revered term *compañero* with these words: "In Nicaragua I believe that only now have Christians recovered the original meaning of charity, the true meaning of sharing (*compañerismo*). This reminds us of the distortion that a high official of the church made recently of the word companion. He said that Christ had called his disciples 'brothers' and he only called as companion, Judas, the traitor. I believe that the person who said that is ignoring or pretending to ignore the true meaning of companion."[20] Borge then went on to suggest that the person who had offered such a critical interpretation of the term *compañero* was probably a "militant counterrevolutionary." In this exchange of verbal attacks no names were used—nonetheless, the principals felt the sting of criticism in the most personal sort of way. As the struggle over the Nicaraguan Revolution became increasingly ideological this personal dimension loomed larger and larger, making compromise all the more difficult.

Preparing for the Papal Visit

From the earliest days of his pontificate John Paul II demonstrated a keen interest in Latin America. It is also clear that revolution and political instability prompted a growing concern in the Vatican over the well-being of the church in Central America. Hence, the announcement that the pope would make a historic pilgrimage through the region, visiting all the nations of Central America, did not come as a surprise. It did, however, provoke an intense mobilization within each country aimed at preparing for the pope's visit so as to maximize its value, including its propaganda value. In a sense all groups sought to gain the pope's blessing, or at the very least to escape his criticism. There were also strenuous efforts in some quarters to "educate" the pope as to the key issues for the church.

One group seeking the pope's ear was the aggressive leadership of CELAM, headed by then-Archbishop Alfonso López Trujillo; another was the Pontifical Commission for Latin America, under the direction of Cardinal Baggio. Offering a different, more moderate perspective was Vatican Secretary of State Cardinal Casaroli. In January 1982 CELAM had published a report highly critical of the religious situation in Nicaragua, perhaps to counter the favorable report on religion and human rights in Nicaragua released by Pax Christi International the previous October. The CELAM report accused the Nicaraguan government of Cubanization and of instrumentalizing religion, of trying to eliminate Catholicism, and of being overtaken by Marxism-Leninism.

Cardinal Casaroli worked within Vatican circles to soften the CELAM interpretation of the Marxist threat to Catholicism in Latin America. To the secretary of state such issues as priests serving in the Sandinista government, while significant, were secondary to the overall question of promoting harmonious church-state relations that assured the autonomy of the church to pursue its religious mission. In Central America the issue was how to relate to a government that was neither a traditional, stable dictatorship nor a liberal democratic regime. Casaroli seemed to feel that precedents might be set in Nicaragua that could be used to improve the church's relations with regimes in Eastern Europe.

Thus, a delicate balance of influences vied to shape the papal perspective and agenda prior to John Paul's visit to Central America. In December 1982 the Vatican announced that the pope would not visit

Nicaragua unless the priest-ministers resigned. This decision, which may well have been encouraged by some members of the Nicaraguan hierarchy, caused genuine consternation within Nicaragua, and a flurry of new negotiations. By late February this obstacle had been surmounted, without the priests' resignation, and Nicaragua was put back on the papal itinerary. In January 1983 Archbishop López Truji- llo, who had pushed an anti-Sandinista line at the Vatican, was named Cardinal.

Pope John Paul II was openly distrustful of Marxist states and skep- tical of their willingness to allow the Catholic church to function freely. It was inevitable that he would bring skepticism, rooted in his own Polish experience, to Nicaragua. When he cautioned Nicaraguan Catholics against "unacceptable ideological commitments," no doubt the specter he saw before him was the dogmatic Marxism of his native Poland. In the same vein, he may have been inclined to see Managua's archbishop, Miguel Obando y Bravo, as a bulwark of Catholic unity against the Marxist Sandinista government, just as Cardinal Josef Glemp represented the church against the Polish regime.

However, our contention is that the real "threat" to the Nicaraguan church was something more fundamental. It had to do with the laity and the changing nature of their role within the institutional church. If the laity were to assume more individual and collective responsibility, all relationships of authority within the church might change: the magisterium might be redefined, including the teaching and pastoral roles of the clergy, so as to accord more authority in these areas to the laity. Such a prospect was particularly upsetting within the context of a revolutionary society where change was already the norm and as- saults on the traditional boundaries of authority in everyday life were becoming routine. As we shall see, Pope John Paul confronted this issue head-on during his visit to Nicaragua. The position he would take, with rather drastic consequences for the Nicaraguan church, was foreshadowed in a letter he sent to the Nicaraguan hierarchy on June 20, 1982, in which he said:

> A "People's Church" opposed to the Church presided over by the lawful pastors is a grave deviation from the will and plan of salvation of Jesus Christ. It is so from the point of view of the Lord's and the apostles' teaching in the New Testament and in the ancient and recent teaching of the Church's solemn magisterium. It is also a principle, a beginning, of fracture and rupture of that

unity which he left as the characteristic sign of the Church itself, and which he willed to entrust precisely to those whom "the Holy Spirit established to rule the Church of God" (Acts 20:20).[21]

Undeniably, Pope John Paul II is strongly committed to defending the dignity of the individual. His forceful denunciation of human rights abuses and his strong pleas for social justice in such countries as the Philippines and Brazil testify to this commitment. Nor has he hesitated to criticize the wealthy for their complicity in the maintenance of widening disparities between rich and poor. Yet, he has been reluctant to connect his general advocacy of social justice to specific political actions. The visit to Nicaragua highlighted this problem. During his sojourn in that country the pope stressed issues of doctrinal orthodoxy, ignoring questions of social justice almost entirely. Even so, his visit inevitably had political repercussions.

During his historic trip through Central America, the pope would refer to himself as an emissary of peace, insisting that his visit was strictly pastoral, not political. But the region was already deeply politicized by the prevailing popular struggles and most Central Americans were looking for signs that the pope sympathized with their partisan views. That is to say, all understood that what the pope had to say was of potential political significance. According to whether they supported or opposed the course of the revolution, undoubtedly many Nicaraguans hoped to receive some sign that the Holy Father also approved or rejected it.

Elaborate preparations were made for the papal visit. But early on, the tensions between church and state made cooperation difficult between the government and the Catholic hierarchy. Again, both the government and the episcopal conference sent delegations to Rome to "brief" the pope and to prepare the way for his visit. The government wished to establish clear guidelines for the itinerary in order to assure strict security measures; moreover, in the face of mounting external aggression, the government viewed the papal mission of peace as especially pertinent to Nicaragua. The bishops, however, sought to minimize any political message the visit might carry. This led to conflict when the bishops tried to insist, as a condition of the papal visit, that the priests resign from the government, and that the pope be officially the guest of church leaders rather than of the government.[22] As writers throughout Latin America have pointed out, this last condition would have distinguished Nicaragua from all other stops on the papal itinerary because he was met consistently by heads of state elsewhere in Central America without accusations of undue partisanship. Had government leaders not been involved in Nicaragua, their absence could have allowed opponents of the revolution to characterize the Sandinistas as indifferent or hostile to the church.[23]

John Paul II in Nicaragua

Pope John Paul II arrived in Central America at the end of February 1983. Huge, adulatory crowds greeted him at his first stop in San José, Costa Rica. San José was to be his base; from there he would fly to each of the other countries. He visited Nicaragua on March 4, spending a little less than twelve hours in country. Although it was a historic moment, fraught with promise and peril, the conduct of neither the pope nor the Sandinista government was notable for its skill or diplomacy. In the government's behalf it can be argued that, since the Sandinistas knew in advance what the pope was going to say, and that he had no words of encouragement for the revolution, they had no reason to be particularly conciliatory toward him. However, junta coordinator Daniel Ortega's welcoming speech at Sandino Airport was quite long and sharply political. The Sandinistas had a legitimate grievance against the United States, and that grievance was clearly articulated in the welcoming speech—but the time to present this grievance was not upon the arrival of a pope who was already uncomfortable with the political tendencies of the Sandinista government, and whose visit had been in doubt several times. A less belligerent welcome, expressing respect for the pope and thanking him for his visit, might have helped to establish a more reassuring and congenial atmosphere.

The most widely reported event that marked the pope's arrival was his rebuff of Ernesto Cardenal, Nicaragua's minister of culture, who was briefly but vigorously scolded by John Paul for his lack of cooperation with church authorities. Unnoticed by the press or the pope, Sandinista leaders and the bishops present embraced and shook hands at the initiative of Comandante Tomás Borge, and to the applause of onlookers; the gesture seemed to symbolize the unity that had been the watchword of the papal visit.[24]

Unfortunately, however, far from healing existing divisions, succeeding events exacerbated them. Here attention will be focused on the mass celebrated in Managua's 19th of July Plaza that afternoon. The crowd exceeded 500,000—about 20 percent of the Nicaraguan population—and included more than half of the nation's clergy. Those unable to attend watched the mass on television. When the pope arrived, dozens of doves were released into the air to symbolize the country's intense desire for peace, while the people waved Sandinista, Nicaraguan, and papal flags. Archbishop Obando y Bravo opened the mass with a welcoming speech that focused on the pope's controversial letter of June 1982. He went on to share an anecdote that compared John Paul's visit to Nicaragua with the visit of Pope John XXIII to the cell of an Italian prisoner who was eventually freed due to papal intervention. The anecdote seemed to suggest that Nicaraguans also were imprisoned, awaiting liberation at the hands of the Holy Father.[25] Even if the analogy seemed appropriate to the archbishop, it violated the hierarchy's own policy of keeping the visit pastoral and spiritual rather than partisanly political.

The pope's homily elaborated at great length on the theme of church unity.[26] The text was highly abstract, and in his manner of delivery John Paul at times seemed distant, at other times emphatic and lecturing. At first his remarks were accompanied by frequent applause from the crowd, but gradually a mood of restlessness developed. Probably few listeners could see the point of the address at first. Eventually, however, they did discern that the Holy Father seemed to be accusing those who supported the revolution of being unfaithful to the church. He insisted vehemently that church unity required strict obedience to the bishops, and he repeated the harsh criticisms of CEBs and other Christian groups supportive of the revolution that he had made the previous summer. In this speech the word "unity" was used fourteen times; the pope spoke of peace only once, and that was in response to the growing chants for peace within the crowd that had begun to interrupt the homily after about half an hour of listening to John Paul read from his prepared text.

What ensued was a spontaneous reaction from the pope's audience. Impatient for him to speak directly to their specific national situation, groups began to shout, chant, and sing—including, in the end, members of the FSLN leadership, who had initially tried to restrain the crowd. John Paul's response to this growing tumult was to repeat the single word "silencio!" Gradually the crowd quieted sufficiently for the pope to go on; he appeared shaken, however, and visibly estranged from his audience. When the mass was concluded he left the stage hurriedly and without the warm and effusive farewell greetings that usually mark his large, open-air masses. As he departed, the strains of the FSLN anthem could be heard in the background.

No aspect of John Paul's Central American trip has been more widely commented on than the stopover in Nicaragua. Much of that commentary, particularly in the United States, was sharply critical of the Sandinistas for allegedly trying to sabotage the visit. At the same time, within Nicaragua allegations were made that the more conservative Nicaraguan Catholics, under the direction of Father Bismark Carballo, had tried to disrupt the crowd and provoke a response from revolutionary Christians. It was also alleged that the pope had been advised, in a briefing paper prepared for the Vatican, that "the Sandinista government is the enemy, any policy of accommodation will fail. . . . A strategy based on strength, unity and firmness will therefore have greater chances of success than others giving first priority to good relations with the government."[27]

Unfortunately, the pope's remarks did not contribute to fostering unity either within the church or between the church and the government. By exhorting the faithful to obey their bishops, most noticeably Archbishop Obando y Bravo, John Paul displayed very little sensitivity to the divisions within the Nicaraguan church—between the bishops and grass-roots Christians, or among the bishops themselves. Even if one were to follow the pope's message and obey the bishops, the question could still be asked: which bishops should be obeyed? Were the laity to follow those bishops who were tolerant of the revolution, or those who were becoming increasingly identified with the opposition?

In his attempt to impose unity upon the Nicaraguan church, John Paul aggravated the institutional crisis of Catholicism as well as the personal crisis of many Nicaraguan Catholics for whom his remarks were not sufficient. Those revolutionary Christians who participated in the CEBs and who were labeled by others as a "People's Church" or a "Parallel Church" could find no solace in the pope's traditional message. Indeed, they were deeply wounded by his criticism of the "People's Church" as "absurd and dangerous." They did not consider themselves a parallel church; in truth, they resented this designation, maintaining that they too were Catholics and that they followed God's law. As a member of the CEB Coordinating Commission from Managua expressed it: "We are part of the church. We are members in good standing, believers, we practice the sacraments. Why should we be called a parallel church?"[28] The previous summer, in response to the pope's June 26 letter to the Nicaraguan bishops, a group of Christians at the grass roots had published an open letter that said:

> The truth is that we do not call ourselves "Popular Church." What has happened is that people have pinned us with this label in order afterwards to say that we are not Christians. But we ourselves have never used the term. When in your letter you described the way ecclesial communities should function, we felt that you were talking about those which already exist here. This is not to say that we are satisfied, that we do everything well, or that we are free from faults. Our ecclesial base communities are far from being truly committed, helpful, and united. But we know that a person is not converted to Christ all at once; instead, each day we must convert ourselves, or as our Bishops have said to us in one of their letters, "we make ourselves Christian by acting as Christians."[29]

It is ironic that a pope who insisted so forcefully that the church's spiritual mission must remain separate from politics would make such a divisively "political" speech in Nicaragua. His attempt to unify the Nicaraguan church by imposing papal authority on existing divisions within the church did not succeed. Indeed, his visit split the Nicaraguan Catholic church more decisively than any other single action. In the short term it also contributed to a measurable weakening of the CEBs. As one priest said: "The Gospels are going in one direction, the Pope in another."[30]

Demobilization and Reorientation of the CEBs

Against this background of church-state conflict and efforts to impose church unity from above, CEBs in Nicaragua struggled to formulate a role for themselves within their country's unfolding revolution. By 1982 church organization at the base level was notably weaker than it had been at the time of the popular insurrection just three or four years earlier. The vitality of the CEBs was slowly but steadily being sapped by the efforts of some bishops to resist the relative autonomy that they had achieved. As we noted in Chapter 8, the removal of priests and religious from parishes that had active CEBs identified with the revolution, only served to break down the link binding the

CEBs to the institutional church. This delegitimation of what might be called progressive CEBs was reinforced by efforts to create new pastoral programs under the direction of priests loyal to the bishops. In this endeavor the hierarchy received financial support from CELAM.

After several years of intense participation in the work of the church and of the revolution, many CEB members began to experience the stresses of overwork. The leadership skills learned at the grass roots made CEB members a logical choice for government service in a period when the tasks of reconstruction were enormous. Many Christians attempted to maintain dual roles in their CEBs and in government service, but found that they could not do both. For many, the political tasks began to overshadow their time commitments to their church. Others managed to perform both these tasks but realized that they had little time in the week to spend with their families. Furthermore, the government selected the most-skilled CEB leaders and sent them to Managua to work, and the priests who worked with the CEBs were transferred to other parishes. All of these factors contributed to the weakened condition of the CEBs by 1982.

By the time of the papal visit a serious self-examination was under way within the CEBs in several parts of Nicaragua. Clergy and lay leaders working with the CEBs were led to reevaluate their commitment to Christianity and reaffirm its importance in their lives. They were keenly aware of the need to strengthen the base of the church once again. Many Christians at the parish level decided to concentrate their activities on the church and to forgo government service, although they still maintained cordial relations with the FSLN.

In several regions schools were established to train additional lay leaders for the CEBs and to begin to develop new pastoral projects. Funded by sympathetic churches in Western Europe, the schools taught volunteers or Christians who were recommended by their peers or priests. The training was intensive and usually took place in the evening after work; the typical course lasted three or four months. The curriculum included lessons in theology, history, interpersonal skills, and leadership; the final examination consisted of a mix of historical and theological questions.

The training schools also made a concerted effort to enroll married couples, in order to encourage a merging of family and religious obligations and to confront the machismo that was a deeply rooted part of marital relations. In Estelí, for example, the training began with separate discussions for men and women in which issues like alcoholism, family relations, and the treatment of women were analyzed in a biblical context. After six weeks of this training, men and women were brought together to discuss interpersonal relations within the family and within God's community.[31] In addition, short courses on the weekends dealt primarily with theology and human relations. The new graduates were then expected to organize new CEBs in their local communities.

Often the lay leaders who agreed to direct these "schools of formation" were persons who had been active in popular organizations in their own towns or districts and who had made a conscious decision to return to the conscientizing work of the church. Meanwhile, throughout the country CEBs were beginning to work together with the mass organizations, such as the CDSs—in the event of natural disaster or Contra attacks, for instance, they would help with the distribution of food and medical supplies, and with rebuilding. Such cooperation served to strengthen ties between the CEBs and popular organizations created by the revolution, without the loss of religious identity in the CEBs so feared by some members of the church hierarchy. As CEB members in Managua pointed out to the authors, on Tuesdays and Saturdays the mass organizations did not schedule activities from 6:00 P.M. to 10:00 P.M. because during those hours the CEBs held their weekly Bible study and reflection meetings.

At the same time that the CEBs were working out their relationship with the CDSs on the local level, they were also trying to formulate a role for themselves with regard to the government. How could they work in the reconstruction process without losing their identity as Christians? In July 1984, Christians active in CEBs throughout Nicaragua organized an annual meeting to celebrate their participation in the first five years of the revolution. Two weeks later the Managua-based leadership met to assess their participation in this anniversary celebration; spontaneously, this second meeting opened up into a general discussion of their role as Christians working within the revolution. At one point the group discussed the slogan that had been so widely used during the pope's visit: "Between Christianity and revolution there is no contradiction." Many still supported this conception, but one member of the group suggested this revision: "Between Christianity and revolution there is no contradiction, but neither is there an identification." This prompted a discussion during which another member of the CEB coordinating committee questioned the suitability of political slogans at religious services. In response a veteran lay worker from the barrio of San Pablo el Apóstol defended the spontaneous use of *consignas* by saying: "the slogans may seem strange to foreigners because they do not know our history." This meeting concluded with the group reaching consensus that they were living in a "delicate moment."[32]

None of this is to say that CEBs in Nicaragua regained the support of their bishops in the months following Pope John Paul's visit. What the pope had really condemned was their independence. What the institutional church sought was direct control over them. The effect of direct control would be to limit the boundaries of pastoral experience, to give up decision-making autonomy, and to restrict, if not sever, ties to the programs of the revolution. The situation was a far cry from the heady days of the honeymoon year, when Christians at the grass roots had played such an active and enthusiastic role in the Literacy Crusade, for example. Now, only three years later, they were struggling to retain their identity and maintain their energy in a hostile religious environment. To do so, they turned inward, seeking personal spiritual succor and renewal. But they also moved cautiously outward to create a structural base that could assure their survival and, they hoped, their long-term vitality. To this end, over the next several years they created a series of regional bodies to facilitate interaction among CEBs all across the country. The most important of these was the National Assembly of Christian Base Communities, which provided a formal structure for contact among CEBs, and between CEBs and other types of popular organizations.

As we turn our attention now to the international arena, focusing particularly on the ideological war waged from Washington, it should be remembered that across the ensuing years these Christians at the parish level often were obliged to refute the many charges of totalitarianism and religious persecution that were made against Nicaragua, not only in Washington but by Catholic church leaders in Nicaragua itself. The irony of their position—denying religious persecution by the government while under severe pressure from their own church—will not be lost on the reader.

The Propaganda War

The Central American policy adopted by the Reagan administration had important implications not only in the international arena but also at home. In Central America the policy led to the creation of the Contra army and the empowering of the CIA to carry the banner of the Reagan Doctrine. At home, the administration had to seize the ideological initiative in forming a national consensus against communism, both in the United States and in Nicaragua; this led to efforts to counter or impede the flow of dissenting information coming from groups that were seen as hostile to the national interest.

Indeed, the Reagan administration engaged in an unprecedented campaign of disinformation within the United States, spearheaded by the White House Office of Media Relations and Planning. This office scheduled regular meetings with leaders of Congress, and with leaders of key interest groups, to convince them of the severe threat posed to U.S. national security by Nicaragua. One group that was lobbied regularly by the White House was the U.S. Catholic Conference of Bishops (USCC). The USCC had been judicious in its evaluation of the Nicaraguan government: at times it had praised actions taken by the Sandinistas; at other times, it criticized them. But a reasoned critique of church-state relations in Nicaragua did not suit the administration. In their determination to portray the Sandinista regime as "totalitarian," Reagan's advisors recognized the importance of influencing the bishops to take a stand against the Nicaraguan government for its persecution of the Catholic church. To this end, the *White House Digest* of February 29, 1984, entitled "Persecution of Christian Groups in Nicaragua," made a strenuous but convoluted attempt to compare the destruction of religion in Communist regimes with the attempt of the "self-admitted Marxist-Leninist leaders in Nicaragua . . . to turn the Catholic church into an arm of the government."[33]

On June 28, 1982, President Reagan told the British Parliament that the United States would launch a major public diplomacy program to help "foster the infrastructure of democracy—the system of a free press, unions, political parties, universities—which allows a people to choose their own way, to develop their own culture, to reconcile their own differences through peaceful means."[34] One tool for achieving these goals would be the newly created quasi-governmental organization called the National Endowment for Democracy (NED). According to the *National Reporter*, the CIA and the National Security Council were involved in the planning of NED, an organization whose program would be part public diplomacy and part covert activity.[35]

The National Endowment for Democracy was funded by an act of Congress in 1983. Its directors included Penn Kemble of the Institute for Religion and Democracy (IRD), William Doherty of the American Institute for Free Labor Development (AIFLD), U.N. Ambassador Jeane Kirkpatrick, former U.S. delegate J. Peter Grace, Michael Novak of the American Enterprise Institute, and Max Singer of the Potomac Organization. By 1985 NED's budget of $18.5 million was channeled through the United States Information Agency, which then funded three major beneficiaries, among which was the AFL-CIO. Labor funds were distributed through the Free Trade Union Institute (of AIFLD), which distributed four million dollars in Latin America during 1985. One of the groups receiving money was PRODEMCA, or Citizens' Committee for the Pro-Democratic Forces in Central America, which was founded in 1981 and openly advertised its support for the Contra rebels. In turn, a beneficiary of PRODEMCA aid was the Archdiocese of Managua, which received funds for the training of lay personnel. In short, as a direct result of U.S. policy to "promote democracy" in Central America, U.S. government funds were flowing into the hands of Catholic church officials who were more and more openly hostile to the Sandinista government.

Much of the funding for PRODEMCA has come from NED. From these funds PRODEMCA has hosted press conferences for the Nicaraguan Democratic Force and given $100,000 to *La Prensa*, an opposition newspaper strongly opposed to the Sandinistas. Also using NED money, PRODEMCA founded the Nicaraguan Center for Democratic Studies headed by Arturo Cruz, who subsequently became a leader of the Contra movement. Still other NED monies channeled through PRODEMCA have funded the Permanent Commission on Human Rights in Nicaragua, a principal source of charges of human rights abuses by the Sandinista government.[36]

All of the organizations discussed so far—the White House Office of Media Relations, the National Endowment for Democracy, and PRODEMCA—were part of an overall Reagan administration drive to shape public opinion in the United States and in Central America. They testify to the "low-intensity" character of the war against Nicaragua. In such warfare, propaganda is a primary weapon; not surprisingly, religion is therefore a primary venue of struggle. Let us look more closely at the propaganda side of the war and its impact on the churches in Nicaragua.

On March 14, 1982, saboteurs trained and equipped by the CIA blew up two vital bridges in Chinandega and Nueva Segovia provinces near the Honduran border. According to a Defense Intelligence

Agency report, "In a 100-day period from 14 March to 21 June, at least 106 insurgent incidents occurred within Nicaragua," including the following types of operations: sabotage of bridges, attempted destruction of fuel tanks, attacks on military patrols, assassination of minor government officials, and burning of a customs warehouse.[37] This rapid escalation of the war caused growing concern in the United States.

By the end of 1982 Congress was becoming increasingly ambivalent about U.S. policy in Nicaragua. On December 21, 1982, Congress passed, and the president signed, the Boland amendment, which restricted the use of government funds for the purpose of overthrowing the Sandinista government. Implicitly, the amendment was designed to curb the activities of organizations like PRODEMCA, thus creating strong tensions within the government of the United States. A year later, in December 1983, the Boland-Zablocki amendment tried to restrict the use of U.S. funds to the interdiction of arms, which was still the official purpose of the Contra policy.[38] But that same year, sabotage operations and the neutralization of "carefully selected and planned targets, such as court judges, *mesta* judges, police, and state security officials," were formalized in a CIA manual entitled *Psychological Operations in Guerrilla Warfare*.[39] The manual was written by a U.S. Army counterinsurgency specialist and was cleared by CIA officials before its release. In essence, it instructed the Contras to employ the selective use of violence against civilians associated with the Sandinista government.

What is less known is the nature of the psychological techniques endorsed in the CIA manual. So-called armed propaganda teams were to be formed, to move about among the populace developing and controlling "front organizations." The propaganda teams would combine political awareness-building with armed aggression in their attempt to recruit the Nicaraguan people to their cause. According to the manual, the FDN should incite people to oppose the Sandinistas by persuading them that membership in the mass organizations had been forced upon them. Yet another tactic was to arouse anxiety about the presence of Cuban teachers in the schools, and to voice "indignation over the lack of freedom of worship, and persecution, of which priests are victims." Special emphasis was placed on the "participation of priests such as Escoto [*sic*] and Cardenal in the Sandinista government, against the explicit orders of his Holiness, the Pope."[40] The manual suggested the use of religious slogans such as "Free Us from the Yoke," and "With God and Patriotism We Will Defeat Communism," in order to disrupt outdoor meetings and incite the populace against the atheistic Sandinista regime.

In addition to the manual for the FDN, the CIA also prepared a manual to be used by anti-Sandinista sympathizers within Nicaragua. A copy of the latter was left behind in the city of Ocotal after a Contra raid in June 1984 (this attack will be described in detail in Chapter 10). Written in a simple, pictorial form, the manual described more than thirty ways to commit minor acts of sabotage that could be attributed to the government or could stop the government from functioning. The suggestions ranged from throwing a typewriter out the window, to constructing a homemade explosive to be thrown at police stations and government buildings.

Nevertheless, despite the continuous flow of U.S. funds to the Contras and the growth of their armed forces to 10,000 men by June 1983, they were incapable of establishing themselves as a viable military or political threat to the Sandinistas.[41] They destroyed villages, health clinics, and schools, but they failed to generate popular support. They were unable to capture any town or village. This brute fact thwarted their desire to declare themselves a provisional government within Nicaraguan territory, which would enable them to request direct U.S. military support or even intervention.

When the Contras had failed to inflict any serious defeat on the Ejército Popular Sandinista, or make any inroads toward bringing down the Sandinista government by 1983, the CIA assumed a more direct role in the war: using operatives recruited in Latin America, it increased the pressure on the Nicaraguan economy by increasing the frequency and intensity of acts of sabotage. One Latin American operative summarized the objective as follows: "Our mission was to sabotage ports, refineries, boats, bridges and try to make it appear that the contras had done it."[42]

In the fall of 1983 two major attacks took place on Nicaraguan port facilities. The first destroyed storage and docking facilities and an underwater oil pipeline at Puerto Sandino. The second, which occurred a month later, hit at Corinto, Nicaragua's largest and most important port: CIA operatives destroyed five oil storage tanks, launched grenades and mortars from a base ship, and burned 3.4 million gallons of fuel. The fire raged out of control for two days, and 25,000 inhabitants had to be evacuated.[43]

In December 1983 President Reagan approved a National Security

Council plan to escalate the level of harassment to include power plants and communications centers. The president also approved a plan devised by an interagency committee representing the departments of State and Defense, the CIA, and the Naval Surface Weapons Center, to mine Nicaragua's harbors with explosives strong enough to destroy small vessels and damage larger ones. Latin commando teams, working from a CIA mother ship, deposited the mines in Nicaragua's harbors on both the Atlantic and Pacific coasts from January through March of 1984.[44] The rationale behind such acts, which were in violation of international law, was to discourage commercial ships from risking damage in Nicaraguan shipping lanes. With no means by which to maintain trade relations, the Nicaraguan economy would be further strained. In a perverse way the mining of the harbors was a prelude to the trade embargo that the Reagan administration was to impose the following year. By April 1984 ten ships from six nations—Nicaragua, Japan, the Netherlands, Liberia, Panama, and the Soviet Union—had been damaged in Nicaraguan waters. The response to this act of sabotage was uniformly critical, both domestically and internationally, and the mood in Congress began to turn against the Reagan policy.

The House and Senate Intelligence Oversight Committees protested that the provisions of the 1980 Intelligence Oversight Act, which obligate the CIA to provide full and current reports of its activities to Congress, had been violated. Six weeks after the first detonations CIA officials offered specific testimony to the Intelligence Committees, detailing the degree of U.S. involvement in the mining. In response, Senator Daniel P. Moynihan, vice-chair of the Senate Select Committee on Intelligence, resigned.[45] In October 1984 the Democratic-controlled House of Representatives refused to approve further aid for the Contra forces, and the Boland amendment, which explicitly barred U.S. intelligence officials from "directly or indirectly" aiding the Contras, was renewed.

The Church and the Contra War

The escalation of the Contra war during 1983 and 1984 further polarized Nicaragua. The state of emergency remained in effect and the nation prepared to defend itself. The October 1983 invasion of Grenada seemed to many Nicaraguans like a preview of the invasion of their own country. While many grass-roots Christians dug in their heels, joined the militia, and excavated trenches around their homes, workplaces, and schools, the Catholic bishops maintained a strict silence about the war. One major source of friction between the base of the church and the hierarchy has been the bishops' refusal to condemn publicly either specific Contra attacks or the general escalation of the war. While North Americans did not learn of the Contra war until 1983, in Nicaragua it was clear that these attacks were mounted by former National Guardsmen who received "covert aid" from the Reagan administration. Italian reporters posed this question to Archbishop Obando in May 1983: "Is it true that there are Somocista guards fighting on the frontier?" The archbishop replied, "Yes, I believe there are Somoza guards, but not only former guardsmen, there are other people. . . . We do not have knowledge of planned aggression of the United States in Nicaragua since we are under a state of emergency which has ended freedom of expression. We only have one version of the truth."[46]

El Nuevo Diario voiced the opinion of many Nicaraguans when it responded to these statements by saying: "The dead are also on one side." While Nicaraguan bishops refused to condemn the war, public criticism did come from Mexican Bishop Sergio Méndez Arceo, who lamented such statements, saying that they "weaken the credibility of the church."[47] Monseñor Obando also remained silent concerning the 1984 mining of Nicaragua's harbors. When asked about the mining he replied, "At this moment, because I do not have my tape recorder, I can't say anything because I will be misquoted."[48] Instead, the hierarchy chose to release two controversial letters, in 1983 and 1984, that further increased the strain in church-state and intrachurch relations. The first was a discussion of the law of Patriotic Military Service, passed by the Council of State in September 1983. The second was the bishops' letter on reconciliation, which was issued during Easter week of 1984.

By mid-1983 the Contra war was making great material and human demands on Nicaragua, and the FSLN determined that the rapid increase in the size of the Contra forces required a larger military mobilization. Much of the fighting at the front was being carried on by militia rather than regular army. Consequently, a bill on patriotic military service was introduced into the Council of State. On August 29, while the bill was still being debated, the church hierarchy issued a letter entitled "General Considerations on Military Service," which was signed only by the secretary of the episcopal conference and was printed in *La Prensa* on September 1.

In a general section on military service, the pastoral letter alluded to the pattern of "all countries with totalitarian governments" wherein the army is used to impose an alien ideology. Such countries seek to establish the "absolute dictatorship of a political party." Arguing from this viewpoint, the letter cited a passage in the bill that said military service would "promote in our young people a sense of revolutionary ethics and discipline." This statement was interpreted to mean that "the army will become an obligatory center for political indoctrination in favor of the Sandinista Party." To forestall such manipulation, the hierarchy urged those who did not share the Sandinista ideology to refuse military service on grounds of "conscientious objection."[49]

A range of Christian groups in sympathy with the revolution responded in *El Nuevo Diario* two weeks later. They argued that in the atmosphere of constant Contra attacks and the escalation of threats from the United States, the hierarchy's message looked like a "call to desertion." They pointed out that the letter was not based on any biblical texts or church documents, and argued that it was the first time in contemporary church history that an episcopal conference had declared obligatory military service illegitimate. Asserting their support for the law, they asked, "What totalitarian state would tolerate . . . the hierarchy publicly proclaiming its illegitimacy and publicly calling on the people to desert it at a time of threat and danger?"[50]

In regard to the unity of the bishops, there is evidence that not all the bishops were present when this communique was discussed and that not all agreed with the contents. Bishop Santi later argued that it was the duty of Christians to defend their nation and that he had not been informed of the communique. Bishop Schlaefer has also stated that Christians have the right to participate in their own national development.[51]

In the Protestant community one could also sense uncertainty about the military service law and its implications. To clarify some of these issues the leadership of CEPAD organized a well-attended nationwide meeting for its membership. This began with a moving homily by Dr. Gustavo Parajón, director of CEPAD, and was followed by a short talk from René Núñez, secretary general of the National Directorate of the FSLN. Mr. Núñez then patiently answered questions for over two hours. He was asked many questions concerning conscientious objection, why women were not also called to serve (he was most uncomfortable with this line of questions), and the status of mothers whose sons were their sole support.[52] This meeting concluded with some fears having been allayed and with the channel of communication still open between these Protestant ministers and the government.

In fact, following the triumph, a constant in the process of reconstruction was the sense of cordiality and dialogue between the government and CEPAD: CEPAD participated in many government-sponsored programs in flood relief, housing construction, and health care. At the same time, it conducted its own health care and rural development program, PROVADENIC, independent of the government. In general, Nicaragua's Protestants were satisfied with the thrust of the government's program of reconstruction and felt that they had a vital contribution to make. Their willingness to work with the Nicaraguan Revolution may be explained by the distinction that CEPAD leaders make between the Nicaraguan and Cuban revolutions. In their view, Christians did not play an initial, important role in the Cuban Revolution because as soon as the revolutionaries attained power, much of the religious community fled. The leadership of CEPAD argued that as Christians they had to stay and influence the revolution. Thus there was clear support for the reconstruction process in word and in deed within the Protestant community, but no loss of Protestant identity.[53]

The flexibility of CEPAD allowed Nicaragua's Protestants to offer support to the government while maintaining the right, if necessary, to offer criticism and advice. It was the host organization for the "Witness for Peace" program, which gave North American Christian witnesses the opportunity to live in communities near the Honduran-Nicaraguan border. At the same time, CEPAD was opposed to the short-lived "taking of the churches" in the summer of 1982. At that time, approximately thirty Protestant churches that were alleged to have been engaged in counterrevolutionary activity were taken over by members of the mass organizations.[54] Several of these churches in the rural areas were at least nominal members of CEPAD. In discussions with the government, CEPAD's leaders took the position that all of the churches should be returned to their pastors. As a result of negotiations carried out at the neighborhood level, CEPAD's member churches, as well as the independent churches, were given back to their pastors. The peaceful resolution of what could have become an ugly crisis was notable because it again demonstrated at the grassroots level the strength and flexibility of popular Christian participation in the revolution, as well as the continuity in the relationship between CEPAD and the Sandinista government. During the insurrection CEPAD had supported the FSLN, and in the 1980s it declared that in the event of invasion its churches would be placed at the service of the government to be used as refugee or first aid centers.

The tense relations that were seriously strained by the release of the bishops' letter concerning military service almost reached the breaking point during Easter week of 1984. While mines damaged ships in Nicaraguan harbors, the episcopal conference released a "Pastoral Letter on Reconciliation" in which they asserted that Nicaraguan society had become subject to a materialistic ideology that repudiated the church "founded by the apostles and their successors, the legitimate bishops." While this viewpoint had been stated before by the bishops (and by the pope in March 1983), what apparently angered many Nicaraguans was the bishops' view that the violence and destruction in Nicaragua were the result of internal causes whose solution must be found in personal reconciliation, and in a dialogue that included those who had taken up arms against the government.

The pastoral letter on reconciliation, like that on compulsory military service, addressed the most explosive issue in Nicaraguan politics, the Contra war—and it generated, not a move toward reconciliation, but intense, divisive controversy. This can be attributed in part to its accusatory tone and content, and in part to what it did *not* say. Commencing at a general, abstract level, the bishops urged that Nicaraguans be open to conversion, live according to Christian standards and values, and "end . . . participation in injustice and violence." They then proceeded to indict the government and its supporters in the church, attacking them for sponsoring "materialist and atheistic education" and for exploiting the Mothers of Heroes and Martyrs[55] to "incite hatred." Christians who supported the revolution were described as having "abandoned ecclesiastical unity and surrendered to tenets of a materialistic ideology." The roots of this situation were traced to "individual sin" and to "political ambition and abuse of power."[56]

The path leading to reconciliation was seen to lie in self-criticism to reveal "our faults," faults that "affront the church." Since only the Sandinistas were criticized explicitly in the letter, it was their conversion to which attention was drawn. This was made explicit in the basis for dialogue laid out by the bishops. The letter characterized the war as a "civil war" and asserted that the Sandinistas were "dishonest to blame internal aggression and violence on foreign aggression." It then called for the incorporation of those "Nicaraguans who have taken up arms against the government" into any dialogue for peace. Indeed, the government was urged to "welcome them with an open heart." The only reference to foreign involvement in the war was as follows: "The great powers, which are involved in this problem for ideological or economic reasons, must leave the Nicaraguans free from coercion."[57]

The letter on reconciliation was quite aggressive, explicitly attacking both grass-roots Christians and the FSLN, and offering an interpretation of the war that made no mention of the U.S. role. It was an interpretation that only a small minority of Nicaraguans would accept. In contrast to the restraint shown by the government when the bishops issued their letter opposing the military draft, the Sandinista response to the letter on reconciliation was an extremely harsh attack on several of the bishops. It was almost as if the bishops had crossed an imperceptible line, which triggered a visceral reaction on the part of the Sandinistas. Daniel Ortega, head of the government and FSLN candidate for president, criticized the bishops because they "refused to talk to us, or to the people but they want dialogue with assassins."[58]

The timing of the bishops' statements, as well as the statements themselves, hastened the deterioration of church-state relations. In December 1983 the Nicaraguan government issued a fairly generous amnesty that excluded only those who participated in the leadership of the counterrevolutionary movements; the bishops' "Letter on Reconciliation" made no mention of this initiative. Moreover, the episcopal conference, which has consistently refused to acknowledge the external involvement of the United States in the "civil" war, maintained a pronounced silence concerning the U.S.-backed mining of Nicaragua's harbors in March–April 1984. At this critical moment in the revolution, the Catholic church in Nicaragua had never been so deeply divided—yet the call for reconciliation did not seem to apply to the church itself.

Ten

Religion, Revolution, and the Reagan Doctrine

War: Reality and Rhetoric

On June 1, 1984, U.S. Secretary of State George Shultz made an unannounced visit to Nicaragua to meet with leaders of the Sandinista government. Shultz was the first cabinet-level figure in the Reagan administration to set foot on Nicaraguan soil. He arrived at the end of a hot and bitter spring in Nicaragua. In Honduras, three successive phases of U.S. military maneuvers, running almost continuously, had been carried out between February and May. A large number of U.S. warships were anchored off Nicaragua's Atlantic coast; to complement this impressive display of naval power, some 30,000 U.S. troops participated in the military exercises, including elements of the 82nd Airborne Division that had been used in the invasion of Grenada the previous autumn. During the exercises two large airstrips were built on Honduran soil to accommodate C-130 transport planes. Throughout Nicaragua there was fear that the exercises were a prelude to a U.S. invasion. It was understood that the airstrips were designed to facilitate such an invasion, as well as to assist in the resupply of the Contras who were now attacking the civilian population from bases in Honduras and Costa Rica. At the end of May the Nicaraguan government announced that Contra attacks in Matagalpa and Jinotega provinces alone had caused 100 million cordobas' worth of damage, not to mention numerous civilian casualties.[1]

Against this background Secretary Shultz came to Managua to explain to the Nicaraguan government why its policies created severe security concerns for the United States. He made two specific demands in this respect. First, he argued, Nicaragua must significantly reduce the size of its army, the very existence of which threatened neighboring countries. Second, Nicaragua must take immediate steps to establish democratic institutions; this democratization, Shultz asserted, was a prerequisite to regional stability and U.S. security.

On the very morning that Shultz arrived in Managua to lecture the Sandinista government about U.S. security concerns, a force of between 600 and 1,000 Contra troops attacked the Nicaraguan city of Ocotal, which lies near the Honduran border. (Ironically, Ocotal is the city where U.S. marines were based in 1927 during the guerrilla war against U.S. occupation led by Augusto César Sandino.) Trained by the CIA, wearing U.S.-made uniforms, and carrying U.S.-supplied weapons, the Contras swept into Ocotal before dawn. Enjoying the benefit of intelligence provided in part by U.S. aerial surveillance, they had pinpointed their targets with precision. They attacked and destroyed a sawmill that employed 250 workers, and indirectly supported another 250 families; they sacked and burned the offices and generating station of the local electrical plant; they severely damaged a coffee-processing plant and storage bins that held a year's supply of basic grains. Including Contra casualties, nearly one hundred Nicaraguans were killed or injured in the attack. Residents of Ocotal later reported that throughout the assault the Contras fired indiscriminately on the civilian population, and that they fired on the hospital during their retreat.[2]

The events to be discussed in the present chapter must be set into this framework of the deepening Contra war. By 1984 the war had become the dominant reality of daily life in Nicaragua. The attack on Ocotal demonstrated that it had become a constant threat to life and limb throughout much of rural Nicaragua, and even the larger cities in the border areas were now subject to attack. Nicaraguans were dying in growing numbers as a result of military actions by CIA operatives, as in the mining of the country's harbors or the bombing of the airport in Managua, and in Contra attacks over which the CIA had financial and operational control.

It was easy enough for the Nicaraguan government, as well as the Nicaraguan people, to connect these attacks to U.S. foreign policy. After all, these spring months of increasing devastation and suffering in Nicaragua were also characterized by a vigorous anti-Sandinista polemic in Washington. A parade of U.S. officials was constantly before the television cameras warning of the dangers posed by the Sandinista Revolution. In May, General Paul Gorman, then-commander of U.S. military forces in the region, pointed to the military build-up in Nicaragua as evidence that the Sandinistas were intent on turning their country into "a Marxist-Leninist garrison state."[3] In a series of speeches General Gorman's own commander-in-chief, President Ronald Reagan, accused the Sandinistas of instituting a "Communist reign of terror" within Nicaragua, and of "supporting aggression and terrorism" against all of their neighbors in Central America.[4] Inside Nicaragua these savage rhetorical attacks on the revolution looked like a justification for the United States' own aggressive actions. Set against the long history of U.S. intervention in Nicaraguan affairs, this combination of rhetoric and military aggression caused the Sandinista government to fear the creation of an "internal front" that could be used to attack their regime from within the country. Given the increasingly vocal opposition to Sandinista policies that was coming from prominent church figures, the religious arena was now seen as a possible source of efforts to undermine the revolution. Hence, tensions between church and state increased sharply during the summer months.

Although church-state tensions reached a crescendo in July 1984, over events to be discussed in a moment, trouble had been brewing for months. A focal point of that trouble was the upcoming national election announced by Junta Coordinator Daniel Ortega on February 21, 1984. In the vigorous rhetorical attacks then being waged against Nicaragua from Washington, the Sandinistas' failure to hold elections was a frequent theme for criticism. The absence of elections was offered as proof of the antidemocratic character of the Sandinista government. The Contra war was also pointed to as evidence of deepening disillusionment with the revolution on the part of the "true democrats" in the original revolutionary coalition. Thus, the increasing pressures being brought to bear on Nicaragua in the international arena, principally by the United States, drew a close connection between the moral and political legitimacy of the Contra war and the absence of elections in Nicaragua.

The National Election of 1984

For its part, the Sandinista Front had already set a timetable for elections. On August 23, 1980, the FSLN announced that "the electoral process would begin in January 1984 and that elections would take place in 1985."[5] The timing of that first announcement was itself of interest, for it coincided with the concluding ceremonies of the National Literacy Campaign. The Sandinista view was that some basic nation-building had to take place before elections could be meaningful as expressions of a democratic process—and a key to nation-building was the basic education of the populace. As the Jesuit priest who directed the Literacy Campaign during the spring and summer of 1980 explained it, "there can be no authentic democracy where more than 50 percent of the populace is illiterate. So, for us, building democracy and promoting economic development must necessarily be based on literacy."[6] To foster such literacy the revolutionary government established the Ministry of Adult Education on the same day that it concluded the Literacy Campaign. Over the next several years a large part of the adult population, including campesinos in the remotest rural areas, were incorporated into the educational system. When elections were held in late 1984, these citizens would be far better prepared for active participation than had ever been the case before in a Nicaraguan election.

In addition to literacy, several other issues had to be addressed before meaningful elections could be held in Nicaragua. The nation needed a legal framework for the conduct of elections. This included the need for a law granting legal status to political parties, guaranteeing their right to organize and offer candidates for election; such a law was passed by the Council of State in August 1983, granting legal standing to a range of political parties for the first time in Nicaraguan history.[7] There was also the need for an electoral law that would establish the legal procedure for elections. In the light of subsequent events, it is ironic that the previous four electoral laws that had functioned in Nicaragua all had had either the active or the tacit approval of the United States: the electoral laws of 1923 and 1928 were actually written by U.S. citizens during periods of U.S. occupation; the 1951 and 1974 laws had been "written to legitimize the Somoza dictatorship in exchange for allowing a certain 'opposition' to 'control' one-third of the Assembly."[8] Although hardly democratic, neither these laws nor the elections held under them had ever been declared by U.S. policy makers to be either grounds for questioning the legitimacy of Nicaragua's government, or a threat to democracy in neighboring countries. With the exception of Archbishop Obando's refusal to endorse the 1974 elections, as discussed above in Chapter 7, neither had any member of Nicaragua's Catholic hierarchy ever criticized these electoral mechanisms.

Nicaragua's new electoral law was approved by the Council of State on March 15, 1984, and signed by the government junta on March 26. On April 2 a three-member Supreme Electoral Council was appointed to administer the electoral process, which included three phases. First there would be a period for the registration of candidates, which was scheduled from May 25 to July 25. Second, voter registration was scheduled from July 27 to July 30. The voter registration drive merits comment as an important example of successful popular mobilization. Registration centers were established in every barrio in cities, towns, and villages throughout Nicaragua. A large pool of people from the mass organizations volunteered their time and energy to make it possible for people to register. Voter registration was complicated by the fact that basic personal records were often nonexistent and census data were hopelessly incomplete and out of date. Many Nicaraguans could not produce proof of age by means of a birth certificate or baptismal registry. In these cases, the individual had to bring another person with him or her who would attest to the identity and age of the person wishing to register; the name of the registered voter and the name of the witness were recorded. Through this vast outpouring of human effort, in the allotted four-day period 93 percent of eligible Nicaraguans registered to vote. In the week following registration, posters appeared proclaiming "Another victory for the Nicaraguan people." This was the first time that many Nicaraguans had bothered to register to vote. As one well-educated Nicaraguan put it, "This time the elections really mean something."[9]

The final phase, the election campaign itself, was to occur between August 8 and October 31.[10] This scheduling meant that, in all, seven months were available in which parties and candidates could prepare for the balloting on November 4, 1984—two days ahead of the elections in the United States. Both external and domestic political factors informed the choice of election date. Speaking of international considerations, one Nicaraguan government official described the nation's forthcoming elections as "a key element in our strategic defense."[11] The underlying rationale was to respond to the Reagan administration's criticism concerning Nicaragua's lack of democracy, as measured exclusively by elections, and to present the United States with an elected government before the presidential elections took place in the United States itself on November 6.

Internally, the FSLN still maintained considerable popular support, yet most party leaders knew that the elections would be a good time to take soundings within the nation in order to identify areas of needed improvement. The FSLN's vice-presidential candidate, Sergio Ramírez, said during the campaign: "We promised the people they would have the right to choose. . . . There's no doubt we will win, but we are establishing a system of choice."[12] At least one member of the National Directorate, Bayardo Arce, expressed dissatisfaction with this approach to the elections: he stated that the elections were "bothersome" and went on to suggest that they might result in "a red constitution and perhaps the removal of the facade of political pluralism and the establishment of the party of the revolution, the single party."[13] Evidently Arce's was a minority viewpoint within the Directorate because the electoral mechanism adopted by the FSLN provided for a system of proportional representation that guaranteed representation in the National Assembly to a multiplicity of parties. It also provided for a Supreme Electoral Council, independent of the junta, that would organize and conduct the elections from beginning to end.

The electoral law assured all parties equal access to public and private communications media during the campaign, and committed the government to providing a minimal base of financing for each registered party.[14] It should also be noted that the electoral law was passed just three months after the Sandinista government had decreed a total amnesty for over three hundred Miskito Indians who had been imprisoned for seditious activities, and had offered amnesty to all Nicaraguans who had left the country after July 1979, including those who were involved with the counterrevolution. The only exceptions were certain top leaders of the armed opposition, meaning the Contras.[15]

On November 4, just over 75 percent of eligible voters turned out to cast their ballots. As expected, the FSLN won the presidency, polling 67 percent of the valid votes cast and 63.5 percent of the National Assembly vote.[16] The Conservative Democratic Party (Partido Conservador Demócrata de Nicaragua, PCD) came in second with 14 percent of the vote, while the Independent Liberal Party (Partido Liberal Independiente, PLI), which probably would have done better had the party not split less than two weeks before the election, came in third with 9.7 percent of the vote. The opposition parties garnered thirty-five seats in the National Assembly, or 36.5 percent of the total. The parties to the left of the FSLN—the Socialist Party (Partido Socialista Nicaragüense, PSN), the Communist Party (Partido Comunista de Nicaragua, PC de N), and the Marxist-Leninist Popular Action Movement (Movimiento de Acción Popular–Marxista Leninista, MAP-ML), which had criticized the FSLN for allowing the private sector to continue functioning—won less than 4 percent of the vote. Numerous observer delegations from western allies of the United States judged the elections to be fair and honest.[17]

The only opposition group that did not participate in the 1984 election was a coalition of small, conservative parties allied with the Superior Council of Private Enterprise (COSEP), which represents many of the largest business firms in Nicaragua. They called themselves the Coordinadora Democrática and their presidential candidate was Arturo Cruz, a former Sandinista ambassador to the United States and later a member of the political wing of the Contras. The Coordinadora requested—and then ignored—several extended deadlines to register and participate in the elections, while claiming that the conditions for elections did not exist in Nicaragua. Both before and after the campaign began, the Coordinadora urged Nicaraguans not to participate in the elections. According to the report of the Latin American Studies Association delegation, Archbishop Obando y Bravo and Bishop Pablo Vega (then-president of the espiscopal conference) "strongly supported the positions taken by the Coordinadora and their views were extensively reported by *La Prensa*."[18] Moreover, before the elections were held in November a senior Reagan administration official admitted to the *New York Times* that "[t]he Administration never contemplated letting Cruz stay in the race because then the Sandinistas could justifiably claim that the elections were legitimate, making it much harder for the United States to oppose the Nicaraguan government." Subsequently, Mr. Cruz joined the leadership of the Nicaraguan resistance movement; by 1987 he resigned from the movement because of the failure of civilian leaders to control the military leadership.[19]

Despite external pressure and internal squabbling, what emerged through the 1984 election process was a new set of rules of the game. Under these rules a loyal opposition was tolerated (albeit nervously), but opposition had clear boundaries: acceptance of the system and the electoral process in which participating opposition parties played a formative role. Under the rules, the large majority of the population was mobilized through the mass organizations, the literacy campaign, the health campaigns, and the Christian base communities. In short, what seemed to be emerging was a unique blend of participatory and representative democracy.

The Church Responds to the Elections

How did the Catholic church hierarchy respond to these steps toward democratizaton undertaken by the Sandinista government? What issues preoccupied the bishops during this period? The answers to these questions help to explain why the conflict between church and state reached such alarming heights in the summer of 1984. From December 1983 to March 1984 the two most visible members of the hierarchy, Archbishop Obando and Bishop Vega, spoke out frequently about the situation in Nicaragua. What was notable was their unwillingness to acknowledge the nature and impact of the Contra war. Neither bishop issued any specific criticism of the CIA mining of Nicaragua's harbors, nor any denunciation of widely reported and thoroughly documented Contra atrocities against the civilian population. Instead, they claimed a lack of knowledge of these events due to the lack of press freedom in Nicaragua.[20]

At one level these bishops seemed to be trying to maintain a nonpartisan position that would enable them to exercise the church's prophetic function evenhandedly. Yet the price of doing so was to ignore the tangible results of U.S. aggression that affected the faithful directly, whether in the loss of lives, the mutilation of bodies, or the destruction of livelihoods. Their statements appeared to put the danger inherent in alien ideologies on a par with the danger of military attacks. Even at that, they were unwilling to associate the military attacks with U.S. sponsorship. In a revealing statement Bishop Vega posed this rhetorical question about Nicaragua's future course under the Sandinistas: "Why should we go from an economic imperialism to one that is even worse; one that is ideological and totalitarian and unites all the vices of absolutism and liberalism?"[21] This equal, if not greater, fear of "ideological aggression" appeared to be rooted in an ongoing conviction on the part of these particular bishops that the Sandinista revolution posed a threat to the church. This was a theme about which Bishop Vega was surprisingly candid and explicit. As he saw it, "The Nicaraguan church is undergoing active ideological persecution by the Sandinista regime. There are many degrees and types of persecution of the Church in Nicaragua, but we have faced them all."[22] This was a claim that Archbishop Obando took to the United States, but more quietly than Vega, in the spring of 1984.

While in New York in early May the archbishop called on a high official of the W. R. Grace Company, seeking financial resources to sustain a variety of pastoral programs that were being developed under his tutelage. The nature of the archbishop's requests and the justification he offered for them were detailed in a private memo to J. Peter Grace, the head of the company. Two things in particular stand out. On one hand, Obando characterized the Sandinista government as consciously and purposefully antichurch, having adopted a "concrete plan" to woo the populace away from the "true church."[23] To meet this threat, Obando had worked for four years and "given all of his resources and skills to developing leaders who can oppose the Sandinistas."[24] Such opposition, based on "orthodox religion" rather than on liberation theology, would not only promote religious freedom and church interests as the archbishop understood them, but would also help to thwart "the present Government's efforts to change the country into a Marxist-Leninist society."[25] In short, in this private conversation with potential North American donors, Archbishop Obando candidly declared that he expected the very worst from the Sandinista government, and that he had long worked to counteract its policies. He also made it clear that he saw the church as a source of *political* opposition.

On the other hand, the archbishop claimed that the Sandinistas had lost most of their original popularity, now that their true colors were clearer for all to see. He declared that the FSLN was unwilling to hold a free election. "The Archbishop said that if a fair election were to be held today, the present administration would be turned out of office. [He] has no hopes that a fair election will be held in the foreseeable future."[26] Given the fact that the Sandinistas had already announced the November elections, Archbishop Obando appears to have judged them out of hand—which may account for why he had so little to say about the elections over the next six months. (When pressed by journalists, Obando and Vega would only say that they doubted whether sufficient conditions existed to hold fair elections in Nicaragua.)

Just prior to the archbishop's trip to the United States, during the celebrations of Holy Week at the end of April, the episcopal conference issued a pastoral letter that had been anticipated by Nicaraguan Catholics for some time. It was expected that the letter would deal with the elections; however, it said nothing about the elections, focusing instead on the theme of reconciliation. This was the pastoral letter on reconciliation discussed at the end of Chapter 9. As we have seen, this pastoral letter caused tremendous controversy because it said nothing about the military attacks on Nicaragua, it called for a dialogue between the Sandinistas and "those Nicaraguans who have

taken up arms against the government,"[27] and it coincided closely
with the public posture of the Reagan administration, which was so
clearly the patron of the Contra army, and of the "right-wing opposition parties."[28] In this context the appeal to reconciliation, ordinarily
an exalted Christian virtue, carried overtones of a highly partisan,
antirevolutionary stand. As such it generated swift and vigorous responses from all across the religious and social spectrum and produced a formal break in relations between church and state.

A number of Sandinista leaders repudiated the call for dialogue
with the Contras, "pointing to it as proof of the hierarchy's links to
reactionary forces."[29] The two dailies sympathetic to the government,
Barricada and *El Nuevo Diario*, exacerbated tensions by running photos
of several bishops that had been taken years earlier—the photos
showed the bishops participating in official state ceremonies and
placed them near the deposed dictator, Anastasio Somoza. This sort
of journalistic treatment of the bishops' letter served only to fan the
flames and increase the estrangement between the Catholic hierarchy
and the revolutionary process.

The response within the church was more measured, but also
highly critical of the bishops' initiative. Catholics at the grass roots
held "hundreds" of meetings to discuss the pastoral letter. This was a
particularly painful experience for the many faithful who had felt the
impact of Contra assaults directly. These Catholics were deeply hurt
by the hierarchy's actions and felt an increasing estrangement from
their own church leaders. Their published replies exhibited both anger and pathos: "The [Contras] did not engage in dialogue with our
parents; they simply tortured them to death. The counterrevolution-
aries do not talk with the campesinos organized in cooperatives; they
kill them. The Catholic bishops do not confer with Catholics at the
grass-roots level; they avoid them. On what, then, do the bishops
base their call for dialogue with criminals?"[30] At the same time, two of
the most prominent religious orders working in Nicaragua—the Jesuits and the Dominicans—issued lengthy statements that questioned
the hierarchy's judgment in issuing the pastoral letter, while also
criticizing the press for its rough handling of the bishops. What was
abundantly clear in the aftermath of these events was that far from
promoting reconciliation, if that had ever been the goal, the bishops'
pastoral letter succeeded only in heightening political and religious
tensions in Nicaragua.

These tensions came to a head in the weeks following Secretary of

State Shultz's visit to Managua and the destructive Contra attack on Ocotal. State security officials, who were investigating a suspected internal front, videotaped a parish priest from the Managua archdiocese transporting arms and explosives. Interior Minister Tomás Borge contacted the papal nuncio and Bishop Vega to request that the priest, Father Amado Peña, be confined to the nunciature while the investigation continued. He also asked that the hierarchy disavow the priest's activities. However, the nuncio and Bishop Vega referred the matter to Archbishop Obando, to whom Father Peña was quite close. Obando refused all cooperation with the government, declaring categorically that Peña was innocent and suggesting that he was the victim of a government frame-up. At this point positions had hardened into sharply confrontational attitudes between a government that felt itself seriously threatened by external aggression and internal subversion, and a church hierarchy that, under Obando's leadership, felt itself persecuted by that same government.

Archbishop Obando seemed determined to make a cause célèbre of Father Peña, who by this time had defied the State Security directive to remain at the nunciature. He had returned to his parish and then, to escape arrest, had fled to the Catholic seminary on the outskirts of Managua. "On July 5, international news cables and the Voice of America radio broadcast announced that 'the first anti-Sandinista demonstration in five years' would take place . . . on July 9."[31] The march was to be a demonstration of solidarity with Father Peña and a protest against government persecution of the church. The government warned Obando that such a march would violate the State of Emergency Law, which was still in effect (although it was soon to be suspended in order to facilitate the impending election campaign). The march, which attracted several hundred people—many of whom were foreign journalists anticipating a dramatic and newsworthy event—took place as planned. Although there were no incidents during the march, that afternoon the government revoked the residency visas of ten foreign priests working in the Managua archdiocese and expelled them from the country.

Among those expelled were several priests who were working in church-sponsored programs that were funded in part by PRODEMCA. This confrontation demonstrated the government's sensitivity to the use of the church in the propaganda war being waged by Washington. While Father Peña was implicated in efforts to form an internal military front against the revolution, some of the expelled priests were implicated in the theological phase of the war inasmuch as they were accepting money from the Reagan administration. From the government's point of view, the expulsions were aimed at driving this point home to church officials.

The immediate response to these expulsions in the international arena was sharply critical of the Nicaraguan government. The Vatican and the episcopal conferences of most Latin American countries condemned the action as excessive and a provocation against the church. In Nicaragua, Archbishop Obando condemned the action strenuously from his pulpit. Denying that the Catholic hierarchy had any intention to overthrow the government, he insisted nevertheless that "it is the church's duty to guide its people." He went on to reinforce his own perspective on the impact the Sandinista Revolution was having in Nicaragua: "The kingdom of heaven is not built with expulsions, with decrees that destroy and asphyxiate individuals, political parties, labor unions and the church."[32] However, there was a notable silence on the part of the rest of the Nicaraguan hierarchy, none of whom made any public statements to back up the archbishop's criticisms. If anything, the expulsions seem to have brought home to many in the Catholic church just how far the mutual provocations between church and state had gone, and to have precipitated a growing awareness that such hostilities were not in the church's interests.

Indeed, one of the more interesting responses to the July expulsions was the thoughtful report generated by U.S. church personnel working in Nicaragua. These church workers, representing sixteen Catholic religious congregations and five Protestant denominations, sought to take seriously the charge of religious persecution by defining what it would entail and then examining the Nicaraguan experience in light of that definition. Among the criteria they specified were mistreatment by government authorities on the basis of religious faith, interference with religious practices and celebrations, restrictions on public expressions of religion, and discrimination against religious education. Measured against such criteria as these, they concluded, there was no government policy of religious persecution in Nicaragua—to the contrary, they found the Nicaraguan government "committed to protecting religious freedom."[33] In support of this conclusion they pointed to dramatic church growth in Nicaragua since the coming of the revolution. In the Catholic church this growth had ranged across the spectrum from CEBs to charismatics: it was not only the grassroots Christian communities generally considered sympathetic to the government that had grown since the triumph, but also Catholic religious movements that were conservative in outlook. Moreover, three new bishops had been ordained and twenty-eight new foreign religious orders had entered the country to take up religious and developmental tasks.

Protestant growth had been equally dramatic, if not more so. Eighty denominations were operating in the country in more than six hundred church buildings, many of these built since the triumph. The distribution of Bibles had increased from about 10,000–15,000 per year during the 1970s, to 136,000 in 1982. New pastors were being trained in all parts of the country through CEPAD's extension courses. "Walking through almost any Managua neighborhood or rural town on any evening of the week, one is sure to pass a small church with its doors and windows wide open, the singing, clapping and spirited preaching floating out to the entire neighborhood."[34]

Finally, with regard to education, the report noted that Nicaragua had 173 church-run schools, most of them Catholic. All had continued to function, and indeed enjoyed the benefit of government subsidies that paid staff salaries and maintenance costs. The major change that had occurred was to make the schools coeducational, tuition free, and open to all students. As then-Minister of Education Carlos Tunnerman put it, "In this way we have made it possible for many poor families to have the famous option of choosing a religious education for their children."[35] In this regard the government's policy toward religious education seemed truly exceptional for a modern revolution. The government not only tolerated religious education, but fostered it.

In the United States, the July expulsion of the ten priests from the Managua archdiocese was a focal point for charges of religious persecution in Nicaragua. The Institute for Religion and Democracy (IRD), a Washington-based lobby group generally supportive of Reagan administration policies, initiated a drive to discourage U.S. churches from aiding the Nicaraguan government. They specifically singled out the Division of Overseas Ministry of the National Council of Churches of Christ (NCCC), claiming that its programs were "pro-Sandinista," even though the Sandinista government had, according to IRD, a deliberate policy of religious persecution. In response to this campaign the NCCC sent a fact-finding delegation to Nicaragua in late August. The delegation met with a broad cross-section of the religious community in Nicaragua, both Catholic and Protestant, as well as with government officials. Their report directly challenged the charges of religious persecution that were then being made so freely in Washington.

This is not to say that the delegation did not find evidence of persecution associated with the practice of religious faith—but its findings cast the whole question in a different light. Seen from a Nicaraguan perspective, the Evangelical churches reported systematic persecution by the Contras. A rapidly growing number of Evangelical churches are in zones penetrated by the Contra forces. Nazarene pastors reported having five churches destroyed in Contra attacks, while the Assembly of God (with 217 congregations, the largest Protestant church in northern Nicaragua) was forced to disband twenty congregations due to Contra activity. Workers and vehicles from CEPAD had also been specifically targeted for attack—one such attack, which cost the lives of a young woman and her six-month-old child, having taken place the very week of the delegation's visit. These same Evangelical pastors repudiated the claim that the Sandinista government engaged in systematic persecution on the grounds of religion. While acknowledging specific instances of conflict, particularly affecting the Moravian church because of its strong presence in the Atlantic Coast region, the pastors denied that these events were part of a pattern of persecution. According to a report prepared by Moravian church leaders, sixty-nine of their congregations had been uprooted, together with a hospital and a seminary; however, this disruption of religious life was attributed by the Moravian pastors themselves to the war between the Contras and the Nicaraguan army. While holding the Nicaraguan government accountable for the mistakes it had made in dealing with the Miskito people, these pastors also credited it with having a growing respect for the Moravian church and a willingness to work with the church on a basis of mutual respect.[36]

Efforts to build a working relationship based on mutual respect were what the NCCC delegation found most notably absent in the atmosphere surrounding the Catholic church hierarchy's relations with the government. Their ninety-minute interview with Archbishop Obando helped to clarify why, from his point of view, this was so. Obando characterized the Sandinista government as a "Marxist-Leninist atheistic government."[37] He went on to portray it as unable to confront the church head-on due to the church's widespread, enduring popularity. Hence, the "FSLN has been forced to choose a strategy of infiltration, subversion and subtle aggression against the church."[38] He suggested that the priests who served in the government and the other clergy and religious women who actively supported the government had been lured into doing so by this subtle strategy. He argued, in other words, that they were naive as to the government's real intentions toward the church.

The Sandinista spokesman on this issue, René Nuñez of the FSLN secretariat, offered a different point of view. He insisted that the FSLN had tried repeatedly to demonstrate its good faith on religious matters, but that some members of the Catholic hierarchy simply would not give credence to any of the government's reassurances or its actions. As he saw it, the conflict was between certain bishops (but not all of them) and the revolution—that is, the conflict was political in origin, not religious. "In Nicaragua, some are with and some are not with the revolutionary process. For many bishops, the revolution means atheism. We have insisted that this revolution is not like that. For many here, faith led to the revolutionary process. . . . But we are not believed."[39]

According to the National Directorate, twenty-nine new religious congregations have entered Nicaragua since July 1979, of which the majority are female. A total of eighty-two religious denominations are working in Nicaragua, and 1,900 priests or brothers spent time in Nicaragua during the first five years of the revolution. The government has also supported religious schools. As of 1984 there were 257 private schools, of which 188 received financial help from the government; of these, 173 were Catholic and the rest were Protestant.[40]

Based on their interviews with a broad cross-section of religious and political actors in Nicaragua, the NCCC delegation concluded that much of the conflict over religion turned on disparate definitions of what constitutes persecution. By and large, Evangelical church leaders saw the Contras as the most serious threat to their religious practices, especially in rural areas. They also tended to see divisions within the Catholic church as more important than government pressures on it. Many Catholics at the grass roots were in agreement with this view, citing in support of their argument the hierarchy's continuing pressure on progressive clergy and religious, including transfers and even expulsions similar to those ordered by the government in July.[41]

Based on their own statements, it seems clear that some Nicaraguan bishops, particularly Archbishop Obando and Bishop Vega, were vehemently opposed to the Sandinista government and questioned its fundamental legitimacy. In a setting where opposition political parties were weak (due to the Somocista legacy, in which party competition meant little in deciding political issues), such outspoken bishops were a vital lightning rod and rallying point for discontent among the organized opposition. Certainly the bishops' criticisms of the Sandinistas provided welcome material for those in Washington, or Miami, or Tegucigalpa who wanted to discredit the Nicaraguan Revolution. Neither Obando nor Vega could have been unaware of this. If their criticisms had been more evenhanded during this period, evincing sensitivity to the suffering caused by the Contra war, there would have been less basis for judging their complaints to be political rather than religious in nature. As it was, their verbal attacks on the Sandinista government had a manifestly political tone. Nevertheless, they were not merely political, as further discussion will attempt to show.

As the year 1984 drew to a close it was clear that the major political issues confronting the nation had not been resolved. Although well received by most international observers, the national elections had been dismissed by the Reagan administration as a "sham." Indeed, in Washington the elections were greeted by a fabricated story about Soviet MIG fighters being shipped to Nicaragua. This false report served to deflect attention from Nicaragua's political accomplishments and to justify continued U.S. hostility. Among Nicaragua's neighbors, presidential elections had been used to justify high levels of U.S. aid on the grounds that they were proof of good-faith efforts to build democracy—but Nicaragua's elections were condemned categorically by U.S. officials, who now moved even more vigorously and openly to provide assistance to the counterrevolution. Thus, Nicaragua continued to live with the reality of war.

In December a Contra attack led to the massacre of thirty employees of the state telephone company.[42] This shocking event provoked the first break in ranks within the episcopal conference over the Contra war. Three bishops from regions of the country where Contra assaults were having the greatest impact issued a public denunciation of the massacre. After more than three years of war and steadily mounting Nicaraguan casualties, this was the first public statement from the Catholic hierarchy condemning Contra atrocities. Two of the bishops went on to call for a renewed dialogue with the government. "Faced with an open break within the hierarchy, Church officials agreed to the dissident bishops' call for a Church-state dialogue."[43] The talks opened on Christmas eve, 1984, and continued, somewhat episodically, through Christmas 1987.

The Nicaraguan Church Gets a Cardinal's Hat

Events in the spring of 1985 demonstrated just how subject Nicaragua was to the pressures of external actors in pursuit of their own interests. The Vatican, the national episcopal conferences of the United States and Brazil, the Reagan administration, and the Contras all played significant roles. But embedded within the layers of conflicting pressures brought by these external actors another, equally important, drama unfolded. It pitted two prominent Nicaraguan Catholics in an increasingly personalized struggle to define the church's proper mission in a revolutionary setting. The principals in this drama were Foreign Minister Miguel D'Escoto and Managua's archbishop, Miguel Obando y Bravo.

At a press conference on January 23, 1985, Bishop Vega announced that the four priests holding ministerial positions in the Nicaraguan government would be suspended "a divinis" from their priestly functions if they did not resign those positions within fifteen days. Each of the priests had been asked by the newly elected government of Daniel Ortega to remain in his post; suspension "a divinis" was in effect a punishment that would prevent them from exercising any priestly responsibilities as long as it was in effect. The suspensions were not long in coming: within two weeks, three of the four priests—Parrales, D'Escoto, and Ernesto Cardenal—had all announced the receipt of suspension notices. Significantly, the orders came directly from Rome rather than through the ordinary channels provided for in canon law. This handling of the suspensions suggested that the Vatican was determined to make a point of its authority over the clergy. In addition, this posture toward the priests serving in the Sandinista government stood sharply in contrast to the attitude displayed toward Archbishop Obando y Bravo. The difference was to be demonstrated in a surprising and telling way a few months later.

On March 2, 1985, Contra leaders associated with the Nicaraguan Democratic Force (FDN) called upon the Nicaraguan government to enter into a national dialogue with the political opposition, including "armed organizations." Their proposal named the Catholic church to set the agenda for such dialogue and to act as mediators. If accepted, this proposal would have given the Contras something they had not yet achieved either on the battlefield or in international opinion: it would have granted them a measure of legitimacy in Nicaraguan politics. Given the Contras' explicitly counterrevolutionary objectives, and the taint of a continuing Somocista element in their ranks, there was little possibility that the Sandinistas would accept this proposal. Three weeks later the episcopal conference issued a communique also urging a national dialogue within the framework of their 1984 pastoral letter on reconciliation. The communique disavowed any intent to choose sides, but the 1984 pastoral letter had called for dialogue with the Contras. Then, just two weeks later, President Reagan put forward a "Peace Plan for Nicaragua" that also pushed the idea of a Sandinista-Contra dialogue mediated by the Catholic bishops. At an evening mass on Holy Thursday the papal nuncio, concelebrating with Monseñor Obando, declared that this dialogue was urged by both the pope and the Nicaraguan hierarchy and, in a veiled reference to Reagan's proposal, he said that "no initiative in favor of peace should be discarded."[44]

Such declarations must have been galling to the Sandinista government and its supporters. As we saw earlier in this chapter, the government had only recently been elected with a 67 percent majority of the national vote.[45] One of the FSLN campaign positions was to defend Nicaraguan sovereignty against the aggressions of the U.S. administration. Throughout the campaign the FSLN had portrayed the Contras as a proxy army, which survived only through U.S. assistance. (Repeated drives by the Reagan administration for Contra aid seemed to bear out this interpretation.)[46] A sizable majority of Nicaraguans had apparently agreed with them. Yet they were being pressured by the church hierarchy to accommodate themselves to the political and military strategy of their enemies. Only a few weeks after this call for reconciliation through dialogue with the Contras, the Reagan administration declared a complete economic embargo against Nicaragua. Directly and indirectly, the administration had all but declared war on the Sandinista government.

Against this background, on April 24, the Vatican announced that Pope John Paul II had named Archbishop Obando y Bravo to be elevated to the College of Cardinals. The appointment took Catholics in Central America by surprise because there were other archbishops in the region who could have been said to have more formidable

credentials. The naming of Obando therefore triggered much speculation as to the pope's motives. Did this appointment signify Rome's
disapproval of the Nicaraguan Revolution? Was it intended to reinforce John Paul's drive to restore the authority of the magisterium
throughout the Roman Catholic church? Whatever the pope's intentions, it is clear that Obando's elevation to cardinal had an immediate
impact in Nicaraguan politics.

On the day of the announcement President Ortega called on
Obando in person to congratulate him, noting that the appointment
was "an honor for all Nicaraguans."[47] The investiture ceremony on
May 25 was broadcast in its entirety on the state-run television network. But it was the most conservative sectors throughout Nicaragua
and Central America who were particularly elated at the announcement, and they were quick to see a political significance in it. On May
27 Costa Rica's right-wing newspaper La Nación editorialized that of all
the appointments to cardinal, "that which provoked . . . the most
interest and is of most relevance, was the nomination of Monseñor
Obando, because of his known relationship to the political vicissi-
tudes of his people and his systematic criticisms of the present regime
in Nicaragua. The nomination was characterized as one of the events
not only of religious but also of tremendous political transcendence.
. . . A deserved action from John Paul II, but also a really magisterial
political attack. . . ."[48]

After the investiture ceremonies Cardinal Obando remained in
Rome for nearly two weeks. He was scheduled to return to Nicaragua
on June 14—however, he chose to pass through the United States
first. Thus he celebrated his first mass as cardinal, not in Nicaragua,
but in Miami, and before a crowd that included the top leaders of the
two principal Contra armies. These leaders, Adolfo Calero of the FDN
and Edén Pastora of the Costa Rica–based ARDE (Alianza Revolucionaria Democrática), were seated as honored guests on the podium.
The rest of the large audience of nearly five thousand people consisted
largely of Nicaraguan and Cuban exiles, including a number of individuals closely associated with the old Somoza regime. After the
mass, Cardinal Obando told reporters: "I do not object to being identified with the people who have taken up arms."[49] The elevation to
cardinal seemed to have fortified the archbishop of Managua, and to
have sealed his resolve to confront the Nicaraguan Revolution even
more directly and vigorously than he had done previously. He was
soon to be called "the Cardinal of Peace" by the opposition, including

the Contras. He appeared to relish the role, and to be determined to push for a political resolution in Nicaragua that met his own political criteria. Very quickly his cardinalate appeared to be heavily politicized.

Cardinal Obando arrived back in Managua on June 14. In the crowd that had gathered to receive him at the airport were "hundreds of right-wing agitators." As a precautionary measure to avoid unnecessary provocations and violence, the government had disarmed the police who were on hand to maintain order. The agitators in the crowd attacked the police, several of whom were injured, one seriously enough to lose an eye. (The incident led Interior Minister Tomás Borge to observe that Nicaragua presented the "unusual spectacle of a repressed police force.")[50] The Cardinal, however, offered no criticism of the violent behavior of his supporters. The next day, during the solemn mass of reception, he chose as his biblical text a passage from Revelations: "Then war broke out in heaven. Miguel and his angels waged war upon the dragon. The dragon and his angels fought, but they had not the strength to win, and no foothold was left to them in heaven. So the great dragon was thrown down, that serpent of old that led the world astray, whose name is Satan."[51] Not only did this text focus attention on violent confrontation rather than peace and reconciliation, it appeared to be a scarcely veiled allusion to Obando's own determination to confront the revolutionary government—and to prevail. This mass was the prelude to a period of intense and high-profile activity by the cardinal.

Two other aspects of that first mass in Managua should also be noted. Although a very large crowd turned out, estimated to be as many as 40,000 persons, there was a conspicuous absence of episcopal representation from other Central American countries. No other archbishop from the region was present, nor were there any representatives at all from the episcopal conferences of Guatemala or Costa Rica. Indeed, even some of Nicaragua's own bishops were absent. The speculation was that the absence of high-ranking church officials from Central America denoted a growing uneasiness over the apparent politicization of the religious situation in Nicaragua. This perception was reinforced by the vigorous way in which the Contra forces now seized upon Obando's appointment as an implicit endorsement of their cause: "Nicaraguan people: let us all stand with our cardinal . . . a new opportunity presents itself for demonstrating that we have not been conquered by the communist enemy . . . united in faith we are invincible."[52] This broadcast over the FDN radio station "15 de septiembre" was echoed by *La Prensa* in a series of editorials exalting Obando as a warrior sent by God. The issue of July 14, for example, proclaimed the following: "One thousand will fall at his right hand and ten thousand at his left hand, but he [the cardinal] will not touch his enemies, for he is a chosen one of the Lord. . . . The life of Cardinal Obando is a mirror where the glory of God is reflected . . . he does not speak in his own name, but through his mouth speaks the Lord."[53]

In late June Cardinal Obando initiated a pastoral tour of the country. Over a period of four months he made some seventy-two visits to parishes throughout the archdiocese. The right-wing political parties cooperated with the archdiocese in organizing these trips, during which Obando stressed the theme of reconciliation. "Each visit was organized as a triumphal procession, with the cardinal displaying his new vestments, then spreading his message that peace can only come when the government agrees to engage in dialogue with the contras."[54] As we suggested above, this position not only contradicted the platform on which the FSLN had won office the previous autumn with a solid majority vote, but it also coincided with the position of the Reagan administration, whose avowed aim was to roll back the Nicaraguan Revolution. To make matters worse, during the cardinal's tour the Catholic radio station, which was run by the cardinal's press secretary, Bismark Carballo, carried appeals urging that young men not accept the military draft. These sentiments were echoed in the hierarchy's new newspaper, *Iglesia*.[55] In the face of mounting Contra aggression, these actions within the Managua archdiocese inevitably took on a strongly partisan political tone.

"La Insurrección Evangélica"

As Cardinal Obando's tour of the archdiocese shifted into high gear, another prominent Nicaraguan Catholic priest undertook his own spiritual initiative. On July 7 the foreign minister, Father Miguel D'Escoto, announced that President Ortega had granted him a temporary leave from his duties in order that he begin a period of fasting and prayer. Father D'Escoto's initiative was called "el ayuno por la paz" (the fast for peace). For the next thirty days he kept vigil in the parish church of the Sacred Heart-of Jesus, which is located in the working-class Managua barrio of Monseñor Lezcano. There he received a steady stream of visitors from all parts of Nicaragua and from around the world.

Father D'Escoto described the fast as an attempt to open up "una nueva trinchera" (a new trench) in the struggle for Nicaraguan sovereignty.[56] He saw it as an act of "creative nonviolence." On the one hand, Nicaragua was obliged to defend itself militarily and the country had been extensively mobilized to accomplish that end. As foreign minister, D'Escoto had spearheaded the country's drive for a negotiated settlement of the military conflict. As a priest, he now chose to dramatize Nicaragua's search for nonviolent avenues of change. As he put it, "we Christians have been unwilling to risk our lives to bring about the conditions for real sisterhood and brotherhood, and to do it nonviolently." D'Escoto later indicated that when he undertook the fast he had worried that the youth of Nicaragua, those who had been called upon to go into combat against the Contras, would not be receptive to his initiative. As it turned out, however, these fears were groundless. Throughout the month-long fast there was a steady stream of young Sandinista soldiers visiting the Monseñor Lezcano parish church. At times "whole contingents of troops just back from the war front" came into the church to pray and to show their solidarity with Father D'Escoto's fast. President Ortega also visited Monseñor Lezcano, where he declared: "I am confident this evangelical act will be supported by Christians in Nicaragua and the U.S. . . . We have confronted U.S. aggression with our combatants, our peasants, militants, workers, youth and with every legal recourse possible. Now there is a new tool in the struggle for peace and we the government support it."[57]

The "ayuno por la paz" generated what Andrew Reding has aptly called "a new form of religious pilgrimage." In contrast to the traditional processions of Nicaraguan folk Catholicism, in which spiritual energies were devoted to the veneration of a series of local patron saints, now "thousands of Nicaraguans from all walks of life streamed in to express their solidarity with a living process."[58] A week after the fast was begun six thousand representatives of Nicaragua's Christian base communities met in León, where they endorsed Father D'Escoto's initiative and discussed ways of implementing it in their own villages and neighborhoods.[59] International support for the "ayuno por la paz" was equally impressive, particularly on the part of human rights groups and church leaders, both Catholic and Protestant. Letters of support came from Catholic bishops in Mexico, Bolivia, Brazil, and the United States. Catholic bishops from Brazil and the United States came to Managua to share directly in D'Escoto's spiritual retreat, as did an Anglican bishop from Britain and a Lutheran bishop from Sweden. Collective fasts of solidarity were held in numerous countries, including Mexico, Panama, France, England, Italy, and West Germany—all nations that were important allies of the United States. The fast's significance for the peace process was highlighted by the visit of the deputy foreign ministers of the Contadora countries.

Among the letters of solidarity from abroad was one from Cardinal Evaristo Arns, archbishop of São Paulo and head of the largest Catholic diocese in the world. Indeed, expressions of solidarity from the Brazilian Catholic church were among the most forceful and significant responses evoked by the "ayuno por la paz." Cardinal Arns's letter said of D'Escoto's fast: "Your prophetic gesture denounces attempts to kill the seed of new life planted by the Sandinista Revolution."[60] Here was a very prominent leader of the Latin American Catholic church not only supporting the "prophetic gesture" of a fellow priest, but acknowledging the legitimacy of the Nicaraguan Revolution. In this respect his letter could be taken as an implicit repudiation of U.S. policy toward Nicaragua, and of the silence of Nicaragua's own hierarchy in the face of the destruction that that policy had wrought. A few days after Cardinal Arns's letter was received in Managua, Bishop Pedro Casaldáliga arrived from Brazil representing, he said, twenty-three of his fellow bishops and some two hundred labor, human rights, and Christian organizations in Brazil. On the day Bishop Casaldáliga arrived, nine Nicaraguan mothers who had been visiting their sons at the front were attacked and murdered by Contra forces; it was he who presided at their funeral in León.[61] These events served to dramatize the chasm that had opened in the Catholic church over the issue of the Nicaraguan Revolution, both at the national level and at the international level.

In one respect the "ayuno por la paz" was clearly aimed at building moral pressure in Nicaragua's behalf against the U.S.-supported aggression of the Contra forces. In Father D'Escoto's hands the "ayuno" was an act of statesmanship. At the same time, it was just as clearly the spiritual act of a believing Christian. But what were its practical implications for the Nicaraguan Catholic church, and for the Christian community? Connor Cruise O'Brien has argued that "the primary target . . . was not Reagan, it was Obando."[62] That is, D'Escoto was trying to push the church hierarchy to express its solidarity with the Nicaraguan people by forcing it to acknowledge that the Contra war not only was destructive but also lacked legitimacy. He wished to mobilize the hierarchy as well as grass-roots Christians to put their spiritual and moral will behind the struggle to preserve Nicaraguan sovereignty. But the effort was likely to be seen by Cardinal Obando more as a public challenge to constituted authority in the church than as an authentic and prophetic religious act. Indeed, while expressions of solidarity were flowing in from church hierarchies in other countries, the Nicaraguan episcopacy kept a studied silence in the first weeks of the fast. No Nicaraguan bishop visited his fellow priest at the parish church in Monseñor Lezcano.

On July 23, after Father D'Escoto had been fasting for just over two weeks, the episcopal conference issued a statement signed only by Bishop Bosco Vivas, the auxiliary of the Managua archdiocese, which was published in *La Prensa*. The communique criticized the government for avoiding dialogue with the bishops and for fostering disrespect toward the church in the popular media. In an oblique reference to the fast, it said: "Regarding supposed pastoral orientations given by individuals to Catholics, the Bishops of Nicaragua reaffirmed once again that only the legitimate authority of the Catholic Church can legislate for its faithful and no other authority or individual can assume the right to order or promote religious activities."[63] Since this communique carried only one signature it may not have reflected a unanimous point of view within the hierarchy. Nevertheless, it did suggest the strength of a continuing preoccupation within the archdiocese over episcopal authority, and the danger of threats thereto. D'Escoto's fast was interpreted in this light, and therefore would not be endorsed in any way by Cardinal Obando or his auxiliary bishop. In the second phase of what came to be known as the "evangelical insurrection," Father D'Escoto's attempt to fortify Nicaraguan Christians and to mobilize opinion in defense of the Nicaraguan Revolution was indeed directed more and more explicitly at the Nicaraguan bishops, and particularly at Cardinal Obando.

On October 15, 1985, the Nicaraguan government renewed the state of emergency that had been suspended more than a year before. From the government's point of view the state of emergency was necessary in order to prevent the formation of an internal military front. During 1985 the Popular Sandinista Army had in fact been quite successful in controlling the military threat posed by Contra units. On the battlefield the tide was running against the Contras. However, the drive by the Reagan administration to destabilize the revolution continued unabated on other fronts: the economic embargo had been declared in May; aid to the Contras had been voted in June; the U.S. military presence in Honduras continued to grow. Perhaps most notably, the rhetorical assaults on Nicaragua being generated in Washington mounted relentlessly. It appeared as though the propaganda war grew in direct proportion to the military failure of the Contra forces in the field.[64]

The War and the Fight for Contra Aid

The Nicaraguan churches were a principal field of struggle in that propaganda war. Members of the Catholic hierarchy continued to voice strident criticisms of the government, while avoiding criticism of the Contras. The hierarchy objected vigorously to the reimposition of the state of emergency; on the other hand, a group of more than one hundred priests and religious signed a declaration stating that the state of emergency was "not for repressing the people, but rather to protect their interests in the face of the dangers that lie in wait for the revolution."[65] These sharply divergent positions reflected the extent of the division that had developed within the Roman Catholic church over the revolution. When the government closed Radio Católica, the radio station of the Managua archdiocese, for refusing to broadcast President Ortega's New Year message as required by law, Cardinal Obando saw the move as one of religious persecution—while Catholics who were sympathetic to the revolution, and who had become increasingly estranged from the archbishop of Managua, saw the incident more in terms of a direct and unwarranted provocation against the government by church officials.

It was against this background of deepening schism within the Catholic church, and the increasingly aggressive propaganda war being waged from Washington, that Miguel D'Escoto launched the second phase of the "evangelical insurrection." On February 14, 1986, the first Friday in Lent, he began a march of the stations of the cross, or "Viacrucis," that would stretch from Jalapa, near the Honduran border, to the capital city of Managua—a distance of more than 300 kilometers. The Viacrucis is a venerable religious celebration in Nicaragua, but is typically carried out within the local community.

D'Escoto's celebratory march would be a "gran Viacrucis por la paz"; that is, it would traverse a large portion of Nicaraguan territory beset by war. It would begin in a town that symbolized Contra aggression and patriotic resistance, for Jalapa had twice been overrun by Contra forces but its citizens had held out, preventing the Contras from gaining a foothold in national territory. And the Viacrucis would end in Cardinal Obando's own diocese, challenging church leaders to stand for peace by standing against the Contra war.

Only Father D'Escoto and a handful of loyal followers walked the entire length of the "gran Viacrucis," but hundreds, and at times thousands, accompanied him on individual legs of the journey. The marchers were predominantly peasants, as were those who greeted them with flowers and holy images along the way. At several points the marchers found the doors of parish churches closed to them; one carried a sign that said: "Don't make politics out of the Viacrucis!"[66] Evidently D'Escoto's dual intent was widely understood. He sought to mobilize religious sentiment by organizing a great expression of popular piety. He also intended to demonstrate the depth of Christian support for the "Sandinista position on peace."[67]

The eighth station of the cross came in Estelí, a city of about 20,000 inhabitants, which had played a crucial role in the popular insurrection of 1978–79. Estelí had a deep identification with the revolution. In a dramatic move Bishop López Ardón ordered the cathedral doors to be opened to the marchers. He welcomed them personally, embracing D'Escoto, blessing him, then kneeling to ask D'Escoto's blessing upon himself. Together they prayed for peace before a crowd of about 20,000 people. As Connor Cruise O'Brien observed, the Viacrucis "had obliged the Bishop of Estelí . . . to stand up and be counted. And he had . . . chosen to be counted on the side of the pilgrims. . . ."[68] As the marchers neared Managua, however, they met a different reception in Tipitapa, the village where General José María Moncada had signed the pact permitting the U.S. occupation of Nicaragua in 1927 that led to Sandino's rebellion. The parish priest, Father Uriel Reyes, threatened his parishioners with possible excommunication if they participated in the Viacrucis, and to ensure that they did not do so, he "surrounded the chapel at the crossroads of San Benito with barbed wire."[69]

The Viacrucis was concluded with a religious celebration on the steps of Managua's ruined cathedral. Some seventy-two priests, or about one-fourth of all priests working in Nicaragua, concelebrated the mass with Father D'Escoto. In his speech D'Escoto appealed to Cardinal Obando to join the Viacrucis. He also voiced open and harsh criticism of the Cardinal's posture toward the war:

> [I]f you are by a television or radio . . . don't turn it off Miguel Obando! The Lord, acting through His humble people, through the campesinos who suffer the aggression of which you have been the principal accomplice, this God, this God of Life, this God of Love and Justice, but also of Compassion, Miguel Obando, has had compassion for you, and has therefore con-vened this people in this moment. . . . there is yet time for repen-tance! . . . All we want is for you to speak in the name of the God of Life, of Love, and of Peace. . . .[70]

These were strong words to speak to the leader of the Nicaraguan church. They would have been unimaginable two decades earlier— but then, the "gran Viacrucis" itself would have been unimaginable before Medellín. In the eyes of Nicaragua's popular church the Contra war called for prophetic action and prophetic denunciation. Miguel D'Escoto, foreign minister and Maryknoll priest, had provided it in the form of an evangelical insurrection. That evangelical insurrection must have looked ominously schismatic to Cardinal Obando.

The cardinal ignored Father D'Escoto's appeal. He and Bishop Vega busied themselves during the spring months traveling outside Nicara-gua, appealing for funds to aid church development and vigorously criticizing the Sandinista government. Their travels in the United States coincided with the Reagan administration's initiation of an in-tense drive to win congressional approval of $100 million in Contra aid. While Cardinal Obando was in New York in late January he denounced the Sandinista government for carrying out a persecution against the church.[71] On March 5, Bishop Vega visited Washington to participate in a seminar on the Central American crisis sponsored by the Heritage Foundation. Other prominent participants were top Contra leaders Arturo Cruz, Adolfo Calero, and former National Guard colonel Enrique Bermúdez.

During the seminar Bishop Vega repeated Cardinal Obando's charges that the Sandinistas engaged in religious persecution. To back up this claim, he stated that the Sandinistas had killed three priests. He went on to describe the Nicaraguan Catholic church as facing a "great dilemma: how to get military support to free people instead of oppressing them, as is happening now."[72] These statements by the president of the Nicaraguan episcopal conference came just one week after President Reagan had sent his Contra aid request to Congress, and after Secretary of State Shultz had justified that aid request before the Senate Foreign Relations Committee with a violent denunciation of the Sandinista government. Repeatedly referring to the Sandinistas as "Communists," Shultz characterized their government as a "new Nicaraguan police state." In support of this claim he charged that the Sandinistas "systematically attacked . . . Catholic and Protestant church leaders," and he held up Contra leaders Arturo Cruz and Adolfo Calero as examples of the sort of Nicaraguan "democrats" the United States should support.[73]

The statements made by Cardinal Obando and Bishop Vega during their visits to the United States were covered extensively in the Nicaraguan press. There was particular outrage over Vega's claim that the government had killed three priests. After returning to Nicaragua he admitted that in fact no priests had been killed. Claiming to have been misquoted, he said his remarks referred to the deaths of three Catholic lay workers; what he did not acknowledge was that the individuals involved were fighting alongside Contra forces and had been killed in battle. This apparent distortion of facts in order to discredit the Sandinista government and buttress the Contra cause only served to deepen the divisions within the Nicaraguan Catholic church. It also heightened the government's suspicions as to the intentions of top church officials.

When President Reagan gave a nationally televised address on March 16 to urge Contra aid, he cited Cardinal Obando's words of late January.[74] This provoked an indignant reaction from church people in Nicaragua, as exemplified in a letter released on April 11 by César Jerez, S.J., the rector of the Central American University in Managua. The letter was addressed to President Reagan and signed by more than 150 priests, members of religious orders, and Protestant pastors, as well as by 800 lay workers. It vigorously contradicted the claims Reagan had made about the religious situation in Nicaragua: "We condemn in the most forceful terms your bold proclamation of yourself as defender of the faith and religion of our people. You, Mr. President, through your 'brothers,' the heralds of terror and death, are the one who is persecuting Christians in Nicaragua. . . ."[75]

This perspective clashed sharply with that of Cardinal Obando, as expressed in an editorial written for the *Washington Post* and published on May 12. In that editorial Obando referred to Christians such as those who had signed the letter to President Reagan as "allies" of "the organizations of the masses in the service of the system." While this language must have seemed curiously oblique and obscure to many U.S. readers, its meaning was clear enough to Nicaraguans. The "system" is the revolution, and the "organizations of the masses" are the popular organizations of campesinos, urban workers, youth, and women that offer critical but reliable support to the Sandinista government. Cardinal Obando was criticizing church people who were identified with these popular organizations on the grounds that they sought "not moral guidance" but rather a "statement to manipulate." As he saw it, their call for a pastoral statement from the bishops on the Contra war was merely an effort to manipulate the hierarchy. If the hierarchy made any statement that indicated support for military aid to the Contras, they would be seen as traitors; if they opposed such aid, on the other hand, "we would be accused of taking sides, which would automatically disqualify us as pastors to all of the people."[76]

In a striking way, Cardinal Obando's argument revealed two major fault lines that have divided the Nicaraguan people since the advent of the counterrevolution. One of those fault lines is theological, involving a question of hermeneutical perspective. Christians who identify with the revolution contend that the Gospel requires the church to take sides in the face of violence and injustice; in their view, the bishops are obliged by their pastoral role to show solidarity with Nicaraguans who are daily being ravaged by the Contra war. Cardinal Obando appealed to a different hermeneutical principle, that of nonpartisanship: he suggested that in order to serve all Nicaraguans, he could not be seen to side with those associated with the mass organizations. His position, however, failed to acknowledge that the Contra war depends on U.S. support, or that the Reagan administration freely utilizes his statements in the partisan cause of making war against Nicaragua.

In fact, Cardinal Obando's editorial made a series of extraordinarily partisan attacks against the Sandinista government. He contended that the Contra war was a "civil war" and rejected the idea that "what is happening is a direct attack by the United States on our country."[77] He went on to assert that the government lacked popular support and even denied that it was "legitimately constituted." Such statements were not only partisan, they bordered on the seditious. In making these statements, the cardinal tried to distinguish his position from that of the U.S. Conference of Bishops, which had consistently criticized the Reagan administration's war against Nicaragua; the U.S. bishops, he maintained, had full access to the media, and their criticisms did "not make them criminals or traitors to their country." However, while the U.S. bishops did vigorously criticize administration policy, they never questioned the government's fundamental legitimacy, as Cardinal Obando did openly in his *Washington Post* editorial.

The second fault line is experiential, and is closely connected to the issue of partisanship and hermeneutical perspective. The Roman Catholic church has always cast its religious appeal across the lines of social class and ethnic diversity. But as we showed in Chapters 5 and 6, historically in countries like Nicaragua the aspiration to appeal to all classes and groups belied two central realities: the church was in fact highly dependent on the state, and closely associated with socioeconomic elites; at the same time, its ties with the mass of people at the grass roots were extremely weak. A major consequence of the conference at Medellín was to reinvigorate contact between the church and the lower classes, but on a new footing. Campesinos and the urban poor came to expect the clergy, including the bishops, to identify with them. In Nicaragua's countryside today this means acknowledging the ravages of war, for war is their daily experience. Since the victims of that war are overwhelmingly campesinos, it is difficult to avoid the class character of the struggle—but by opting for "nonpartisanship," that is precisely what Obando appears to do, thus denying the experiential base from which campesinos interpret the demands and promises of their Christian faith. For them the Contra war is an attack on the poor. It is unjust because, in attacking farming cooperatives, health clinics, and schools, it is aimed at destroying the biblically promised Jubilee.

To peasant Christians in Nicaragua the programs of the revolution represent first steps to a more just sharing of the nation's wealth. One woman, an original member of the Solentiname community founded by Ernesto Cardenal in 1966, expressed her view of these programs by saying, "the revolution never promised us that we would be rich, but if we all shared the poverty no one would be dirt poor."[78] To the poor the revolution's programs are an affirmation of life and of human dignity. As such, they are in conformity with God's promises. In short, their experience with the revolution conforms to the way they read the Bible. Cardinal Obando's experience and reading of the Gospel are quite different. Hence, there is a great divide separating

Nicaraguan Christians from one another—but the divide is owing to religious experience and biblical interpretation rather than to governmental authoritarianism or religious persecution.

The Expulsion of Bishop Vega

In early March 1986, as we have seen, Bishop Pablo Vega traveled to Washington to participate in a seminar devoted to airing the Contra perspective on the war in Nicaragua. While there, he asserted that the Sandinista government was persecuting the church.[79] Back in Managua on March 13, Bishop Vega claimed that he had been misquoted in the U.S. press, and that his intention was to foster a clearer analysis of the Nicaraguan situation. The next day Contra units operating near the mining town of Siuna in northeastern Nicaragua attacked and destroyed the residence of the Missionaries of Christ Sisters. They burned down a dispensary and a sewing workshop that served the peasants of the area.[80] Two days later, in a major televised speech urging Contra aid, President Reagan drew on remarks Cardinal Obando had made in January to the effect that the church suffered persecution under the Sandinista government.

The congressional vote for President Reagan's Contra aid request was scheduled for June 25. On June 5, as the debate grew more and more intense, Bishop Vega again traveled to Washington, this time at the request of PRODEMCA. Once again he appeared with Contra leaders, making public statements that seemed to endorse the Contra cause. Speaking of the armed struggle against the Sandinista government, he asked: "What other solution remains for a people that is repressed, not only politically but militarily?"[81] The night before the vote President Reagan, making one last appeal for aid, quoted Bishop Vega: "Pablo Vega said that in Nicaragua they [the Contras] are defending the right of man to exist."[82] Whatever their intentions may have been, the public declarations of the two Nicaraguan bishops who are best known outside the country were made in settings that linked them to the Contra cause in a highly partisan way. And they were seized upon avidly by the Reagan administration to justify the war against Nicaragua.

On June 25 the House of Representatives voted approval of the president's $100 million aid request. A week later Bishop Vega gave a press conference in Nicaragua in which he bitterly criticized the

Sandinista government, calling it "a government of the extreme left." He appeared to say also that a U.S. invasion was inevitable due to the Soviet presence in Nicaragua and the government's indifference to the popular will.[83] On July 4, Nicaraguan government officials escorted Bishop Vega to the Honduran border and expelled him from the country.

The expulsion of Bishop Vega[84] marked the nadir of church-state relations in Nicaragua since the triumph of the revolution. The Sandinistas received considerable criticism in the international media, and in the U.S. press. Pope John Paul II vigorously condemned the action, while Reagan administration officials seized upon it as proof of their repeated allegations about religious persecution. What was surprising was how little reaction these measures provoked within the wider Nicaraguan Christian community.[85] While it is reasonable to suppose that few Christians welcomed the action, it is also likely that they had come to regard open identification with those making war on the country as neither nonpartisan nor properly pastoral behavior for Catholic leaders. Many may well have sympathized with the position of the government, as expressed by President Ortega in a speech at Riverside Church in New York City on July 28:

> It is true. We acted against a bishop. We did so because this bishop did not . . . want to heed the laws of our country. Bishop Vega actually lobbied the U.S. Congress on behalf of the $100 million. An organization [PRODEMCA] affiliated with the U.S. government brought Bishop Vega to Washington . . . in the weeks just prior to the vote in Congress. . . . [G]oing over the boundary of the law, siding with those who are committing an aggression against our country is punishable in Nicaragua or in any other country.[86]

Whatever the popular mood in Nicaragua may have been, there is little doubt that by the spring of 1986 the Vatican was quite concerned about the status of church-state relations in that country. The papal nuncio in place at that time, Archbishop Lanza di Montezemolo, was thought to have very strained relations with Cardinal Obando, who may have pushed for his removal. The question was, what attitude would the new nuncio take toward the now-open clash between the church and the government? When Bishop Paolo Giglio arrived in Nicaragua on July 28, he immediately made clear his intention to work toward lessening tensions both between Nicaragua and the United

States, and between the Catholic church and the Sandinista government. He also staked out positions that were notably different from those taken so publicly by Cardinal Obando and Bishop Vega during the preceding year. Of Nicaragua's relations with the United States he said, "up to now the refusal to dialogue has not come from Nicaragua, but from Reagan." He went on to say that the church had an obligation to "test all the ways of creating conditions so that a dialogue can take place."[87] Such remarks seemed to repudiate not only the bellicosity of Washington's policy toward Nicaragua, but also the Nicaraguan hierarchy's unwillingness to stand against it.

But Bishop Giglio went further, making statements that seemed to speak directly to the church's posture toward the Sandinista government. He said, for example: "The mission of the church is to form good citizens, to instruct our Catholics to love their country. . . . What makes a good Christian? To fulfill one's duty, to obey the laws of the country. To love God, to love the country, to love one's neighbor. . . ."[88] The fact that the nuncio chose to stress the Christian duty to obey the law was perceived in Nicaragua as an effort to pull back from the confrontational posture of Obando and Vega. Did the Vatican's policy imply sympathy for the theological and pastoral positions of those Catholics who openly supported the government? Did it, for example, imply solidarity with Father D'Escoto's "evangelical insurrection"? There is little likelihood that it meant either of these things. It is far more likely that the policy was rooted in a pragmatic concern for the interests of the institutional church.

By the time of Bishop Vega's expulsion from Nicaragua, the political positions adopted by him and by Cardinal Obando had put a great distance between them and the hierarchies of other nations in the hemisphere. The United States Catholic Conference had spoken repeatedly against aid to the Contras and in favor of a negotiated settlement to the conflict between Nicaragua and the United States. The Brazilian bishops had strongly expressed their solidarity with Nicaragua. The World Court had concluded Nicaragua's suit against the United States by declaring the United States guilty of violating international law in its support of the Contra war. Latin American sentiment as a whole, as embodied in the Contadora peace process, had coalesced in favor of diplomatic solutions in Central America. Against this expression of international opinion, the Nicaraguan hierarchy stood increasingly isolated.

Moreover, the confrontation with the state was not being "won" by the church. A number of clergy had been expelled from the country. The Catholic media were now severely restricted because, in the government's eyes, they had been used in a highly partisan and even disloyal way during a time of war. Political confrontation was undercutting the church's ability to carry out its pastoral functions. In short, it was adverse to the church's interests.

These circumstances would help to account for the fact that one of Bishop Giglio's first acts as nuncio was to reactivate the church-state dialogue, which had been discontinued when tensions began to mount in the fall of 1985. President Ortega had proposed resumption of the talks in July; after the nuncio's arrival, the talks were in fact scheduled for September. The first meeting, held on September 27, produced agreement to reinstitute the dialogue commission and a commitment from both sides to work toward creating an atmosphere conducive to the resolution of differences.[89] During the fall and early spring the Church-State Dialogue Commission met a number of times, and there was a slackening of tensions. In November U.S. Attorney General Edwin Meese announced the Justice Department's investigation of illegal funding of the Contras. Both for the Nicaraguan nation and for the Nicaraguan Catholic church, these events signaled the hope for a season of peace and reconciliation.

Eleven

Conclusion

L atin America was deeply affected by the Second Vatican Council. The initiatives taken in religious life and thought at Vatican II seized hold of the Christian churches throughout the continent, precipitating demands for change that have not yet entirely run their course. Central America shared fully in this dynamic process. Religious change revitalized the Catholic church and challenged the Protestant churches to live up to their Reformational heritage. Indeed, we would characterize the postconciliar period in Central America as one of "Reformational changes."

The churches took a preferential option for the poor. In Central America, this implied an identification with the vast majority of the populace. Assuming that church leaders grasped the implications of such an option, how could an institutionally weak church carry it out? One possibility was to organize the poor so that they could meet some of their own religious needs. The key to this endeavor was the Christian base community and its lay leaders, the Delegados de la Palabra. The hub around which CEB activity revolved was study of the Bible. In the view of dictatorial regimes, the prophetic emphasis given to Bible study made it appear dangerously subversive in a society so marked by inequality and injustice. Religious activism spilled over irresistibly into the political arena.

During the period examined in this book a number of countries in Central America were particularly susceptible to the influence of religious change due to the weakness and illegitimacy of existing regimes. For example, the political system of El Salvador eroded severely during the 1970s. The narrowly based system of oligarchical rule had become totally dependent on the military for its survival; this system of "reactionary despotism" was maintained only through violent repression of the myriad demands for change being voiced within the country.[1] In Nicaragua the Somocista regime was gravely weakened by a series of events during the 1970s—including the 1972 earthquake, Somoza Debayle's heart attack, and the Carter administration's human rights policy—over which it had little control. It was also particularly vulnerable to the criticisms of mobilized Christians. In fact, *Somocismo* made Nicaragua unique, even within Central America. The regime's peculiar characteristics, such as the extreme concentration of power in the hands of a single family, and that family's identification with the National Guard and dependence on U.S. support, facilitated a sustained popular mobilization that swept the Somoza dynasty from power in 1979. As we have shown, Christians organized to play a key role in these events.

It is clear, then, that the political crisis of Somocista Nicaragua derived in important ways from the prophetic reorientation of the Christian churches. Religious energies encouraged the creation of an institutional network at the grass roots. *Delegados* and CEBs became integral and important elements of a broader structure of rebellion. Viewed in the larger perspective of modern Western history, Nicaragua shows remarkable similarities to the English and American revolutions. In each of these revolutions it was a popular demand for rights justified by religious principles that fueled the movement for change. Above all, the Reformational doctrine of the "priesthood of all believers" supported the demand for individual political rights. At the same time, the congregational model of church membership, based on the principle of voluntarism, strongly suggested that legitimate authority in government should derive from the consent of the governed.

In Nicaragua, too, powerful claims to individual dignity raised a strong challenge to autocracy. That impulse came as much from the churches, and from new accents of religious faith, as from any other source. Postconciliar theology in Central America, which was worked out as much in CEBs as in seminaries or universities, helped to spread the ideas of individual dignity and equality of rights among a populace suffering ever more acutely from economic and social dislocation. The religious environment in Nicaragua during the 1970s resembled that of England in the 1640s, and that of America after 1740. It is also true that in all three cases political developments overtook changes in the religious sphere. However, the effect was not to suppress religion but to sharpen and "politicize" the more radical religious ideas by applying them to political problems.

Thus, for example, in seventeenth-century England, the Civil War and the New Model Army organized the religious and political grievances of disenfranchised groups, fostering a sense of class consciousness and solidarity among them. The counterparts to these phenomena in the Nicaraguan Revolution were the popular insurrection and the Sandinista Front of National Liberation. To carry the analogy one step further, the English Civil War brought together groups with divergent interests, united only by their common grievances against the king; their coalition disintegrated after the military defeat of the Royalist forces. Similarly, the Nicaraguan insurrection produced a broad coalition of groups opposed to Somoza, but that coalition broke down soon after the triumph—not only pitting former political allies against one another, but producing a serious schism within the Christian churches. In this regard, at least, the Nicaraguan Revolution was quite unlike its predecessors in Mexico and Cuba. In those cases the churches uniformly opposed the revolution, and religious teachings were, from the very beginning, used to justify that opposition.

We have pointed to three aspects in particular that the Nicaraguan Revolution shares with those now-distant revolutions in England and America. First, we have stressed the enormous impact that prophetic renewal in religious life had in stimulating and sustaining the struggle for change. Through the historic meeting of Latin American bishops at Medellín, the Second Vatican Council initiated a series of changes in religious thought and practice that had revolutionary implications for Central America. We have argued that these changes were Reformational in two broad senses. First, the bishops at Medellín insisted that Christians were responsible for the world around them; seeing that Latin America had fallen into a "state of mortal sin," there was much to be done to rectify the evils. Second, the churches were obligated to judge and denounce "systemic poverty." Perhaps the central teaching of Medellín was that the churches had to show their solidarity with the poor, not in word only, but in deed. This meant repudiating a history of social and political exploitation that the church itself had often supported, at least tacitly.

The Medellín conference called the church to conversion. Its new, prophetic interpretation of the faith rejected the old dualisms that had separated the spiritual from the profane. Medellín refocused the notion of salvation to encompass the whole person in the fullness of life. While the primacy of faith was reasserted, emphasis was shifted from the mere acceptance of established dogma to a trust in the active presence of the Holy Spirit. Christian truth had to do with living in conformity with the Gospel, even in the midst of an unjust, violent society. Medellín called the churches to be servants of the people. This implied that the religious authority of the churches would be a function of their faithfulness in pursuing the integral development of the people rather than in preserving the continuity of their ancient and venerable institutions.

As it turned out, efforts to implement the preferential option for the poor had powerful repercussions for the institutional church, particularly in Roman Catholicism. The critique of systemic injustice strained the Roman church's ties to established elites. The creation of CEBs and the promotion of Bible study dramatically altered the teaching function of the church. A form of popular education emerged, which aimed at dignifying and mobilizing the poor. The remarkable success of this pastoral mission rejuvenated the church at the grass roots. It also produced a "praxis" that overtook the theory, much as had happened in Reformational Europe. Luther had liberated the German peasant from the control of the priest, for example, only to discover that reading the Bible made that peasant want to be an independent and self-directing individual. Access to the Bible in a context of religious and political authoritarianism could have a disturbingly democratizing effect on common people. Nicaragua illustrates this outcome in the most extraordinary way.

The second aspect shared by the Nicaraguan, English, and American revolutions is, then, the drive for democratization. Our book has placed strong emphasis on this theme. In particular, we have attempted to highlight the dramatic growth in the demand for participation that swept through Central America in the 1970s. This demand for a voice in the public councils was increasingly effective as it was more and more coherently organized. In the Central American milieu, as illustrated by our study of Nicaragua, the popular voice was organized through an unprecedented collaboration of religious reformers and political revolutionaries.

The reader should bear in mind that the superficial forms of democratic government have long been in place in Central America. Political parties existed, they offered candidates for election, and the elections took place more or less routinely. But from the viewpoint of the campesino majority, electoral campaigns debated issues that were entirely secondary. They did not articulate the political interests of the poor, much less address fundamental questions having to do with the legitimacy of regimes. Elections only thinly masked the de facto rule of the oligarchy and the military, a system of elite rule personified literally in Nicaragua by *Somocismo*. An important function of "elections" in Somocista Nicaragua was to limit and control popular participation.

For these reasons popular mobilization within the Roman Catholic church, which was Medellín's great legacy, presented a revolutionary challenge to the political systems of Central America. Religion and politics underwent a sharp realignment as Christians at the parish level began to question the "natural hierarchies" of the old order, and to challenge the concentration of power that made for antidemocratic politics. In Nicaragua the churches exposed human rights violations by the Somoza regime, and individual clergy played key roles in such opposition movements as Los Doce, which attacked and weakened the regime's credibility. At the same time, CEBs coordinated their energies with those of other popular organizations to create a potent resource for political struggle at the grass roots.

This democratizing effect was felt within the churches as well, especially in the Catholic church. Herein lies a third theme we have stressed in this book. The challenge to authoritarianism in politics had implications for the church. By giving the poor a voice of their own, the church had set loose a questioning and critical spirit that soon asked: "What is the church?" Gradually two distinct views emerged—or, more precisely, a new perception emerged to challenge the traditional view.

On the one hand there was the conception of the church as the institutional expression and embodiment of the Christian faith. This view placed supreme importance on the role of the magisterium in defining the church and its mission. It was the authority of the hierarchy that gave definition, weight, and purpose to the "church." But out of the CEBs came another view, one that developed in tension with the first even though it was rooted in the postconciliar teachings of the hierarchy. The newer view, which was articulated primarily at the lower levels of the institutional church, tended to define the "church" as a historical community of believers, or the "people of God." This shift in emphasis corresponded directly to the growth of participation. The broadening of access to God's word created a mood in which it seemed natural that the church should behave as a more representative institution. This view did not imply a rejection of the magisterium but rather an insistence that the hierarchy take account of, and be accountable to, the entire community of the faithful.

We have shown how untenable this new conception was for the Catholic church hierarchy. A major focal point of conflict in the Nicaraguan Revolution has been the struggle to realize, or to contain, this new conception of the church. Pope John Paul II focused his own visit to Nicaragua on precisely this issue, throwing his weight decisively on the side of the more traditional view, which exalts the authority of the clergy, especially the bishops, and leaves little scope for the laity to define the church's mission. This approach clashes both with the experience of Christians at the grass roots and with the spirit of a revolution that seeks to enhance popular participation. Therefore, the proper role of Christians in the church, and of the church in the revolution, will continue to be at issue in Nicaragua for the foreseeable future. This situation creates the curious paradox that efforts to express the needs and will of popular majorities are labeled "sectarian," while what is sometimes scornfully called the "popular church" is seen as schismatic. It follows logically that high church officials are suspicious of political leaders who appeal to those popular majorities, as the Sandinistas do—and, indeed, as they must.

These thoughts return our attention to the issue of democracy. The goal of building democratic institutions has been loudly proclaimed but poorly defined in the debate over Central America. The Reagan administration's single-minded pursuit of the Contra war, and its disingenuous efforts to portray the Contras as a "democratic resistance," have generated widespread skepticism about the U.S. commitment to democratic values in that particular area of the world. Two points should be kept in mind. First, Nicaragua is still in the early stages of nation-building. Second, Nicaragua is unlikely to replicate the developmental path of seventeenth-century England or eighteenth-century North America. If Nicaragua is to develop a democratic form of politics, it must do so in the general context of late dependent development. Within the more specific setting of Nicaragua's Sandinista Revolution, the nation-building process will have to accommodate aspects of Marxism—including especially the importance accorded to a vanguard party—the demand for mass popular participation, aspects of representative democracy, Sandino's nationalistic legacy, and the dynamic mix of religious values discussed in this book. It would be naive to think that these competing tendencies can be harmonized easily into a working democratic polity. But it would be arrogant and cynical to insist that Nicaraguans are incapable of integrating this plurality of claims into a viable political system.[2]

At least with respect to its attitude toward religion, we conclude that the Nicaraguan Revolution is highly unusual, if not unique. The

Sandinista government not only recognizes but embraces the importance of religion in Nicaraguan society. Although the churches and the government have had conflicts during the nearly ten years of the revolution, these conflicts have not arisen because of a conscious effort on the part of the government to eliminate, or even restrict, religious practice. Since the signing of the Esquipulas peace accords in August 1987, the Nicaraguan government has worked hard to open a political path to peace. The Sandinistas have reached out to church leaders for help in promoting negotiations to end the Contra war, naming Cardinal Obando to head the national commission on reconciliation. It now remains to the churches to draw on their own moral authority and spiritual resources to advance the cause of peace. Within that process, a major piece of unfinished business is the reconciliation of the prophetic and traditional currents that have divided the religious community itself.

Notes

Chapter 1

1. Three excellent sources on the history of U.S. intervention in the Caribbean Basin are Cole Blasier, *The Hovering Giant: U.S. Response to Revolutionary Change in Latin America* (Pittsburgh: University of Pittsburgh Press, 1976); James Chace, *Endless War* (New York: Vintage Books, 1984); Walter LaFeber, *Inevitable Revolutions: The United States in Central America* (New York: W. W. Norton, 1984).

2. Blasier, *The Hovering Giant*, makes this very clear in the case of Mexico; see pp. 64–68, 101–28. For the Cuban case see Edward González, *Cuba Under Castro: The Limits of Charisma* (Boston: Houghton Mifflin, 1974), esp. pp. 27–76. On Nicaragua see John A. Booth, *The End and the Beginning: The Nicaraguan Revolution* (Boulder: Westview Press, 1982), esp. pp. 41–46, 137–52.

3. For an interesting comparison of the revolutionary approaches of Cuba and Nicaragua, see Max Azicri, "A Cuban Perspective on the Nicaraguan Revolution," in *Nicaragua in Revolution*, ed. Thomas W. Walker (New York: Praeger, 1982), pp. 345–73. Azicri stresses the more pluralistic nature of the Nicaraguan Revolution.

4. Daniel Ortega, "Nicaragua's View of Nicaragua," in *Nicaragua: Unfinished Revolution*, ed. Peter Rosset and John Vandemeer (New York: Grove Press, 1986), p. 5.

5. Ibid., p. 8.

6. A penetrating and illuminating discussion of the historical origins and ideological character of *Sandinismo* is Donald C. Hodges, *Intellectual Foundations of the Nicaraguan Revolution* (Austin: University of Texas Press, 1986). Hodges demonstrates that *Sandinismo* is an eclectic ideology that incorporates liberal elements in its commitment to human rights, religious elements in its active collaboration with revolutionary Christians, and Marxist elements in its determination to end class-based exploitation. From Sandino himself *Sandinismo* has inherited an anarchist impulse that coexists in creative tension with its Marxist principles. Hodges's analysis makes it clear that the Nicaraguan Revolution is different in important ways from the Cuban Revolution. See esp. chap. 8 and the conclusion.

7. E. Bradford Burns, *At War in Nicaragua: The Reagan Doctrine and the Politics of Nostalgia* (New York: Harper and Row, 1987), p. 20.

8. Many main-line Protestant denominations in the United States have adopted resolutions opposing U.S. intervention in Nicaragua. In support of

these resolutions the denominations have disputed the Reagan administration's portrayal of the Sandinistas as totalitarians who oppose religious faith and persecute the churches. For an example, see "Our Nation is Providing Support for the Powers of Death in Central America," *Report to Presbyterians from Washington* 5 (January 1984): 1–4. The United States Catholic Conference has taken similar positions.

9. See Betsy Cohn and Patricia Hynds, "The Manipulation of the Religious Issue," in *Reagan versus the Sandinistas: The Undeclared War on Nicaragua*, ed. Thomas W. Walker (Boulder: Westview Press, 1987), pp. 106-10.

10. Donald E. Smith, *Religion and Political Development* (Boston: Little, Brown, 1970), p. 24.

11. Ibid., p. 51.

12. The quotation is from Scott Mainwaring, *The Catholic Church and Politics in Brazil, 1916–1985* (Stanford: Stanford University Press, 1986), p. 11. See also chap. 2 of Daniel H. Levine, *Religion and Politics in Latin America* (Princeton: Princeton University Press, 1981); and Brian H. Smith, "Religion and Social Change: Classical Theories and New Formulations in the Context of Recent Developments in Latin America," *Latin American Research Review* 5 (Summer 1975): 3–34.

13. Hans Gerth and C. Wright Mills, eds., *From Max Weber: Essays in Sociology* (New York: Oxford University Press, 1958), pp. 61–66.

14. Ibid., p. 63.

15. The phrase comes from Christopher Hill, *The World Turned Upside Down* (New York: Penguin Books, 1975).

16. Booth, *The End and the Beginning*; Walker, *Nicaragua in Revolution*.

Chapter 2

1. The most exhaustive treatment of the U.S. role in creating the National Guard, and of Somoza control of the Nicaraguan political system through the National Guard, is Richard Millett, *Guardians of the Dynasty* (Maryknoll, N.Y.: Orbis Books, 1977). See also John A. Booth, *The End and the Beginning: The Nicaraguan Revolution* (Boulder: Westview Press, 1982), esp. pp. 51–60.

2. For a discussion of the Carter administration's response to the Nicaraguan Revolution and the alteration of the Carter policy by the Reagan administration see William M. LeoGrande, "The United States and Nicaragua," in *Nicaragua: The First Five Years*, ed. Thomas W. Walker (New York: Praeger, 1985), pp. 425–46.

3. "Text of Reagan Address on Central America," *Congressional Quarterly* 41 (April 30, 1983): 853–54.

4. Langhorne A. Motley, *Democracy in Latin America and the Caribbean*, Cur-

rent Policy Paper no. 605, U.S. Department of State (Washington, D.C.: August 1984), p. 8.

5. Remarks of President Ronald Reagan during a weekly radio broadcast aired December 14, 1985.

6. Motley, *Democracy*, p. 4.

7. President Ronald Reagan, "America's Foreign Policy Challenge in the 1980s" (Address to the Center for Strategic and International Studies, Washington, D.C., April 6, 1984), p. 5.

8. Motley, *Democracy*, p. 3.

9. Ibid.

10. Ibid., p. 2.

11. Ibid.

12. Reagan, "America's Foreign Policy," p. 5.

13. Quoted in Motley, *Democracy*, p. 8.

14. Detailed discussions of religious involvement in political conflict are provided by Phillip Berryman, *The Religious Roots of Rebellion: Christians in the Central American Revolutions* (London: SCM Press, 1984), esp. part 2; Jorge Cáceres et al., *Iglesia, política y profecía* (San José, Costa Rica: Editorial Universitaria Centroamericana, 1983); and Penny Lernoux, *Cry of the People* (New York: Penguin Books, 1982), pp. 61–123.

15. "Persecution of Christian Groups in Nicaragua," *White House Digest*, February 29, 1984, p. 1.

16. "Church Says Sandinistas Try to Discredit It," *Washington Post*, July 11, 1984.

17. As reported on ABC television news, April 20, 1984.

18. "Church Says Sandinistas."

19. "Response to Address by President Reagan to Joint Session of Congress by U.S. Religious Personnel in Nicaragua" (Managua, April 29, 1983, Mimeo).

20. "A Pastoral Letter from CEPRES to the Nicaraguan People and Churches" (Managua, March 15, 1984, Mimeo).

21. "Christians Speak about the Electoral Process: A Message from Grassroots Christian Lay People" (Managua, March 7, 1984, Mimeo).

22. John Plamenatz, "The Uses of Political Theory," in *Political Philosophy*, ed. Anthony Quinton (Oxford: Oxford University Press, 1967), pp. 19–31; and George Orwell, "Politics and the English Language," in *Prose Models*, ed. Gerald Levin, 3d ed. (New York: Harcourt Brace Jovanovich, 1975), pp. 181–94.

23. Probably the best-known reference to the greatness of Athenian democracy as a system of internal politics is the admittedly idealized portrait given in Pericles's "Funeral Oration," as reported in Thucydides, *History of the Peloponnesian War*. See also M. I. Finley, *Politics in the Ancient World* (Cambridge: Cambridge University Press, 1983), esp. pp. 70–84.

24. Our discussion here owes much to the stimulating essays of M. I. Finley; see his *Democracy, Ancient and Modern*, rev. ed. (New Brunswick, N.J.: Rutgers University Press, 1985), pp. 12–34.

25. *Politics of Aristotle*, trans. Ernest Barker (Oxford: Oxford University Press, 1952), pp. 124–25.

26. Ibid., p. 126.

27. Finley, *Democracy*, pp. 23, 70.

28. See J. Roland Pennock, "Responsiveness, Responsibility, and Majority Rule," *American Political Science Review* 46 (September 1952): 790–807.

29. Peter Laslett, ed., *Two Treatises of Government*, rev. ed. (New York: Mentor Books, 1963), p. 324. Interesting in this connection is John Plamenatz's critique of Locke, which demonstrates that Locke himself did not argue for democracy, although he did argue for responsible—i.e., limited—government; see John Plamenatz, *Man and Society*, 1 (New York: McGraw Hill, 1963), 209–41.

30. R. R. Palmer, "Uses of the Word Democracy," *Political Science Quarterly* 68 (March–June 1953): 203–26.

31. Alexander Hamilton, James Madison, and John Jay, *The Federalist* (Washington, D.C.: National Home Library Foundation, 1937), pp. 58–59.

32. Finley, *Democracy*, p. 5.

33. Richard Wollheim, "Democracy," *Journal of the History of Ideas* 19 (January 1958): 225–42; George Sabine, "The Two Democratic Traditions," *Philosophical Review* 61 (October 1952): 451–74.

34. Plamenatz, *Man and Society*, pp. 220–41.

35. Sabine, "The Two Democratic Traditions," p. 459.

36. Carole Pateman, *Participation and Democratic Theory* (Cambridge: Cambridge University Press, 1970).

37. *Fort Worth Star-Telegram*, February 29, 1984.

38. Author interview, Managua, August 6, 1980.

39. Many short magazine and newspaper articles about some aspect of church life in Nicaragua have appeared in recent years, but few longer studies. One book-length account that has received notice is Humberto Belli, *Breaking Faith: The Sandinista Revolution and Its Impact on Freedom and Christian Faith in Nicaragua* (Westchester, Ill.: Crossway Books, 1985). This book is a highly polemical and tendentious account of church involvement in the Nicaraguan Revolution. Its manifest aim is to discredit the Sandinista government by trying to prove that the Sandinistas are antireligious, and to discredit Christians who support the revolution by persuading the reader that they are dupes of Marxism. However, apart from its Manichean vision of "good progressives" and "bad radicals," the book suffers from two other grave deficiencies. First, it focuses almost exclusively on elites, above all on the episcopate. Second, it ignores the history of religious renewal at the grass roots that explains, as we intend to show in the present book, why large numbers of

poor Christians supported the revolution and professed loyalty to the Sandinistas.

40. For discussions of the counterinsurgency policy and its impact on Nicaragua, see E. Bradford Burns, *At War in Nicaragua: The Reagan Doctrine and the Politics of Nostalgia* (New York: Harper and Row, 1987), esp. pp. 48–79; Peter Kornbluh, *Nicaragua: The Price of Intervention* (Washington, D.C.: Institute for Policy Studies, 1987); and Gordon Spykman et al., *Let My People Live: Faith and Struggle in Central America* (Grand Rapids: William B. Eerdmans, 1988), pp. 136–70.

Chapter 3

1. Howard Shaw, *The Levellers* (New York: Harper and Row, 1968), p. 99.

2. Ibid., p. 9.

3. Thomas W. Walker, *Nicaragua: The Land of Sandino* (Boulder: Westview Press, 1981), pp. 47–58.

4. William Haller, *Liberty and Reformation in the Puritan Revolution* (New York: Columbia University Press, 1955), p. 11.

5. Shaw, *The Levellers*, p. 12.

6. Ibid., p. 541. See also Peter Porner and Rodolfo Quirós, "Institutional Dualism in Central America's Agricultural Development," *Journal of Latin American Studies* 5 (1973): 217–32.

7. Lawrence Stone, *The Causes of the English Revolution: 1549–1642* (London: Routledge and Kegan Paul, 1972), p. 112.

8. Christopher Hill, *The World Turned Upside Down* (New York: Penguin Books, 1975), pp. 44–45.

9. See Michael Walzer, *The Revolution of the Saints* (Cambridge, Mass.: Harvard University Press, 1965).

10. Hill, *The World*, p. 48.

11. Haller, *Liberty and Reformation*, p. 15.

12. Stone, *The Causes*, p. 102.

13. Shaw, *The Levellers*, p. 3.

14. Haller, *Liberty and Reformation*, p. 136.

15. Hill, *The World*, p. 143.

16. Ibid., pp. 92–93 (emphasis in original).

17. Quoted in Stone, *The Causes*, p. 101.

18. Hill, *The World*, p. 95.

19. Stone, *The Causes*, pp. 12–13.

20. Ibid., p. 113.

21. Shaw, *The Levellers*, p. 25.

22. Ibid., p. 103.

23. Austin Woolrych, "The English Revolution: An Introduction," in *The*

English Revolution: 1600–1660, ed. E. W. Ives (London: Edward Arnold, 1968), pp. 11–15.

24. Ibid., pp. 17–20.

25. Ibid., pp. 21–23.

26. Austin Woolrych, "Puritanism, Politics and Society," in Ives, *The English Revolution*, p. 95.

27. Shaw, *The Levellers*, p. 25.

28. Woolrych, "The English Revolution," p. 25.

29. Hill, *The World*, p. 26.

30. Woolrych, "Puritanism," p. 95.

31. Shaw, *The Levellers*, p. 26.

32. G. P. Gooch, *English Democratic Ideas in the Seventeenth Century* (London: Cambridge University Press, 1927), p. 256.

33. Joseph Frank, *The Levellers* (New York: Russell and Russell, 1969), pp. 25–28.

34. Gooch, *English Democratic Ideas*, p. 198.

35. Ibid., p. 25.

36. H. N. Brailsford, *The Levellers and the English Revolution*, ed. Christopher Hill (Nottingham: Russell Press, 1983), p. 255.

37. Ibid., pp. 261–62.

38. Brian Manning, "The Levellers," in Ives, *The English Revolution*, p. 145.

39. Brailsford, *The Levellers*, p. 274.

40. Ibid., pp. 275-76.

41. Gooch, *English Democratic Ideas*, p. 139.

42. Manning, "The Levellers," p. 151.

43. Ibid., p. 156.

44. Frank, *The Levellers*, p. 181.

45. Woolrych, "The English Revolution," p. 28.

46. Shaw, *The Levellers*, p. 3.

47. Ibid., p. 4.

48. Lawrence Stone, "The Results of the English Revolutions of the Seventeenth Century," in *Three British Revolutions: 1641, 1688, 1776*, ed. J. G. A. Pocock (Princeton: Princeton University Pres, 1980), p. 35.

49. Christopher Hill, "The Norman Yoke," in *Puritanism and Revolution* (London: Panther Books, 1968), p. 64.

50. Stone, "The Results," p. 35.

51. Hill, "The Norman Yoke," p. 81.

52. Stone, "The Results," p. 37.

53. Ibid., p. 61.

54. Ibid., p. 99.

Chapter 4

1. An exhaustive treatment of the Monroe Doctrine and its historical usage to explain and justify U.S. intervention in Latin America is T. D. Allman, *Unmanifest Destiny: American Nationalism in the Third World* (Garden City, N.Y.: Dial Press, 1984). See also Dexter Perkins, *A History of the Monroe Doctrine* (Boston: Little, Brown, 1955).

2. Quoted in Harold Molineu, *U.S. Policy Toward Latin America: From Regionalism to Globalism* (Boulder: Westview Press, 1986), p. 28.

3. The term *fragment society* is borrowed from Louis Hartz, and our discussion of colonial North and South America owes a great deal to his pathbreaking work. See Louis Hartz, *The Founding of New Societies* (New York: Harcourt, Brace and World, 1964), esp. chaps. 1, 2, 4, and 5.

4. Ibid., pp. 6–10.

5. Richard M. Morse, "The Heritage of Latin America," in Hartz, *The Founding*, pp. 140, 152.

6. Claudio Véliz, *The Centralist Tradition of Latin America* (Princeton: Princeton University Press, 1980), pp. 43, 52–69.

7. Charles L. Thompson, *The Religious Foundations of America* (New York: Fleming H. Revell, 1917), p. 123.

8. Ibid., p. 131.

9. Bruce Catton and William B. Catton, *The Bold and Magnificent Dream* (Garden City: Doubleday, 1978), pp. 86–94.

10. Alice M. Baldwin, *The New England Clergy and the American Revolution* (Durham, N.C.: Duke University Press, 1928), p. 25.

11. Thompson, *Religious Foundations*, p. 145.

12. Catton and Catton, *Bold and Magnificent*, p. 171.

13. Ibid., p. 177.

14. Baldwin, *The New England Clergy*, p. 49.

15. Ibid., p. 57.

16. Catton and Catton, *Bold and Magnificent*, p. 182.

17. Baldwin, *The New England Clergy*, p. 80.

18. Ibid.

19. William G. McGloughlin, "The Role of Religion in the Revolution," in *Essays on the American Revolution*, ed. Stephen G. Kurtz and James H. Hutson (Chapel Hill: University of North Carolina Press, 1973), pp. 202, 207.

20. Baldwin, *The New England Clergy*, p. 98.

21. Ibid., pp. 120–26.

22. Ibid., p. 168.

23. Bernard Bailyn, *The Ideological Origins of the American Revolution* (Cambridge, Mass.: Harvard University Press, 1967).

24. Hartz, *The Founding*, pp. 73–77.

25. Bailyn, *The Ideological Origins*.

26. Ibid.

27. Louis Hartz, *The Liberal Tradition in America* (New York: Harcourt, Brace and World, 1955).

28. Bailyn, *The Ideological Origins.*

29. Véliz, *The Centralist Tradition*, pp. 35–37.

30. Ibid., p. 40.

31. J. Lloyd Mecham, *Church and State in Latin America*, rev. ed. (Chapel Hill: University of North Carolina Press, 1966), p. 11.

32. Ibid., p. 12.

33. Véliz, *The Centralist Tradition*, p. 43.

34. Ibid., pp. 25–26; see also Morse, "The Heritage," pp. 147–50.

35. Stanley J. Stein and Barbara H. Stein, *The Colonial Heritage of Latin America* (New York: Oxford University Press, 1970), p. 76.

36. Mecham, *Church and State*, p. 34.

37. Ibid., p. 37.

38. James Lockhart and Stuart B. Schwartz, *Early Latin America: A History of Colonial Spanish America and Brazil* (Cambridge: Cambridge University Press, 1983), p. 12.

39. John Leddy Phelan, *The Kingdom Of Quito in the Seventeenth Century* (Madison: University of Wisconsin Press, 1967), p. 81.

40. Ibid., p. 82.

41. Véliz, *The Centralist Tradition*, p. 191.

42. Lockhart and Schwartz, *Early Latin America*, p. 413.

43. Véliz, *The Centralist Tradition*, p. 192.

44. Mecham, *Church and State*, p. 62.

45. Véliz, *The Centralist Tradition*, p. 194.

46. Christian Lalive d' Espinay, *Haven of the Masses* (London: Lutterworth Press, 1969), as quoted in José Míguez Bonino, "Protestantism in Latin America" (unpublished paper).

47. Wilton M. Nelson, *Protestantism in Central America* (Grand Rapids: Erdmans, 1984), p. 11.

48. Ibid., p. 14.

49. Ibid., p. 30.

50. James C. Dekker, "North American Protestant Theology: Impact on Central America," in *Occasional Essays of CELEP* (Centro Evangélico Latinoamericano de Estudios Pastorales; San José, Costa Rica: December 1984), p. 65.

51. Ibid., p. 66.

52. Nelson, *Protestantism*, pp. 45–47.

53. John Stam, "Missions and U.S. Foreign Policy—A Case Study From the 1920s," *Evangelical Missions Quarterly* 15 (July 1979): 167–75.

54. Dekker, "North American Protestant Theology," pp. 59–77.

55. Nelson, *Protestantism*, p. 56. According to Nelson: "To calculate the

'Protestant community' it is customary to multiply the number of communicant members by three."

56. Ivan Vallier, *Catholicism, Social Control and Modernization in Latin America* (Englewood Cliffs, N.J.: Prentice-Hall, 1970), p. 7.

57. Marcos McGrath, CSC, "Church Doctrine in Latin America after the Council," in *The Church and Social Change in Latin America*, ed. Henry A. Landsberger (Notre Dame: University of Notre Dame Press, 1970), p. 107.

Chapter 5

1. Thomas F. O'Dea, *The Catholic Crisis* (Boston: Beacon Press, 1968), p. 43.
2. Ibid., p. 49.
3. Ibid., pp. 54–55.
4. Brian H. Smith, *The Church and Politics in Chile* (Princeton: Princeton University Press, 1982), p. 16.
5. Anne Fremantle, ed., *The Papal Encyclicals in Their Historical Context* (New York: Mentor Books, 1960), p. 167.
6. Donal Dorr, *Option for the Poor: A Hundred Years of Vatican Social Teaching* (Maryknoll, N.Y.: Orbis Books, 1983), p. 12.
7. Anne Fremantle, ed., *The Social Teachings of the Christian Church* (New York: Mentor-Omega Books, 1963), p. 21.
8. Dorr, *Option*, p. 15.
9. François Houtart and André Rousseau, *The Church and Revolution*, trans. Violet Nevike (Maryknoll, N.Y.: Orbis Books, 1971), p. 95.
10. Ibid.
11. Fremantle, *The Papal Encyclicals*, p. 168.
12. Ibid., p. 175.
13. Ibid., p. 167.
14. Ibid., pp. 173–74.
15. Ibid., p. 186.
16. Ibid., p. 192.
17. Gordon A. Craig, *Europe Since 1815* (New York: Holt, Rinehart and Winston, 1961), pp. 345–50.
18. Dorr, *Option*, p. 27.
19. Ibid., p. 31.
20. Juan Kessler and Wilton M. Nelson, "Panamá 1916 y su impacto sobre el protestantismo latinoamericano," in *De Panamá a Oaxtepec: El protestantismo latinoamericano en busca de unidad, Pastoralia*, Año 1, no. 2 (November 1978): 7. (*Pastoralia* is a journal published by CELEP, San José, Costa Rica.)
21. Ibid., p. 13.
22. Ibid., pp. 42–48.
23. Ibid., p. 10.

24. Ibid., p. 13.

25. Ibid., p. 7.

26. Rubém Alves, "Protestantism in Latin America: Its Ideological Function and Utopian Possibilities," *Ecumenical Review* 22 (January 1970): 11.

27. Ibid., p. 12.

28. H. Richard Niebuhr, *The Social Sources of Denominationalism* (New York: Henry Holt, 1929), p. 19.

29. Ibid., pp. 20–21.

30. Ibid., pp. 22–23.

31. See, for example, chap. 10, "What Ever Happened to Evangelicalism?" in Donald W. Dayton, *Discovering an Evangelical Heritage* (New York: Harper and Row, 1976), pp. 121–37.

32. Ibid.

33. Ernest R. Sandeen, *The Origins of Fundamentalism* (Philadelphia: Fortress Press, 1968), p. v.

34. Ibid., p. 3.

35. Lecture by Gustavo Gutiérrez, Ann Arbor, Mich., November 10, 1986.

36. Karl M. Schmitt, ed., *The Roman Catholic Church in Modern Latin America* (New York: Alfred A. Knopf, 1977), p. 22.

37. Ibid., p. 25.

38. Dorr, *Option*, p. 118.

39. Phillip Berryman, "What Happened at Puebla?" in *Churches and Politics in Latin America*, ed. Daniel H. Levine (Beverly Hills: Sage, 1980), p. 58.

40. Dorr, *Option*, pp. 106–7.

41. Walter M. Abbott and Joseph Gallagher, *The Documents of Vatican II* (New York: Guild Press, 1966), p. 202.

42. Ibid., p. 228.

43. Ibid., p. 244.

44. Ibid., p. 281.

45. Ibid., p. 201.

46. *Mater et Magistra* (Washington, D.C.: National Catholic Welfare Conference, 1961), p. 66.

47. Abbott and Gallagher, *The Documents of Vatican II*, p. 203.

48. Ibid., p. 491.

49. Ibid., p. 490.

50. Edward L. Cleary, O.P., *Crisis and Change* (Maryknoll, N.Y.: Orbis Books, 1976), p. 22.

51. Ibid., pp. 32–33.

52. Phillip Berryman, *Liberation Theology* (New York: Pantheon Books, 1987), p. 23.

53. Joseph Gremillion, *The Gospel of Peace and Justice* (Maryknoll, N.Y.: Orbis Books, 1976), p. 446.

54. Ibid., p. 457.

55. Dorr, *Option*, p. 138.

56. Gremillion, *The Gospel*, p. 472.

57. Ibid., p. 447.

58. Ibid.

59. Ibid., p. 452.

60. Ibid., p. 461.

61. Ibid., p. 453.

62. Ibid., p. 456.

63. Ibid., p. 460.

64. For a succinct discussion of the influence of Pope Paul VI on the Medellín conference see Dorr, *Option*, chap. 8.

65. Gremillion, *The Gospel*, p. 461.

66. See Dorr, *Option*, chap. 8 for a full discussion of the impact of Medellín.

67. CELA I was held in Buenos Aires in 1949, CELA II in Lima, Peru, in 1961, and CELA III in Buenos Aires in 1969.

68. Wilton M. Nelson, "En busca de un protestantismo latinoamericano: De Montevideo 1925 a La Habana 1929," in *De Panamá a Oaxtepec, Pastoralia* (see above, n. 20).

69. Interview with Sidney Rooy, professor of church history at the Protestant seminary ISEDET in Buenos Aires, concerning the CELA conferences and the formation of ISAL (San José, Costa Rica, January 1987).

70. José Míguez Bonino as quoted in T. S. Montgomery, "Latin American Evangelicals: Oaxtepec and Beyond," in Levine, *Churches and Politics*, p. 95.

71. See, for example, Orlando E. Costas, *Crossroads Theology: Latin America* (Amsterdam: Rodopi, 1976), and José Míguez Bonino, "Protestantism in Latin America" (unpublished paper).

72. Costas, *Crossroads Theology*, p. 87.

73. Ibid., p. 86.

74. Ibid., p. 87.

75. Ibid., p. 94.

76. Ibid., pp. 89–91.

77. Orlando E. Costas, "Una nueva conciencia protestante," in *De Panamá a Oaxtepec, Pastoralia*, p. 56.

78. Costas, *Crossroads Theology*, p. 97.

79. Costas, "Una nueva conciencia protestante," p. 61.

80. Montgomery, "Latin American Evangelicals," p. 96. For a full discussion of the Majority Youth Report see Costas, "Una nueva conciencia protestante."

81. Costas, *Crossroads Theology*, p. 107.

82. Costas, "Una nueva conciencia protestante," p. 69.

83. Interview with Sidney Rooy, San José, Costa Rica, January 1987. According to Rooy, UNELAM tried to please everyone and as a result pleased no one.

84. Montgomery, "Latin American Evangelicals," p. 98.

Chapter 6

1. Three major encyclicals of the twentieth century were written to commemorate and extend the teachings of *Rerum Novarum*: *Quadragesimo Anno* (1931), *Octogesima Adveniens* (1971), and *Laborum Exercens* (1981).

2. Joseph Gremillion, *The Gospel of Peace and Justice* (Maryknoll, N.Y.: Orbis Books, 1976), p. 514.

3. Ibid., pp. 516–17.

4. Donal Dorr, *Option for the Poor: A Hundred Years of Vatican Social Teaching* (Maryknoll, N.Y.: Orbis Books, 1983), pp. 186–90.

5. Pope Paul VI, *On Evangelization in the Modern World* (Washington, D.C.: United States Catholic Conference, 1975), p. 21.

6. Ibid., p. 23.

7. Dorr, *Option*, p. 197.

8. Pope Paul VI, *On Evangelization*, p. 24.

9. Ibid., p. 25.

10. Dorr, *Option*, p. 200.

11. Author interviews, Cuernavaca, Mexico, June 1973 and July 1975.

12. See the extensive documentation in Penny Lernoux, *Cry of the People* (New York: Doubleday, 1980).

13. Marcos McGrath, CSC, "The Impact of Gaudium et Spes: Medellín, Puebla and Pastoral Creativity," in *The Church and Culture Since Vatican II*, ed. Joseph Gremillion (Notre Dame: University of Notre Dame Press), pp. 61–74.

14. See Quentin L. Quade, ed., *The Pope and Revolution: John Paul II Confronts Liberation Theology* (Washington, D.C.: Ethics and Public Policy Center, 1982). This work is a good example of neoconservative arguments against liberation theology, which rely heavily on the teachings of John Paul II.

15. Jon Sobrino, "The Significance of Puebla for the Catholic Church in Latin America," in *Puebla and Beyond*, ed. John Eagleson and Philip Scharper (Maryknoll, N.Y.: Orbis Books, 1979), p. 299.

16. Ibid, p. 295.

17. Quade, *The Pope and Revolution*, p. 53.

18. Ibid., pp. 53–54.

19. Ibid., p. 57.

20. Ibid., p. 58.

21. *Evangelii Nuntiandi* as quoted in Quade, *The Pope and Revolution*, p. 67.

22. T. S. Montgomery, "Latin American Evangelicals: Oaxtepec and Beyond," in *Churches and Politics in Latin America*, ed. Daniel H. Levine (Beverly Hills: Sage, 1980), p. 87.

23. Ibid., p. 103.

24. Carmelo Alvarez, "El papel de la iglesia en América Latina," in *De Panamá a Oaxtepec: El protestantismo latinoamericano en busca de unidad*, Pastoralia, Año 1, no. 2 (November 1978): 110.

25. Montgomery, "Latin American Evangelicals," p. 103.

26. Ibid., pp. 100–101.

27. Plutarco Bonilla A., "Melbourne y Pattaya: Cuatro años despues," in *La década de los ochenta: En busca de la misión de la iglesia, Pastoralia,* Año 5, nos. 10–11 (July–December 1983): 6.

28. Mr. Palau, an Argentinian of British-Italian descent, was once considered to be the heir apparent to North American evangelist Billy Graham.

29. As quoted in Plutarco Bonilla A., "Melbourne y Pattaya," p. 27.

30. Montgomery, "Latin American Evangelicals," p. 104.

Chapter 7

1. "The Catholic Church in Nicaragua," Report of the U.S. Catholic Press Association, 1962, p. 18.

2. The concept of a prophetic church is discussed at length in Michael Dodson, "Prophetic Politics and Political Theory," *Polity* 12 (Spring 1980): 388–408.

3. In Argentina, they called themselves the Movement of Priests for the Third World; in Chile, the Christians for Socialism; in Colombia, Golconda; in Peru, the National Office of Social Information (Oficina Nacional de Información Social, ONIS).

4. *The Church in the Present Day Transformation of Latin America in Light of the Council* (Washington, D.C.: United States Catholic Conference, 1968), pp. 80–82.

5. The English term *consciousness-raising* is not normally associated with the development of political awareness and has a more individualist orientation than does the Spanish term *concientización*. The latter term implies group process and political action, so we use it throughout, translating it as "conscientization."

6. The reference to Christian communities throughout this chapter reflects the language used by Nicaraguans themselves to refer to the fluid, decentralized nature of church experience between 1968 and the revolutionary victory of 1979. Much of the prophetic action of the church took place in small communities at the local level without the sponsorship or, in some cases, even the awareness of the official church hierarchy. Many formal Christian base communities were established, but many more grew up spontaneously, carrying Christians into the revolution without formal church approval.

7. The term *pastoral* is widely used in Latin America to refer to all aspects of the priestly or ministerial function of evangelizing. Its Spanish meaning is thus broader than the English usage. We use the Spanish sense of the term throughout this book.

8. It is important to note that during this period the actual number of

Christian communities in Nicaragua developing along the lines of Medellín was small. Initially only a dozen or so parishes were involved in the process described in the text—but these parishes played a crucial role in the popular insurrection ten years later. Moreover, the change to increasingly explicit emphasis on social concerns created conflict within the Christian communities between those who followed Medellín on one side, and charismatics, or groups that persisted in their attachment to popular religious practices, on the other. This conflict was never resolved and it continued into the 1980s.

9. "Declaración de sacerdotes nicaragüenses," *Cuadernos de Marcha* 17 (September 1968): 31–32.

10. Interview by T. S. Montgomery, Managua, February 27, 1980.

11. Pablo Richard and Guillermo Meléndez, eds., *La iglesia de los pobres en América Central* (San José, Costa Rica: DEI, 1982), pp. 156, 165; and author interview with Father Uriel Molina, parish priest in Barrio Riguero, July 1980.

12. "Climate of Violence Hits Nicaragua," *National Catholic News Service* (Washington, D.C.: U.S. Catholic Conference), October 1, 1970, p. 2.

13. Interview with Peggy Dillon, M.M., Ciudad Sandino, Nicaragua, July 29, 1980.

14. Interview with Ricardo Chavarría, Managua, August 11, 1980.

15. John A. Booth, *The End and the Beginning: The Nicaraguan Revolution* (Boulder: Westview Press, 1982), pp. 82–83.

16. Yvonne Dilling et al., *Nicaragua: A People's Revolution* (Washington, D.C.: EPICA Task Force, 1980), p. 23.

17. The case of El Salvador is documented by T. S. Montgomery in her book *Revolution in El Salvador* (Boulder: Westview Press, 1982), pp. 103–5. The case of Honduras was detailed for the authors in interviews with Honduran clergy in La Trinidad, Honduras, on February 4, 1987.

18. Teófilo Cabestrero, *Revolutionaries for the Gospel*, trans. Phillip Berryman (Maryknoll, N.Y.: Orbis Books, 1986), pp. 48–49.

19. Ibid., p. 50.

20. A moving example of this dialogue appears in Ernesto Cardenal, *The Gospel in Solentiname*, vols. 1 and 2 (Maryknoll, N.Y.: Orbis Books, 1977, 1978).

21. This discussion of the religious and political situation in Zelaya is based on author interviews with the Capuchin fathers in Managua, during August 1980.

22. Interview with Padre Vásquez in Matagalpa, July 1980.

23. "Mensaje de la conferencia episcopal de Nicaragua renovando la esperanza cristiana al iniciarse el año de 1977," Managua, January 8, 1977, p. 3.

24. These data were supplied by CEPAD leaders during interviews conducted in Managua in February 1980.

25. Ibid.; CEPAD's 1980 membership included thirty-four denominations and four organizations, representing approximately eight hundred churches with 250,000 members, or 96 percent of the Evangelicals in the country and 10

percent of the population—an extraordinarily high figure for Latin America.

26. "Los evangélicos en Nicaragua: Juicio y mensaje a la nación," document signed November 24, 1976, and adopted by the CEPAD Directorate on June 7, 1977.

27. The process for Evangelicals was slower than for many Catholics, in part due to far lower levels of education and theological training. Many pastors had only a grade-school education.

28. Interview with Ricardo Chavarría, August 11, 1980.

29. Interview with Peggy Dillon, M.M., July 29, 1980.

30. Ibid.

31. Ibid.

32. Interview with Benjamin Cortes, Managua, February 1980.

33. Interview with Peggy Dillon, M.M., July 29, 1980.

34. "Declaración de los 500," II Retiro Interdenominacional de Pastores Evangélicos de Nicaragua (RIPEN II) (October 5, 1979, Mimeo).

35. Ibid.

36. Subsequently, the Federation of Christian Businessmen, without CEPAD's knowledge or permission, promoted CEPAD for membership in the Council of State, a move from which CEPAD publicly disassociated itself, meanwhile reaffirming "our militant participation in the revolutionary process" (Letter to the junta, published in *El Nuevo Diario*, August 1980).

Chapter 8

1. For a thorough description of the original Sandinista program, see George Black, *Triumph of the People* (London: Zed Press, 1981), pp. 121–22.

2. "Nicaraguan Bishops Speak to Catholics and All Nicaraguans," *LADOC* (Latin American Documentation) 10 (November–December 1979): 20–23.

3. Black, *Triumph*, pp. 107–18.

4. Phillip Berryman, *The Religious Roots of Rebellion: Christians in Central American Revolutions* (Maryknoll, N.Y.: Orbis Books, 1984), p. 235.

5. "Hablan los obispos de Nicaragua," *Cuadernos de capacitación*, no. 5 (Lima: CELADEC, 1979), p. 21.

6. The bishops said: "Our process will be something creative, original, profoundly national and not imitative. Because, like the majority of Nicaraguans, what we want is a process toward a society that is authentically Nicaraguan, not capitalist, nor dependent, nor totalitarian" (*Compromiso cristiano para una Nicaragua nueva*, November 17, 1979, n.p., p. 9).

7. Ibid., pp. 8–9.

8. This reference to Sandino comes from a 1980 speech given in Managua by Minister of the Interior Tomás Borge.

9. Referring to this position paper, one Sandinista cabinet minister said,

"just as the church had its dogmatists we have ours too" (author interview, Managua, July 25, 1982).

10. See the excellent summary of church sponsorship of CEBs provided by Scott Mainwaring, *The Catholic Church and Politics in Brazil, 1916–1985* (Stanford: Stanford University Press, 1986), pp. 178–80. See also Thomas C. Bruneau, "Brazil: The Catholic Church and Basic Christian Communities," in *Religion and Political Conflict in Latin America*, ed. Daniel H. Levine (Chapel Hill: University of North Carolina Press, 1986), pp. 106–23.

11. For an interesting discussion of the relative impact of CEBs in several countries of Latin America, see the essays by Mainwaring, Berryman, Dodson, and Levine in the *Journal of Inter-American Studies and World Affairs* 26 (February 1984).

12. According to several charismatic critics, the government tried to change the Catholic meaning of Christmas and they could not do it; to do so they would "have to destroy Christianity and create another religion" (interview with Enrique A. Montalban, Managua, July 13, 1982).

13. *El Nuevo Diario*, November 26, 1980, p. 10.

14. *La Barricada Internacional*, December 30, 1982, p. 3.

15. The *purísima* is a festival to Mary that takes place during the Christmas celebration and lasts for twelve days. During this time, Catholic families construct altars to Mary, and children visit homes in their neighborhood and receive candies, fruits, or gifts from each house they visit. The holiday begins with a traditional *gritería* (a call and a response in honor of the Immaculate Conception of Mary).

16. *La Prensa*, November 29, 1980, p. 2.

17. Interview with James Goff, Managua, April 13, 1983.

18. Berryman, *The Religious Roots*, pp. 71, 231.

19. José Revelas, "López Trujillo envía conquistadores: El clero local firme en el gobierno," *Proceso*, May 26, 1980, pp. 2–3.

20. *Los cristianos están con la revolución* (San José, Costa Rica: DEI, 1980), pp. 9–14.

21. Thomas C. Bruneau, "The Catholic Church and Development in Latin America: The Role of the Basic Christian Communities," *World Development* 8 (1980): 538.

22. Phillip Berryman, "Latin America: La iglesia que nace del pueblo," *Christianity and Crisis* 41 (September 21, 1981): 239–40.

23. Interview with a CEB organizer, Estelí, January 27, 1987.

24. Interview with Pablo Schmidt, Managua, November 26, 1981.

25. For a detailed discussion of the role of the church in El Salvador see T. S. Montgomery, *Revolution in El Salvador* (Boulder: Westview Press, 1982), esp. chap. 4.

26. Interview with a CEB leader, Estelí, January 27, 1987.

27. Alexander Wilde, "Ten Years of Change in the Church: Puebla and the

Future," Working Paper no. 36 (Washington, D.C.: The Wilson Center, 1979), p. 5.

28. We do not contend that the bishops were of one mind on these issues. There is diversity of opinion among the bishops with regard to the revolution. However, the emphasis on church unity so devoutly encouraged by Pope John Paul II has forced a closing of ranks in public, resulting in the surface appearance of unity.

29. Daniel Levine, "Colombia: The Institutional Church and the Popular," in Levine, *Religion and Political Conflict*, pp. 192–96.

30. Quoted during national CEB meeting in Masaya, July 1982.

31. Educating citizens to a new level of civic consciousness and pride, including a greater concern for the well-being of others, has been an important theme in the Sandinista revolutionary program—a theme that has been strongly echoed in the CEBs.

32. Carlos Nuñez Tellez, "El papel de las organizaciones de masas en el proceso revolucionario," Serie Orientación Sandinista, no. 3 (1980), p. 9.

33. Author interview with PDC leaders, Managua, July 1982. For an excellent discussion of the role of the Council of State in the national political system prior to the 1984 elections, see John A. Booth, "The National Governmental System," in *Nicaragua: The First Five Years*, ed. Thomas W. Walker (New York: Praeger, 1985), pp. 35–37.

34. *Sacerdotes en el gobierno nicaragüense: Poder o servicio?* (San José, Costa Rica: DEI, n.d.), p. 9.

35. As reported on Nicaraguan television, October 20, 1980.

36. "Comunicado pastoral de la conferencia episcopal de Nicaragua," *Iglesia de Nicaragua: Tiempo de discernimiento y de gracia*, MIEC-JECI (Movimiento Internacional de Estudiantes Católicos [Pax Romana]–Juventud Estudiantil Católica Internacional), no. 25 (July 1981): 13–15.

37. See "Primera respuesta de sacerdotes," ibid., pp. 19–20.

38. See "Comunidad de cristianos en la revolución se refieren al reciente comunicado pastoral de la conferencia episcopal," ibid., pp. 23–24.

39. "Comunicado oficial de la dirección nacional del FSLN sobre la religion," *Barricada*, October 7, 1980, p. 3.

40. Ibid.

41. *Nicaragua: La hora de los desafíos* (Lima: Centro de Estudios y Publicaciones, 1981), p. 119.

42. Ibid., pp. 121–22.

43. *El Nuevo Diario*, July 17, 1981, p. 1.

44. *Barricada*, July 16, 1981, p. 1.

45. *Nicaragua: La hora*, p. 121.

46. *Jesucristo y la unidad de su iglesia en Nicaragua* (Managua: Editorial Union, 1980), p. 3.

47. See the testimony of Bishop López Ardón in *Pax Christi International*

Human Rights Reports of the Mission: Nicaragua (Antwerp: Omega Books, 1981), p. 98.

48. Interview with Father Antonio Castro, Managua, June 2, 1983.

49. "La iglesia en Nicaragua," *CELAM* 19 (December 1981): 11–21.

50. This controversy received extensive coverage in all three Nicaraguan dailies. See *El Nuevo Diario*, August 19, 20, 24, 27; *La Prensa*, August 24, 25, 27; and *Barricada*, August 26, 1981.

51. "Problems with the Church in Nicaragua," *Envío* (Instituto Histórico Centroamericano), no. 4 (September 1981), p. 2.

52. *Amanecer*, no. 12 (September 1982), pp. 4–5.

Chapter 9

1. *New York Times*, March 17, 1982.

2. "America's Secret War," *Newsweek*, November 8, 1982.

3. *Wall Street Journal*, March 5, 1985.

4. *New York Times*, April 7, 1983.

5. Ibid.

6. Francis Bouchey et al., *A New Inter-American Policy for the Eighties* (Council for Inter-American Security, Washington, D.C., 1980, Mimeo), pp. 45–46.

7. Ibid.

8. Mary Vanderlaan, *Revolution and Foreign Policy in Nicaragua* (Boulder: Westview Press, 1986), pp. 101–2.

9. The photograph actually showed the Red Cross burning the cadavers of persons killed by the National Guard during the insurrection.

10. Philippe Bourgois, "Ethnic Minorities," in *Nicaragua: The First Five Years*, ed. Thomas W. Walker (New York: Praeger, 1985), p. 204.

11. Statement of the Episcopal Conference of Nicaragua, February 18, 1982.

12. The government's position was subsequently supported by the reports of investigations carried out by the Americas Watch Committee (May 1982) and by Amnesty International (December 1982).

13. Archbishop Obando refused to specify who the informants were or how they had obtained their information (author interview, Managua, July 10, 1982).

14. Ibid.

15. See the coverage in *El Nuevo Diario*, August 24, 1982. Apparently, Horacio Ruiz of *La Prensa* first alleged that Bishop Schlaefer had been imprisoned; when Ruiz was questioned, he stated that the archbishop had given him this information. See *El Nuevo Diario*, August 20, 1982.

16. For an extended discussion of freedom of the press see L. N. O'Shaughnessy, "The Contradictions of Liberal and Participatory Democracy in Nicaragua," unpublished paper, 1984.

17. *La Prensa*, June 29, 1982, p. 1.

18. *La Prensa*, July 31, 1982.

19. No printed copy of this sermon could be found in Nicaragua, but author interviews confirmed that it had been delivered.

20. "The Revolution Fights against the Theology of Death," *Informes* (Managua: Centro Antonio Valdivieso), June 14, 1982.

21. "Leamos 'La carta del papa,'" Conferencia Episcopal de Nicaragua, June 29, 1982.

22. Adolfo Aguilar Zinser, "El acierto del papa," *Uno Mas Uno*, February 20, 1983, p. 11.

23. See, for example, Tomás Gerardo Allas, "Conflicto de poderes clérigos —Estado ante la proximidad de la visita papal," *Proceso*, February 20, 1983, pp. 40–45.

24. "Juan Pablo II en Nicaragua," *Envío* (Instituto Histórico Centroamericano), no. 21 (March 1983), pp. 7–20.

25. The authors were not present at the papal mass in Managua but have seen a videotape of the mass and discussed the event with Nicaraguans who did attend.

26. "Juan Pablo II en Nicaragua," p. 15.

27. *Latin American Weekly Report* 83, no. 35 (September 1983): 11.

28. Author interview in Masaya, June 10, 1982.

29. "Open letter to Pope John Paul II from Catholics in Nicaragua," August 15, 1982, in "Church and Revolution in Nicaragua," *Central America Update* (Toronto: LAWG [Latin American Working Group], November 1982), pp. 9–12.

30. *New York Times*, March 6, 1983, p. 14.

31. Interview with Rodolfo Rodríguez, head of the Diocesan Lay Council of Estelí, in Estelí, August 1984.

32. Author notes from participation in CEB meeting, Managua, August 2, 1984.

33. *White House Digest*, February 29, 1984, p. 1.

34. Tom Barry and Deb Preusch, eds., *The New Right Humanitarians* (Albuquerque: Resource Center, 1986), p. 57.

35. *National Reporter* 10, no. 1 (Summer 1986): 23.

36. Barry and Preusch, *The New Right Humanitarians*, p. 58.

37. Peter Kornbluh, "The Covert War," in *Reagan versus the Sandinistas: The Undeclared War on Nicaragua*, ed. Thomas W. Walker (Boulder: Westview Press, 1987), p. 25.

38. *In Contempt of Congress*, Report by the Central America Crisis Monitoring Team (Washington, D.C.: Institute for Policy Studies, 1986), pp. 11–22.

39. *Psychological Operations in Guerrilla Warfare: The CIA's Nicaragua Manual*, as quoted in *In Contempt of Congress*, p. 22.

40. *Psychological Operations in Guerrilla Warfare: The CIA's Nicaragua Manual*

(New York: Random House, 1986), p. 62.

41. Kornbluh, "The Covert War," p. 21.

42. Ibid., p. 24.

43. *Washington Post*, April 18, 1984.

44. *Newsweek*, April 23, 1984.

45. *In Contempt of Congress*, p. 21.

46. *El Nuevo Diario*, May 25, 1983.

47. Ibid.

48. *Barricada*, April 14, 1984.

49. "Conferencia episcopal sugiere 'objeción de conciencia': Nadie puede ser obligado a tomar armas por un partido," *La Prensa*, September 1, 1983, p. 1.

50. "Al pueblo de Nicaragua y al mundo," *El Nuevo Diario*, September 13, 1983, p. 2.

51. *El Nuevo Diario*, September 6, 1983.

52. Notes from attendance at this meeting by L. N. O'Shaughnessy, August 1983.

53. This analysis of CEPAD is based upon interviews with Gilberto Aguirre, Gustavo Parajón, Sixto Ulloa, and Benjamin Cortes, as well as informal conversations with CEPAD members at several CEPAD-sponsored meetings from 1981 through 1984.

54. See Michael Dodson and Laura Nuzzi O'Shaughnessy, "Religion and Politics," in Walker, *Nicaragua: The First Five Years*, p. 139.

55. The name given to mothers whose sons and daughters have died in Contra attacks. Such mothers now number in the thousands.

56. "Pastoral Letter on Reconciliation from the Nicaraguan Bishops," trans. U.S. Department of State (April 22, 1984), pp. 3, 6, 7.

57. Ibid., pp. 9–12.

58. *Barricada*, April 25, 1984.

Chapter 10

1. "Defense in All Spheres: Requisite for Survival," *Envío* (Instituto Histórico Centroamericano) 3 (June 1984): 2a.

2. Author interviews, Ocotal, July 1, 1984; see also "Bitter Witness: Nicaraguans and the 'Covert' War," Witness for Peace Documentation Project (Santa Cruz, Calif.: October 1984), pp. 155–60.

3. Gen. Paul F. Gorman, "The Caribbean Basin and the U.S. National Interest," Speech to the Council of the Americas, Washington, D.C., May 8, 1984.

4. President Reagan's televised address on Central America, May 9, 1984.

5. "The Electoral Law: Another Step toward Institutionalizing the Revolution," *Envío* 3 (April 1984): 3b.

6. Author interview, Managua, January 14, 1987.

7. "The Electoral Law," p. 3b.

8. Ibid., p. 4b.

9. Author interview with Ricardo Chavarría, Managua, July 29, 1984.

10. "Defense in All Spheres," p. 7a.

11. Latin American Studies Association delegation interview with Alejandro Bendaña of the Nicaraguan Ministry of Foreign Relations, Managua, November 1984. Michael Dodson was a member of the delegation.

12. As quoted in *Wall Street Journal*, October 11, 1984.

13. As quoted in *Miami Herald*, August 8, 1984.

14. "The Electoral Law," p. 6b.

15. "The Right of the Poor to Defend Their Unique Revolution," *Envío* 4 (July 1984): 26.

16. Wayne A. Cornelius et al., *The Electoral Process in Nicaragua: Domestic and International Influences* (Austin, Tex.: Latin American Studies Association, 1984), p. 17.

17. See ibid.; Thom Kerstiens and Piet Nelissen (official Dutch government observers), "Report on the Elections in Nicaragua, 4 November, 1984" (photocopy); Irish Inter-Party Parliamentary Delegation, *The Elections in Nicaragua, November, 1984* (Dublin: Irish Parliament, 1984); Parliamentary Human Rights Group, "Report of a British Parliamentary Delegation to Nicaragua to Observe the Presidential and National Assembly Elections, 4 November 1984" (photocopy); and Willy Brandt and Thorvald Stoltenberg, "Statement [on the Nicaraguan Elections in behalf of the Socialist International]," Bonn, November 7, 1984.

18. *The Electoral Process in Nicaragua*, p. 9.

19. *New York Times*, October 21, 1984; March 10, 1987.

20. Michael Dodson and Laura N. O'Shaughnessy, "Religion and Politics," in *Nicaragua: The First Five Years*, ed. Thomas W. Walker (New York: Praeger, 1985), pp. 137–40.

21. "Break-Off or Break-Through? The Catholic Church in Nicaragua," *Envío* 4 (August 1984): 4c.

22. Ibid., as quoted in the December 29, 1983, issue of the Honduran daily, *La Prensa*.

23. "Memorandum to Mr. J. Peter Grace," May 9, 1984, p. 3.

24. Ibid.

25. Ibid., p. 4.

26. Ibid.

27. Quoted in "Two Models of the Church: Chronology of the Catholic Church in Nicaragua," *Envío* 5 (August 1985): 8b.

28. "Break-Off or Break-Through?" p. 6c.

29. Philip J. Williams, "The Catholic Hierarchy in the Nicaraguan Revolution," *Journal of Latin American Studies* 17 (1985): 367.

30. "Break-Off or Break-Through?" p. 7c.

31. Ibid., p. 9c.

32. Juan O. Tamayo, "Sandinistas, Catholic Hierarchy Swap Accusations, Escalate War of Words," *Miami Herald*, August 1, 1984.

33. Howard Heimer, "Is There Religious Persecution in Nicaragua? An Open Letter to the American People," Ecumenical Committee of U.S. Church Personnel in Nicaragua (September 21, 1984, Mimeo), p. 8.

34. Ibid.

35. Ibid.

36. Ronald Taylor et al., "Report of Delegation to Investigate 'Religious Persecution' in Nicaragua" (n.d., Mimeo), pp. 5–9.

37. "Nicaragua: NCC Probes Church-State Tension," *Latinamerica Press* 16 (October 4, 1984): 1–2.

38. Taylor et al., "Report of Delegation," p. 11.

39. Ibid., p. 15.

40. Interview with Leana Nuñez, office of the National Directorate of the FSLN, Managua, August 17, 1984.

41. "Church and Politics: Internal Upheaval and State Confrontation in Nicaragua," *Update* 5 (January 21, 1986): 2–3.

42. Ibid., p. 6.

43. Ibid.

44. "Two Models of the Church," p. 10b.

45. Cornelius et al., *The Electoral Process in Nicaragua*, p. 1.

46. See Christopher Dickey, *With the Contras: A Reporter in the Wilds of Nicaragua* (New York: Touchstone, 1987), esp. pp. 131–72.

47. "Two Models of the Church," p. 10b.

48. Pablo Richard, "The Church of the Poor in Nicaragua: July 1979–April 1986," Mimeo, p. 4.

49. Connor Cruise O'Brien, "God and Man in Nicaragua," *Atlantic Monthly*, August 1986, p. 51.

50. Andrew Reding, "Seed of a New and Renewed Church: The 'Ecclesiastical Insurrection' in Nicaragua," *Monthly Review* 39 (July–August 1987): 27.

51. Ibid.

52. Richard, "The Church of the Poor," p. 4.

53. Ibid.

54. Reding, "Seed," p. 29.

55. "Church and Politics," p. 6.

56. Author interview, Managua, January 14, 1987.

57. "Two Models of the Church," p. 12b.

58. Reding, "Seed," p. 44.

59. Richard, "The Church of the Poor," p. 9.

60. Ibid.

61. Reding, "Seed," p. 45.

62. O'Brien, "God and Man in Nicaragua," p. 64.

63. "Two Models of the Church," p. 13b.

64. See Peter Kornbluh, *Nicaragua: The Price of Intervention* (Washington, D.C.: Institute for Policy Studies, 1987), esp. pp. 160–98.

65. Their declaration was published in *Amanecer*, no. 38–39 (December 1985), pp. 10–12.

66. O'Brien, "God and Man in Nicaragua," p. 64.

67. Ibid.

68. Ibid.

69. Reding, "Seed," p. 48.

70. Ibid., pp. 48–49.

71. *Mesoamerica* 5 (February 1986): 7.

72. Joseph S. Mulligan, S.J., "Nicaraguan Bishops Continue Opposition Role; Other Catholics Support Sandinista Government," Central American Historical Institute (March 1986), pp. 1–2.

73. *Nicaragua: Will Democracy Prevail?* U.S. Department of State Bulletin (April 1986), p. 34.

74. "Nicaraguan Bishops and Christian Activists Issue Letters for Peace," *Update* 5 (May 1, 1986): 2.

75. Ibid., p. 3.

76. Miguel Obando y Bravo, "Nicaragua: The Sandinistas Have 'Gagged and Bound' Us," *Washington Post*, May 12, 1986, p. A15.

77. Ibid.

78. Interview with Olivia Guevara, Managua, July 1983.

79. "Nicaraguan Bishops and Christian Activists," p. 2.

80. Ibid., p. 3.

81. *Barricada*, June 6, 1986, p. 5.

82. "Chronology of Bishop Vega" (n.d., Mimeo), p. 15.

83. Ibid.

84. At the same time that Bishop Vega was expelled, Father Bismark Carballo, Cardinal Obando's press secretary, was refused permission to reenter Nicaragua. He had been traveling in Europe, where he made strongly partisan accusations against the Sandinista government.

85. "In the Eye of the Hurricane," *Envío* 5 (September 1986): 11.

86. Remarks by President Daniel Ortega at Riverside Church, New York City, July 28, 1986.

87. "New Mood in Church-State Dialogue," *Central America Report* 13 (October 31, 1986): 333.

88. "In the Eye of the Hurricane," p. 12.

89. "New Mood in Church-State Dialogue," p. 333.

Chapter 11

1. The term is taken from Enrique Baloyra, *El Salvador in Transition* (Chapel Hill: University of North Carolina Press, 1982).

2. It is not the task of this book to reconcile these differing components of the Sandinista system; we refer the reader to other works that have attempted to do so: José Luis Coraggio, *Nicaragua: Revolution and Democracy* (Boston: Allen and Unwin, 1986); Dennis Gilbert, *Sandinistas: The Party and the Revolution* (New York: Basil Blackwell, 1988); Donald C. Hodges, *Intellectual Foundations of the Nicaraguan Revolution* (Austin: University of Texas Press), 1986; Carlos Vilas, *The Sandinista Revolution: National Liberation and Social Transformation in Central America* (New York: Monthly Review Press), 1986.

Index

AFALIT, 131
Agrarian reform, 29, 94–95, 157, 166
Agreement of the People, 44–46
Aguirre, Gilberto, 131
AIFLD (American Institute for Free Labor Development), 195; Free Trade Union Institute of, 195
Algerian Revolution, 4
Alliance for Progress, 50
Alvarez, Carmelo, 113
Alves, Rubém, 83, 84, 115
American Revolution, 7, 25, 46, 58–61; drive behind, 9; theory of society connected with, 28; distinction between Nicaraguan Revolution and, 30–32; and English revolution, 48, 49, 58; and Enlightenment thought, 65
Anabaptism, 74
Anglican church, 10, 48; and Puritans, 36–39, 41, 54, 58; in England's North American colonies, 56, 58, 59
Arbenz, Jacobo, 15
Arce, Bayardo, 209
ARDE (Alianza Revolucionaria Democrática), 222
Argentina, 117, 118, 177–78
Argüello, Álvaro, 153
Argüello, Roberto, 168, 171, 182
Arias Caldera, José, 175
Aristocracy, 10, 28
Aristotle, 23–24, 26
Arminians, 41
Arns, Paulo Evaristo, 226
Assembly of God, 217

ATC (Asociación de Trabajadores Campesinos), 125, 126, 139
Athens: democracy in, 23, 25, 26
Authoritarianism, 10, 21, 74, 84; in seventeenth-century England, 33–34, 49; and the Reformation, 143; and CEBs, 159

Bailyn, Bernard, 60
Baldwin, Alice M., 58
Baltodano, Emilio, 171
Baptist Convention of Nicaragua, 20
Baptists, 56; and missionary activity in Latin America, 81, 82, 87
Barni, Julián, 172, 173, 182
Barricada, 169, 172, 213
Barrientos, Alberto, 114
Barrios, Justo Rufino, 67
Batalla, Manuel, 174
Batista, Fulgencio, 3
Bay of Pigs invasion (1961), 3–4, 50, 116, 178
Belzúnegui, Pedro, 174
Bermúdez, Enrique, 230
Berryman, Phillip, 156
Bible, 37–39, 47, 55, 57; distribution of, 66, 81, 216; authority of, 86; Catholics and reading of, 88, 144; Protestants and reading of, 97, 99; Revolutionary Christian Movement and study of, 122, 238, 241
Bill of Rights (England), 48
Boland amendment, 196
Boland-Zablocki amendment, 196
Bonafacio, Father, 119
Borge, Tomás, 30, 183, 187, 214

Bosanquet, Bernard, 27
Brailsford, H. N., 44
Brazil, 150, 151, 186, 220; CEBs in, 155–56
Britain. *See* England

Calero, Adolfo, 230, 231
Call to Action, 102
Calvinism: and English revolution, 37, 41, 42, 43–44, 46–47; and colonial American religion and society, 55, 57
Campesino groups, 138, 144, 165, 233
Capitalism, 35, 98, 105
Capuchin Fathers, 127–28
Carazo, 125, 128, 135
Carballo, Bismark, 189, 224, 267 (n. 84)
Cardenal, Ernesto, 119, 167, 187, 220, 233
Cardenal, Fernando, 133, 154, 167
Caritas, 135
Carter administration, 5, 16, 176–77; and human rights abuses, 17, 178, 239
Casaldáliga, Pedro, 226
Casaroli, Agostino, 171, 182, 184
Castro, Emilio, 114
Castro, Fidel, 3, 116, 117
Catholic church: and Mexican Revolution, 3, 144; and Cuban Revolution, 3–4, 5, 116; traditional and prophetic forces within, 8–13, 76–101; and French Revolution, 28; and popular mobilization, in Central America, 28–32, 74, 116–39; predominance of in Nicaragua, 31; and Somoza regime, 34; and colonization of Latin America, 51, 53, 62–69; and challenge of modernity, 76–80; and "Christian Commitment for a New Nicaragua,"

147–48; and "popular" church, 159–60; and Nicaraguan elections of 1984, 211–20
14 de Septiembre (Managua barrio), 119, 121, 133
Catton, Bruce, 56–57
CAV (Centro Antonio Valdivieso), 153, 169
CDSs (Comites de Defensa Sandinista, Sandinista Defense Committees), 152, 192
CEBs (*comunidades eclesiales de base*, Christian base communities), 11, 36, 215, 238–39, 241–42; meetings of, 12; declaration of members of, 20; creation of, 108, 119, 129, 257–58 (n. 8); and Puebla conference, 109; as hope of the church, 111; popular religiosity in, 120; and grass-roots change, 121; and Revolutionary Christian Movement, 121–22; and *delegados*, 126; and renewed interest in the church, 144; and church hierarchy, 148, 150–51, 154–62; reorientation of, 190–98
CELA (Conferencia Evangélica Latinoamericana, Latin American Evangelical Conference), 97–101, 114
CELAM (Consejo Episcopal Latinoamericano, Latin American Bishops' Conference), 111; and Nicaraguan Revolution, 171, 174, 184; and CEBs, 191. *See also* Medellín conference; Puebla conference
Central American Constitution, 66
Central American Mission, 67
Central American University (Universidad Centroamericana, UCA), 121, 152–54
CEPA (Comité Evangélico de Promoción Agraria), 124–25; training seminars of, 128; and campesino

development, 138; and CAV, 153; and Nicaraguan Revolution, 154, 160; and church hierarchy, 169

CEPAD (Comité Evangélico Pro-Ayuda al Desarollo), 12, 119, 131, 217, 258–59 (n. 25); and evangelicals, 132, 138; and September insurrection, 135; relations with Sandinistas, 200, 201–2; extension courses of, 216

Chamorro, Pedro Joaquín, 134, 147

Chamorro, Violeta, 167

Charles I (king of England), 36, 40–42

Charles IV (king of Spain), 65

Chile, 4, 17, 69

Chinandega, 12, 195

Christ: message/image of and social justice and change, 56, 79, 94, 99, 110, 122, 138, 172–73; evangelization in name of, 104, 110; Sandino and, 149

Christianity: and Marxism, 7; spread of to New World, 51; and Sandinista Revolution, 107; institutionalization of, 143. See also specific churches and organizations

Christian Youth Movement, 133–34

Church of England. See Anglican church

Church-state relations, 77, 84, 165–72

CIA (Central Intelligence Agency) (U.S.), 50, 196–98; Reagan authorizes Nicaraguan activities of, 176–78; and mining of Nicaragua's harbors, 198, 199, 211; and attack on Ocotal, 205

Ciudad Sandino. See OPEN 3

CLAI (Consejo Latinoamericano de Iglesias, Latin American Council of Churches), 113–15

Cleary, Edward, 91–92

CNPEN, (Consejo Nacional de Pastores Evangélicos de Nicaragua, National Council of Evangelical Pastors), 12

Coffee, production of, 35, 36

Cold War, 31, 32

Colombia, 117, 118

Colonization, 9, 13, 51; English, 53–58; Spanish, 61–65, 66, 93

Committee of Santa Fe, 178

Communism, 20, 26. See also Marxism; Socialism

Compañero: meaning and interpretation of term, 183

CONELA (Confraternidad Evangélica, Latin American Evangelical Confraternity), 114, 115

Congregationalists, 54, 55–56, 58

Congress (U.S.), 16, 196, 198, 231, 234

Congress of Panama, 80–83, 97

Conscience: role of in religious belief, 37, 57, 77

Conscientization, 119, 120

Consent, doctrine of, 24, 27–28

"Constantinianism," 76

Contra war, 12, 176–203, 204–37, 243–44; onset of, 11; attack on Ocotal, 12, 205, 214; and tension in the church, 146; struggle for aid for, 228–34

Conversion: importance of in religious experience, 54, 94, 110

Coolidge, Calvin, 68

Copyholders, 34

Córdoba Rivas, Rafael, 167, 172

COSEP (Consejo Superior de la Empresa Privada), 167

Costa Rica, 67, 82, 113, 223; CEBs in, 156; John Paul II's visit to, 187; and the Contra war, 204

Costas, Orlando E., 98, 100

Cotton, John, 55

Cotton, production of, 35, 36

Council of State, 166–67, 199, 207
Covenants: as basis for establishing
    churches, 42, 55
CRISOL, 135
Cromwell, Oliver, 40, 41, 42, 44, 46
Cruz, Arturo, 210, 230, 231
Cuba, 115, 156; and FSLN, 20; U.S.
    economic blockade of, 138, 164;
    and Soviet Union, 179. *See also* Cu-
    ban Revolution
Cuban Revolution, 3–4, 5, 16; Ro-
    man Catholics and, 31, 116, 144;
    Kennedy and, 50–51; and Nicara-
    guan Revolution, 144, 240

Declaration of Independence (U.S.),
    25, 58, 61
Declaratory Acts, 60
Delegados de la Palabra, 36, 124–30,
    156–57, 238, 239
Dell, William, 42, 44
Democracy, 12, 194, 243–44; and
    Marxism, 6, 7; promotion of, 15,
    17–22; and religion, 21–22; forms
    of, 22–28; Aristotle on, 23–24, 26;
    language of, and the Nicaraguan
    Revolution, 28, 208. *See also* De-
    mocratization
Democratization, 9, 13, 25, 157–58;
    and U.S. intervention, 15–16, 18–
    22; and the Somocista system, 30;
    and Puritanism, 37–38; of polity in
    England, 44–49; and Calvinism,
    55; and socialism, 78
D'Escoto, Miguel, 167, 220, 224–30
Díaz, Porfirio, 3
Dictatorships, 18, 20, 100
Dispensationalism, 86
Doherty, William, 195
Dorr, Donal, 88, 106
Dualism, 84

Earthquake, in Managua (1972), 118,
    122–24, 126, 128, 130; first anniver-
sary of, 132–33; and weakening of
    Somocista regime, 238
Economic models, 94–95
Education, 73, 82, 96; moral, 24, 28;
    reform of, 98, 119; of CEB leaders,
    191–92
Egalitarianism, 55, 59, 78
Elective affinity, 9
Electoral process, 26–27, 29–30, 206–
    20, 241–42
Elizabeth I (queen of England), 34,
    36
El Nuevo Diario, 172, 199, 200, 213
El Salvador, 5, 18, 21, 28, 82, 238;
    victimization of religious persons
    in, 19; revolutionaries in, 156, 177;
    CEBs in, 158
El Tayacán, 12
Encomienda, 63, 64
England, 81; and colonization of
    North America, 52, 53–58. *See also*
    Anglican church; English revolu-
    tion
English revolution, 7, 28, 56, 59; cir-
    cumstances and course of, 9–10,
    33–49; and Nicaraguan Revolu-
    tion, 30–32, 34, 239–40, 243; au-
    thoritarianism and, 84
Enlightenment, 65
EPS (Ejército Popular Sandinista),
    179
Equality, 46–47; natural, principle of,
    56
Eschatology: and democratization,
    37–38; and liberation/salvation, 104
Esquipulas peace accords, 244
Estelí, 12, 128, 139, 154, 229; CEBs
    in, 156–57, 159, 191–92
Evangelicals, 130–32, 138
Evangelii Nuntiandi, 103, 104–5, 107,
    109–10
Evangelism in Depth, 98–99
Evangelization, 67, 104, 143

Fagoth, Steadman, 179–80
Falkland Islands, 178
Fascism, 26, 87
FDN (Fuerza Democrática Nicara-
  güense, Nicaraguan Democratic
  Force), 179, 197, 220–21, 222, 224
Federalist Papers, 25
Ferdinand I (king of Spain), 61, 62
Ferdinand VI (king of Spain), 65
Foreign policy, U.S., 5–8, 15, 164,
  245 (n. 8); Bay of Pigs invasion, 3–
  4, 50, 116, 178; and promotion of
  democracy in Latin America, 17–
  22; and lack of historical perspective, 33; and common heritage of
  the Americas, 50; economic blockade of Cuba, 138, 164. *See also*
  Reagan administration
Fragment societies, 51–53
Freedom, religious, 6, 19, 28, 215;
  and democracy, 22; and Leveller
  movement, 43; and colonization of
  North America, 54–58; Protestant,
  84; in FSLN *Official Communique
  Concerning Religion*, 169–70
French Revolution, 7, 26, 28, 46; and
  the English revolution, political
  ideas of, 48; and Enlightenment
  thought, 65; and Constantinianism, 76; anticlericalism of, 79
FSLN (Frente Sandinista de Liberación Nacional, Sandinista Front of
  National Liberation), 14, 20, 118–
  19, 130, 133–34, 139, 147, 151, 240;
  and Marxism, 4; Reagan's characterization of, 17; and grass-roots
  movements, 122, 124; and ATC,
  125; and CEPA, 125; García and,
  127; and CEBs, 129, 158, 191; and
  Evangelicals, 132, 135; the church
  as mediator between government
  and, 133; and RIPEN II, 138; and
  church hierarchy, 145–52, 157,
  170–72, 218; ideology of, 149; *Offi-*

*cial Communique Concerning Reli-
  gion*, 150, 169–70, 172–73; and pastoral option for the poor, 160; and
  ruling junta, 166; and Miskitos,
  179; and Contra war, 179, 183, 189,
  191, 199, 202–3; and Obando y
  Bravo, 183; and national election
  of 1984, 206–10, 212, 221, 224
Fundamentalist churches, 83, 86

García, Edgardo, 126
García Laviana, Gaspar, 130
Gaudium et Spes (Pastoral Constitu-
  tion on the Church in the Modern
  World), 88, 89–90, 92, 93–94
Giglio, Paolo, 235, 236, 237
Glemp, Josef, 185
Glorious Revolution of 1688, 48, 53
God: and individual believer, 57, 242;
  as source of public authority, 80;
  dispensationalist view of, 86; and
  poverty, 94; and liberation/salva-
  tion, 104; activist view of, 122
Gooch, G. P., 45
Gorman, Paul, 205–6
Grace, J. Peter, 195, 211–12
Great Awakening, 56–57, 58
Grenada, 161, 198, 204
Guatemala, 17, 18, 67, 161, 223

Haig, Alexander, 180
Hartz, Louis, 52, 59, 61
Havana Conference, 98
Heritage Foundation, 230
Hill, Christopher, 35, 36, 37–38, 43;
  47
Hill, John, 67
Hobbes, Thomas, 38, 45
Honduras, 82, 177–78, 195, 204, 228
House of Commons (British Parlia-
  ment), 44, 45
Human rights abuses, 96; Carter ad-
  ministration and, 17, 178, 238–39;
  Catholic student protests against,

122; and RIPEN I, 132; and church hierarchy, 181

Iberia, 52, 53; colonization from, 62, 64. *See also* Spain
Iglesia, 224
Immortale Dei, 80
Independents (English Civil War), 42, 44, 48
Individualism, 35, 38, 98, 105
Industrialization, 76, 80
Intervention, U.S.. *See* Foreign policy, U.S.
IRD (Institute for Religion and Democracy), 216
Ireton, Henry, 40, 42, 45, 48
Isabella I (queen of Spain), 61
ISAL (Iglesia y Sociedad en América Latina, Church and Society in Latin America), 98, 100, 115
Islas de Solentiname, 119, 121
Islas Malvinas, 178

James I (king of England), 33
Jara, José de la, 119
Jefferson, Thomas, 61
Jesuits, 119. *See also* Central American University; CEPA
Jinotega, 129, 204
John XXIII (pope), 87–90
John Paul I (pope), 108
John Paul II (pope), 104, 221–22; at Puebla, 109; and CEB concept, 155; visit to Central America, 182–83, 184–90, 193
Jornada Navideña, 151–52, 153
Julius II (pope), 61–62
Justice in the World, 103

Kemble, Penn, 194
Kennedy, John F., 50, 51
Kirkpatrick, Jeane, 195

La Hoja Dominical, 12, 182
Lamennais, Robert de, 77
Land reform, 94–95
La Prensa, 149, 165, 182, 195, 200, 210, 224, 227
La Purísima, 151–52, 260 (n. 15)
Laud, William, 36, 40, 41
Leo XIII (pope), 69, 76, 77–79, 80, 102
Levellers, 42, 43–48, 53, 54, 56
Levine, Daniel H., 8, 159
Liberalism, 79
Liberation, 103–5, 107; John Paul II's view of, 109–10, 111. *See also* Liberation theology
Liberation theology, 74–75, 111, 212. *See also* Liberation
Lilburn, John, 43
Literacy, 10, 30, 37, 131, 157; Sandinista campaign for, 154, 193, 206–7, 210
Locke, John, 24, 27, 47, 59, 61
Long Parliament, 41, 44
López, Julio, 149–50
López Ardón, Rubén, 157, 172, 173, 229
López Fitoria, Leovigildo, 172
López Trujillo, Alfonso, 171, 184, 185
Loyalists (American Revolution), 31
Lumen Gentium (Dogmatic Constitution on the Church), 90
Luther, Martin, 74
Lutherans, 81

McGrath, Marcos, 69
Madison, James, 25–26, 27–28
Mainwaring, Scott, 8
Majority: tyranny of, 27; logic of, 29
Managua, 12, 15, 121, 135; occupation of cathedral in, 122; and struggles between barrio and government, 134; CEBs in, 157–58; Lay Commission in, 173. *See also*

Earthquake, in Managua; specific barrios

MAP-ML (Movimiento de Acción Popular–Marxista Leninista, Marxist-Leninist Popular Action Movement), 209

Marx, Karl, 9, 80

Marxism, 3–7, 120, 212, 243; and Christianity, 7, 138; and opposition to Somoza, 10, 118; and Catholicism, 19, 128, 184–85; and totalitarianism, 22; as tool for social analysis, 92; cultural values of, 105; and Sandinista Revolution, 107. *See also* Communism; Socialism

Maryknoll Missionaries, 123–24, 133, 134

Masaya, 125, 135; CEB conference held in, 161–65

Massachusetts Bay Colony, 54–55

Matagalpa, 12, 129, 204

Mater et Magistra, 89, 90

Materialism, historical, 9

Mayhew, Jonathan, 58

MDN (Movimiento Democrático Nacional, Democratic National Movement), 167

Mecham, J. Lloyd, 62

Medellín conference (CELAM II), 20, 21, 73, 74, 75, 90–96; challenge and response following, 102–15, 117; documents issued by, 106, 107, 108, 165; calls for reform at, 119, 144, 240–41; influence of, 120, 121, 124; *delegados* and teachings of, 127, 128; and church-state relations, 165

Medrano, Luis, 174

Meese, Edwin, 176, 237

Méndez Arceo, Sergio, 106–7, 112, 199

Methodists, 81

Mexican Revolution, 3, 4–5, 7, 144, 240

Mexico: Nicaragua as threat to, 15; visit of John Paul II to, 109; CEBs in, 156. *See also* Mexican Revolution

Míguez Bonino, José, 84, 98, 115

Miranda, Otilio, 174

Miskito Indians, 172, 179–83, 209

Missionaries, 66–67, 68; in heyday of "Manifest Destiny," 80–83. *See also* specific churches and organizations

MISURA (Unidad de los Miskitu, Sumu, y Rama), 179–80

Modernists, 86

Modernization, 66, 76–80, 87; and "trickle-down" perspective, 98

Molina, Uriel, 161

Moncada, José María, 229

Monimbó, 135, 158

Monroe Doctrine, 50

Monseñor Lezcano (Managua barrio), 174, 225, 227

Montezemolo, Lanza di, 235

Montgomery, T. S., 113

Morality, 8, 24, 28, 77, 79, 89

Motley, Langhorne, 16, 17, 18

Moynihan, Daniel P., 198

Naseby, battle of, 41, 42

National Directorate (FSLN), 166, 218

National Guard (Nicaragua), 5, 10, 177, 239; brutality of, 14, 127–28, 129; and ruling elite, 30; protests against presence of, 122; and *delegados*, 127–28, 129, 156; and peasants, 130; and commemoration of first anniversary of earthquake, 133; and September insurrection, 135; and efforts to undermine Sandinista government, 178, 199

National Reporter, 194
National Security Council (U.S.), 177, 194, 197–98
NCCC (National Council of Churches of Christ), 216–18; Division of Overseas Ministry of, 216
NED (National Endowment for Democracy), 194–95
New Model Army, 38, 40, 42, 43, 44, 239–40
Niebuhr, H. Richard, 85–86
Novak, Michael, 195
Novedades, 130
Nueva Segovia, 195
Nuñez, René, 172, 200

Oaxtepec, meeting in (1978), 112–14, 115
Obando y Bravo, Miguel, 19, 73, 116, 220–22, 236; and Somoza, 120, 129; and grass-roots movements, 122; defense of in *Novedades*, 130; and commemoration of first anniversary of earthquake, 133; and relationship of church to revolution, 137, 168, 171, 173, 174, 182; and FSLN, 147, 183; and the CEB conference in Masaya, 161; CELAM report on, 174–75; and Contra war, 181, 199, 230, 231–33, 234, 244; Holy Week sermon by, 183; and John Paul II, 184, 188, 189; and national election of 1984, 210, 211, 212, 214, 215, 219; and Viacrucis, 230; *Washington Post* editorial, 231, 233; and Lanza di Montezemolo, 235
O'Brien, Connor Cruise, 226, 229
Ocotal, 12, 205, 214
Octogesima Adveniens, 102
Oligarchy, 4, 10, 15; in England, 34, 46
OPEN 3 (Managua barrio, now Ciudad Sandino), 123–24, 133–34, 158

Ortega, Daniel, 154, 220, 237; on Marxism, 4–5; on democracy, 29; and national elections, 29, 206; and Permanent Commission for Dialogue, 172; welcoming speech to John Paul II, 187; and church and Contra war, 203; announcement of national election, 206; and Obando y Bravo's appointment as cardinal, 222; and D'Escoto, 224; New Year message of, 228; speech at Riverside Church, 235
Overton, Richard, 47

Palau, Luis, 114
Palmer, R. R., 25
Papal authority, 102
Papal Infallibility, 77
Parajón, Gustavo, 130, 200
Paris Commune, 79–80
Parliament (England), 10, 34, 39, 45; Independents in, 42, 48; and powers of the king, 53; sovereignty of, 60
Parrales, Edgard, 152, 167
Pastora, Edén, 222
Paul VI (pope), 96, 102–6, 111; death of, 108; and CEB concept, 155
PCD (Partido Conservador Demócrata de Nicaragua, Conservative Democratic Party), 209
PC de N (Partido Comunista de Nicaragua, Communist Party), 209
Peasantry, 34, 35, 74, 95, 130. *See also* Campesino groups
Peña, Amado, 214
Pentecostalism, 68, 98, 100, 112
Permanent Commission for Dialogue, 172
Peters, Hugh, 42
Philip II (king of Spain), 63
Pilgrims, 54
Pius IX (pope), 77
Pius XI (pope), 76

Pius XII (pope), 76
PLI (Partido Liberal Independiente, Independent Liberal Party), 209
Pluralism, religious, 6, 59, 91, 102, 143
Polk, James K., 50
Poor, church's option for, 103–6, 112, 159, 160
Populorum Progressio, 96, 106, 107
Presbyterian church, 41, 42, 47, 56, 87
Princeton theology, 86
PRODEMCA (Citizens' Committee for the Pro-Democratic Forces in Central America), 195, 196, 214, 234, 235
Property rights, 3, 26, 27; in England, 40, 45, 48
Protestantism, 65, 66–69; and English and American revolutions, 31; and Congress of Panama, 80–83; anomaly of, 83–87; and CELA, 97–101, 114. *See also* Protestants
Protestants, 3, 10, 12, 225; in seventeenth-century England, 35; among North American colonists, 51, 55; search for unifying directive among in Latin America, 97; and 1978 Oaxtepec meeting, 112–14; and emergency relief, 123. *See also* Protestantism
PROVADENIC, 131, 201
PSN (Partido Socialista Nicaragüense, Socialist Party), 209
Puebla conference (CELAM III), 20, 104, 106–12, 115; attention given to CEBs at, 155, 159; and church-state relations, 165, 169
Puritanism, 33–39, 40, 41, 42, 46, 74; and Leveller movement, 43; and English colonization of North America, 52–58; and CEBs, 155
Putney, debate at, 44–46, 48

Quakers, 56

Radicalism, religious: and political radicalism in seventeenth-century England, 43, 48; John Paul II's view of, 109–10; origins of in Nicaraguan church, 117–22; and Nicaragua's Evangelicals, 130–32. *See also* CEPA; Delegados de la Palabra
Rainsborough, Thomas, 44, 45
Ramírez, Sergio, 172, 209
Reagan, Ronald, 194, 231, 232; speech on Central America to joint session of Congress (1983), 16, 19–20; characterization of Sandinista regime by, 16–17, 18, 20, 206; and CIA assistance in Contra war, 176–77, 197–98; proposes "Peace Plan for Nicaragua," 221; televised speech urging Contra aid (1986), 234. *See also* Reagan administration
Reagan administration, 5, 75, 204–37; and "public diplomacy" campaign, 6; and "rollback policy," 15; and human rights abuses, 17; views Central America through East-West lens, 20–21; and Contra war, 176–78, 180, 193–98, 243. *See also* Reagan, Ronald
Reagan Doctrine, 32, 194, 204–37
"Red Christmas" campaign (1981), 179–80
Reformation, Protestant, 9, 13, 31, 65; and U.S. political heritage, 33; and Puritanism, 35, 37; and colonization of North America, 53; and evolution of the church in Latin America, 73, 74, 241; and "Constantinianism," 76; and Catholic Church, 87; and authoritarianism, 143
Rerum Novarum, 69, 76, 77–80
Revolutionary Christian Movement, 121–22, 124, 238, 241

Revolutions: Aristotle on, 21; Locke on, 27. *See also* specific revolutions

Reyes, Uriel, 229

Rights, 29, 58, 239; property, 3, 26, 27, 40, 45, 48; "natural," 56, 57, 59, 79. *See also* Freedom, religious

Riguero (Managua barrio), 121–22, 133

RIPEN (Retiro Interdenominacional de Pastores Evangélicos de Nicaragua, Interdenominational Retreat of Evangelical Pastors): I, 132, 137; II, 137–38

Robelo, Alfonso, 167

Romberg, Alan, 19

Rousseau, Jean Jacques, 26, 27

Rump Parliament, 46

"Sainthood." *See* Conversion

Saltmarsh, John, 42, 44

Salvation: and authority, 8; and liberation, 103–4, 105

Sandeen, Ernest R., 86

Sandinismo, 245 (n. 6). *See also* FSLN

Sandinistas. *See* FSLN

Sandino, Augusto César, 149, 205, 245 (n. 6)

San Judas (Managua barrio), 123, 133, 174

San Pablo el Apóstol, 121

Santi, Carlos, 182, 200

Schaull, Richard, 115

Schlaefer, Salvador, 128, 172, 181

Schumpeter, Joseph, 26–27

Sectarianism, 143–44, 243

Shaw, Howard, 34

Shultz, George, 204–5, 214, 231

Singer, Max, 195

Sisters of the Assumption, 123, 174

Smith, Brian H., 8

Sobrino, Jon, 108

Socialism, 4, 78; as threat to the church, 79–80; false vs. humanistic types of, 148–49. *See also* Communism; Marxism

Social justice, 74, 78; and Congress of Panama, 82–83; and Vatican II, 88–89; and CELAM II, 93, 96; and peace, 96; the church's response to reality of, 103–4; CEBs and struggle for, 144

Somocismo, 29–30, 124, 239, 241–42; Catholic opposition to, 128, 134; armed revolution against, 136; and *Sandinismo*, 149. *See also* Somoza Debayle, Anastasio; Somoza regime

Somoza Debayle, Anastasio, 5, 14, 115, 130, 213; compared to Charles I, 41; and Obando y Bravo, 120, 129; and commemoration of first anniversary of earthquake, 132–33; persecution by, 139; and church hierarchy, 156; and Carter administration, 178. See also *Somocismo*; Somoza regime

Somoza regime, 3, 10, 74, 112, 144, 219, 222, 238; U.S. support for, 5; brutality of, 14, 127–28, 129; and Catholic church, 34, 117; final assault on, 115, 145, 146; celebration of triumph over, 116; disillusionment with after 1972 earthquake, 118; and FSLN, 119; and relief supplies, 124; and *delegados*, 126–27; loyalty to, 129; collapse of, 178. *See also* National Guard; *Somocismo*; Somoza Debayle, Anastasio

Soviet Union, 16, 20, 178, 198

Spain, 52, 61–65, 66, 93

Spanish Inquisition, 63, 66

Stamp Act, 58, 60

Star Chamber, Court of, 41

State Department (U.S.), 6

Stewart, Bill, 14

Stone, Lawrence, 36, 39, 48
Strachan, Harry, 67–68
Strachan, Susan, 67–68
Syllabus of Errors, 77
Synod of Bishops, 103, 169

Taxation, 39, 41
Tenant farmers, 34
Third World, 88, 106
Thucydides, 23
Tipitapa, 174, 229
Toleration Act, 48
Totalitarianism, 22, 170, 200, 246
   (n. 8)
Trade unions, 107
Tunnerman, Carlos, 182, 216

UNAG (Unión Nacional de Agricul-
   tores y Ganaderos), 161, 163
UNELAM (Movimiento Latino-
   americano Pro-Unidad Evangélica,
   Latin American Protestant Unity
   Movement), 100, 113
United Brethen, 81
USCC (U.S. Catholic Conference of
   Bishops), 194

Vásquez, Miguel, 129
Vatican, 111, 168, 170, 215, 220–24,
   236; and John Paul II's visit to Cen-
   tral America, 184, 185, 189
Vatican I, 77
Vatican II, 73, 74, 80, 87–90, 91; and

Catholic renewal in Latin America,
   97, 117, 120, 124, 238; loss of vital-
   ity prior to, 143–44; revolutionary
   implications of, 240
Vega, Pablo, 210, 211, 212, 214, 219,
   220; and Contra aid, 230, 231; ex-
   pulsion of, 234–37
Véliz, Claudio, 64
Viacrucis: D'Escoto's 1986 celebra-
   tion of, 228–30
Vigil, Miguel Ernesto, 171, 182
Vílchez, Pedro, 182
Violence, 105–6, 107, 130
Vivas, Bosco, 175

Walwyn, William, 43
Washington Post, 19, 231, 233
Waspam, 179
Weber, Max, 9
Whig ideology, 48, 57, 61
White House Digest, 19, 194
Whitefield, George, 56
Wilde, Alexander, 159
Wildman, John, 44
Winthrop, John, 55
World Council of Churches, 99
World Mission, 99
W. R. Grace Company, 211

Yalí, 129
Youth Commission (CELA III), 100

Zelaya, 127, 154, 156–57, 179